Digital Classics Outside the Echo-Chamber: Teaching, Knowledge Exchange & Public Engagement

Edited by
Gabriel Bodard and Matteo Romanello

]u[

ubiquity press
London

Published by
Ubiquity Press Ltd.
6 Windmill Street
London W1T 2JB
www.ubiquitypress.com

First published 2016

Cover design by Amber MacKay
Front cover image: *The end of the tunnel* by Conan, licensed under CC-BY 2.0
Background cover image: mikegi / Pixabay, licensed under CC0

Printed in the UK by Lightning Source Ltd.
Print and digital versions typeset by Siliconchips Services Ltd.

ISBN (Hardback): 978-1-909188-46-4
ISBN (Paperback): 978-1-909188-48-8
ISBN (PDF): 978-1-909188-47-1
ISBN (EPUB): 978-1-909188-61-7
ISBN (Mobi/Kindle): 978-1-909188-62-4

DOI: http://dx.doi.org/10.5334/bat

The full text of this book has been peer-reviewed to ensure high academic standards. For full review policies, see http://www.ubiquitypress.com/

To read the free, open access version of this book online, visit http://dx.doi.org/10.5334/bat or scan this QR code with your mobile device:

In memoriam Sebastian Rahtz (1955–2016)

We dedicate this volume to our colleague, collaborator and friend Sebastian—scholar, archaeologist, humanist, geek— whose life and work always exemplified the openness, interdisciplinarity, curiosity and generosity with which we hoped to infuse this book.

El futuro no te sera indiferente, amigo.

Table of Contents

Acknowledgements

The editors would like to thank the following colleagues who gave feedback on one or more chapters: Elton Barker, Aurélien Berra, Barbara Bordalejo, Tom Brughmans, Paul Caton, Mark Depauw, Sebastian Heath, Timothy Hill, Fabian Körner, Undine Lieberwirth, Pietro Liuzzo, Franco Luciani, Marcus Neuschäfer, John Pearce, Elena Pierazzo, Jonathan Prag, Allen Riddell, Eleanor Robson, Charlotte Roueché, Wolfgang Schmidle, Martina Trognitz, Charlotte Tupman, Raffaele Viglianti, Jane Winters and those we have inevitably forgotten! The quality of the book was also enhanced by the insightful peer-review comments from Monica Berti and one anonymous reviewer.

Contributors

Bridget Almas (bridget.almas@tufts.edu) has worked in software development since 1994 in roles which have covered the full spectrum of the software development life cycle, focusing since 2007 in the fields of language study and digital humanities. In her current role at Tufts University, Bridget is the lead software developer and architect for the Perseus Digital Library, currently serving as technical lead on the Perseids Project. She was also one of the primary programmers on the open source Alpheios Project, whose goal is make reading and learning mankind's most beautiful and significant classical languages as easy and enjoyable as possible.

Marie-Claire Beaulieu (marie-claire.beaulieu@tufts.edu) is an Assistant Professor of Classics at Tufts University. Her research centers on Greek religion and Digital Humanities. In Greek religion, she has published on various aspects of Greek cults and myths, especially centering on myths of the sea. She has just published a book titled *The Sea in the Greek Imagination* (University of Pennsylvania Press). In Digital Humanities, she is the co-director of the Perseids Project, a collaborative online environment in which users can edit, translate, and produce commentaries on a variety of ancient source documents, including inscriptions, medieval manuscripts, and texts transmitted through the manuscript tradition.

Gabriel Bodard (gabriel.bodard@sas.ac.uk) is Reader in Digital Classics at the Institute of Classical Studies, University of London. After a PhD in Classics, he worked for nearly fifteen years in Digital Humanities, where he specialised in text encoding, digital editing, and linked open data for ancient texts and objects. He has contributed to several online corpora of inscriptions and papyri, is one of the lead authors of the EpiDoc Guidelines for XML encoding of ancient source texts, and is the principal investigator of the Standards for Networking Ancient Prosopographies project.

James Brusuelas (jbrusuel@gmail.com) is Researcher in Papyrology and Digital Philology in the Faculty of Classics at the University of Oxford. His research focuses on Greek literature and papyrology, ancient comedy, and Greek philosophy and science. As the principal creator and project manager for numerous digital initiatives at Oxford, he is currently developing applications that facilitate the creation of born-digital critical (and thus citable) editions of Greek and Latin literature. For ancient books and fragmentary manuscripts in general, he is also designing new models for virtual museums that have impact on non-academic communities and especially the tourism industry.

Alberto Campagnolo (alberto.campagnolo@gmail.com) trained as a book conservator in Spoleto, Italy and has worked in that capacity in various international institutions, including the Vatican Library. He studied Conservation of Library Materials (BA Hons) at Ca' Foscari University Venice and then Digital Culture and Technology (MA) at King's College London. His doctoral research, at the Ligatus Research Centre, University of the Arts London, focussed on automatically visualizing historical bookbinding structures. He is interested in building a dialogue between the world of conservation in memory institutions and that of digital humanities, and in the digital representation of physical aspect of books.

Stella Dee completed her masters in Digital Humanities at King's College London, examining the pedagogical construction of online resources for TEI XML encoding. Stella studied international comparative studies at Duke University, with a focus on Fulfulde literary history. Through the Robertson Scholars Program, she completed a second major in archaeology at the University of North Carolina, Chapel Hill. Her interests include the intersections and shaping forces of language, power, and education.

Maryam Foradi (maryam.foradi@uni-leipzig.de) graduated from Shahid Beheshti University, Tehran, with a masters in Teaching German as a Foreign Language, as well as a bachelor's degree in Translation Studies. Her working languages as a professional translator include Farsi (L1), German and English. A longstanding focus on language instruction and translation led her to her current position as a doctoral student whose dissertation will focus on pedagogical issues of using translation alignment tools for Classical Persian.

Alejandro Giacometti (alejandro.giacometti@gmail.com) has a PhD in Image Analysis from University College London, and an MA in Humanities Computing from University of Alberta. His PhD consisted of an evaluation of image processing methodologies for recovering writing from multispectral images of damaged manuscripts. He worked in the Department of Digital Humanities at King's College London creating digital platforms to organise and explore datasets such as classical inscriptions and historical prosopographies. His research interests include multispectral imaging, data science, and humanities data visualisation. In particular, he is interested in how computational and machine learning methodologies can aid and complement traditional humanities expertise.

Simon Mahony (s.mahony@ucl.ac.uk) is Associate Director for Teaching at the UCL Centre for Digital Humanities and Senior Teaching Fellow at the Department of Information Studies, where he is Programme Director for the MA/MSc

in Digital Humanities. He has research interests in the application of new technologies to the study of the ancient world; using web based mechanisms and
digital resources to build and sustain learning communities, collaborative and
innovative working; the development of education practice and the use of new
tools and technologies to facilitate this. He is also an Associate Fellow at the
Institute of Classical Studies.

Francesco Mambrini (francesco.mambrini@dainst.de) obtained his PhD in
Classical Philology from the University of Trento (Italy) and EHESS, Paris
in 2008. Since then he has specialised in Computational Linguistics and the
Ancient Greek language. He has edited the annotation of the tragedies of
Aeschylus and Sophocles for the Ancient Greek and Latin Dependency Tree-
bank (Perseus Project). Currently, he works as a research fellow for the German
Archaeological Institute. He is one of the promoters and co-chairs of the
bi-annual workshop Corpus-Based Research in the Humanities.

Silvia Orlandi (silvia.orlandi@uniroma1.it) is Associate Professor of Latin
Epigraphy at Sapienza University of Rome. Her main research interests are
the inscriptions of Late Antique Rome (with special attention to the sena-
torial inscriptions of the Colosseum) and the history of epigraphy, including Renaissance forgeries. Since 2012 she has been responsible, together with
Silvio Panciera, for the Epigraphic Database Roma (edr-edr.it) and scientific
coordinator of the European project EAGLE (Europeana network of Ancient
Greek and Latin Epigraphy:eagle-network.eu). She is currently member of
the Pontificia Accademia Romana di Archeologia and President of the charity
Terra Italia Onlus.

Matteo Romanello (matteo.romanello@gmail.com) is a post-doctoral
researcher at the German Archaeological Institute in Berlin and at the Digital
Humanities Laboratory of the École Polytechnique Fédérale de Lausanne. He
recently completed a PhD in Digital Humanities Research at King's College
London under the supervision of Willard McCarty. His experience and research
interests include the automatic extraction and analysis of bibliographic references from large corpora of publications, and issues of semantic interoperability and usability within digital research infrastructure projects.

Jeff Rydberg-Cox (rydbergcoxj@umkc.edu) is a Professor in the Department
of English, Director of the Classical and Ancient Studies Program, Director of
the Liberal Studies Program and an affiliated faculty member with the School
of Computing and Engineering at University of Missouri-Kansas City. His
research focuses on digitization methodologies, multispectral analysis of manuscripts and early printed books, and statistical analysis of Ancient Greek texts.

Filip Šarić (fsaric@hrstud.hr) obtained his BA in Communication Sciences
and Latin in 2011 at University of Zagreb's Centre for Croatian Studies (grad-
uation thesis on "Analysis of Attractio Modi in Lealius"), and graduated in

Croatian Latinity with a thesis on "Marulić's Latin" in 2014. Since 2015 he works in Digital Humanities at the University of Leipzig as a researcher in the field of treebanking and is an assistant professor at Centre for Croatian Studies. Currently he is a PhD candidate at the Faculty of Humanities and Social Sciences' Linguistics department at University of Zagreb, mainly working with syntactical phenomena.

Simona Stoyanova (simona.stoyanova@kcl.ac.uk) graduated in Classics from Sofia University, Bulgaria, holds an MA in Classics and is currently a part-time PhD student in Digital Humanities and Classics, King's College London. She has worked at the Humboldt Chair of Digital Humanities, Leipzig as a research associate, is currently a research assistant on Ancient Inscriptions of the Northern Black Sea (IOSPE), and provides TEI XML and EpiDoc consultancy for digitisation and electronic publishing of Ancient and Mediaeval primary sources. Her experience and research interests include digital scholarly editing and textual criticism, digital epigraphy and papyrology, linked open data, and academic crowdsourcing.

Ségolène Tarte (segolene.tarte@oerc.ox.ac.uk) is a Senior Research Fellow at the University of Oxford's e-Research Centre (UK). A multi-disciplinary scholar with a background in Mathematics (MSc; Grenoble, F) and Image Processing (PhD; Bern, CH), and with a general interest in creative, collaborative, and cross-disciplinary research, her work focuses on scholarship in palaeography— the art of identifying, reading, and interpreting scripts to study the circulation of ideas and knowledge in their historical and sociocultural contexts. Her Digital Humanities research is underpinned by an effort to find complementarities between the cognitive dimensions of human expertise and the power of computational processing.

Valeria Vitale (valeria.vitale@kcl.ac.uk) is completing her PhD in Digital Humanities and Classics at King's College London. Before starting her academic career, she worked for several years as public engagement and digitisation specialist in museums and cultural institutions. Currently, her research focuses on the use of Open Linked Data to document 3D visualisation of ancient artefacts, and the drafting of a dedicated field ontology. Her interest covers the methodological and technological issues related to the visual representations of objects and places that belong to the past.

Introduction

Matteo Romanello and Gabriel Bodard

Prelude

Situated within the broader field of Digital Humanities, Digital Classics is concerned with the application of computational methods and theories to the study of the Greco-Roman and wider ancient world. Over the last decade or so, a decentralised and international community of researchers in this area has emerged, centred around the *Digital Classicist*. In addition to curating a wiki, and conversations over discussion lists in two languages, this community has been organising several seminar series aimed at providing a venue for discussion of work in progress. Indeed, some of the chapters in this collection arose from papers given at the Digital Classicist seminars in Berlin or London, although the majority were conceived or commissioned afresh for this publication. The scholarly community in the context of which this volume is coming into being, however, has been formed around both sets of seminars (plus those in Leipzig, Tufts and Göttingen), a series of conference panels, and previous volumes arising from them that were published by the *Digital Medievalist* journal, by Ashgate Press, and as a supplement to the *Bulletin of the Institute of Classical Studies* respectively.[1]

How to cite this book chapter:
Romanello, M and Bodard, G. 2016. Introduction. In: Bodard, G & Romanello, M (eds.) *Digital Classics Outside the Echo-Chamber: Teaching, Knowledge Exchange & Public Engagement*, Pp. 1–11. London: Ubiquity Press. DOI: http://dx.doi. org/10.5334/bat.a. License: CC-BY 4.0.

All of the chapters in this volume are significant scholarly contributions in their own right, presenting research questions in Classics or Digital Humanities (or in many cases both). They are all also examples of work within one of the most important area of academia today: scholarly outputs that address an audience other than the colleagues who work down the corridor (or at the other end of a VOIP call), be they our students, academics in very different fields from our own, commercial partners, or the broader public. As Gregory Crane has argued, collaboration, particularly with better-funded and more high-tech disciplines, is essential to Digital Humanities and even more so to Classics.[2] Such collaboration and sharing of values and outputs requires us to consider research outputs to be more than simply peer-reviewed papers—or rather, for us to recognise as peers and readers a much wider range of interests than we might traditionally have done.

As scholars, we have always recognised the need to do better at communicating with less-specialist audiences: those who do not necessarily share our educational privilege and cultural capital; those who may not understand our jargon or swim in the same sea of acronyms and camelCase shorthand. It is our duty, as academics and public servants, to communicate the value and the results of our research to the public, as well as to scholars and practitioners to whom it is already obvious *why* we would study the impact of Linked Open Data on the collection of onomastic data on people two thousand years dead. Perhaps even more importantly, we have not only the responsibility, but the existential need, to communicate the relevance of our place in the academy, and the very academy in the wider world, to an audience beyond the comforting echo chamber. The digital tools, methods and approaches that we implement and develop in our field offer new potential for communicating in new ways, through new media, and to new audiences. We have tools for asking new or more sophisticated questions of our ancient sources, and methods for studying texts, objects and data at scales previously impossible; similarly, information and communication technologies allow us to tell stories in ways, and accessible to people, that we have heretofore neglected.

Especially in the current climate of challenges to academic budgets and resources, the importance of engaging with audiences outside of our own discipline is clear, both in terms of academic survival and for meeting the criteria of academic role descriptions, promotion review panels or institutional assessments: criteria which include 'impact', engagement, teaching and environment, as well as conventional research output. The international perspectives on these issues are especially valuable in an increasingly connected, but still institutionally and administratively diverse, world.

This volume is accordingly offered to an audience that, yes, includes scholars in the various fields of Classics, Archaeology and History covered by the chapters (from epigraphy, papyrology and manuscripts, via Greek language, linguistics and literature, to imaging and modelling of artefacts and architecture);

and, indeed, includes academics in digital humanities, library and information science, informatics, and pedagogy whose domains of expertise are relevant to the technologies and methods further applied and discussed in the individual chapters. But we also hope that the pedagogical discussions will be accessible to students, as well as teachers; that the accounts of collaboration and cross-sector sharing will be of interest to our non-academic partners; and that the arguments around public engagement, reception, crowdsourcing and citizen science speak to those contributing or interested citizens, as well as the scientists who run the projects attempting to engage them.

We hope this book as a whole will be of value beyond the scholarly interest in individual chapters. For example, much of the discussion herein will be of practical and specific value to educators who might be looking for ideas to engage their students or the wider public in looking at, working with or contributing to digital resources for antiquity. There is also value to participants in large and highly collaborative projects that involve humanists and scientists or commercial developers, in papers that share insights into issues and pitfalls involved in crossing different disciplines, and ways in which we need to interact and negotiate between research cultures. The public engagement discussion inevitably also intersects with important conversations around the importance of the Humanities and the contribution of Digital Humanities in communicating this value both to the academy and to the community at large.

This book is divided into three sections.

Section 1: Teaching will discuss the contribution of digital humanities to pedagogy, teaching and learning in the classics, archaeology or digital humanities—including the creation of classroom or online materials for the study of languages, texts, or topics in ancient history and archaeology, and the teaching of digital humanities techniques such as text encoding and linguistic analysis. All of the chapters in this section acknowledge that the division between digital methods for teaching, and research into digital tools is a porous one, and that digital approaches are helping to break down the divide between the researcher and the student.

Section 2: Knowledge Exchange will focus on digital research projects or activities that bring together scholars or practitioners from outside of the traditional disciplines classicists and digital humanists are used to working with, or from outside of academia altogether. Collaborations with the medical sciences, with library and cultural heritage institutions, and with media and gaming industries all benefit both parties, with expertise and new insights into research questions moving in both directions.

Section 3: Public Engagement will discuss issues such as crowdsourcing or 'citizen science,' which serve not only to harvest the expertise or enthusiasm of non-specialists on a large scale, but arguably even more profitably engages the crowd with scholarly materials in a way that they might never have considered before. We also address publications of classical material that are targeted at a non-academic audience: popular books, documentaries, games, open access publications that are available far beyond the university library. Considering that the research that enables the production of such scholarly materials is often made possible thanks to public funding, we believe that more attention could profitably be paid to reflecting on the extent to which the wider public is aware of and benefits from—and even is able to contribute to—such materials.

Teaching

One recurring characteristic of the application of digital technologies to teaching and learning is the disruption of barriers and requirements to accessing knowledge that are set by more traditional curricula. What emerges from several chapters in this and in the Knowledge Exchange section, is a willingness to open up resources and communicate knowledge to all "regardless of native language, background and level of expertise".[3] With regards to teaching, this means imparting a subject or set of skills to an audience with no prior familiarity with it, such as teaching ancient Greek to absolute beginners or digital editing of texts by means of structured markup to students and scholars with little or no computing background.

The image of students that emerges from several chapters in this section is that of learners and, at the same time, content producers. Interestingly the Ancient Greek Treebank, which is central in Chapter V, was created with an essential contribution by students in classrooms. This is made possible also by the existence of tools such as SoSOL or Perseids, discussed in Chapter IX, that engage students, in addition to a more general public, in the creation and improvement of digital resources. From this perspective, digital scholarly editing becomes an invaluable pedagogical tool for learning to encode texts by means of markup, and also empowers students to make an original research contribution while learning.

Moreover, the use of digital technologies in teaching prompts a reflection on the added value of using these technologies, and a more general reflection on how there is no need to treat the acquisition of digital skills as an extraordinary topic, needing to be taught separately from non-digital subjects such as epigraphy or ancient languages. By the same token, the same digital research outcomes and methods should not be considered as separate from the pedagogical needs to which they are so well suited to contribute.

In Chapter I, Dee et al. consider the theory and practice of a 'learning by doing' approach to the encoding of texts by means of XML markup following the Text Encoding Initiative (TEI) guidelines. This chapter reviews the theory behind digital pedagogy and contains a useful review of several resources, informed by different pedagogical models, for learning. The authors also give an example of the issues that are raised by the creation of truly multilingual user interfaces that would allow for moving outside the echo chamber of Euro-American academia. Such issues in the visual display of right-to-left scripts emerged as a scholar was working on a Farsi translation of an ancient Greek text within the Perseids platform.

The focus on the creation of open resources for teaching is even more central in Chapter II, in which Mahony considers the creation and availability of Open Education Resources (OERs) for the teaching of Classics, with a specific focus on the situation in the UK. His discussion of specific issues related to OERs, such as the choice of distribution formats or the importance of repositories where these resources can be openly shared, is interwoven with a review of past projects aimed at increasing awareness around OERs and their reuse. The author also presents the results of a search for OERs for the teaching of Classics across UK repositories. The picture that emerges is not particularly encouraging and highlights the need for the practice of creating, sharing and re-using such resources to become embedded in teaching habits at every level, starting with the training of new teachers.

Chapter III focusses on the experience of teaching EpiDoc (TEI markup for epigraphy and papyrology) to an audience of classicists and historians over the past decade. The first part of the chapter is dedicated to describing the history of these training events, their structure and the content that is taught at (or omitted from) them. Based on the feedback received by workshop participants, Stoyanova and Bodard discuss some new models that could be integrated into the teaching of EpiDoc in the future. In the second part of the chapter the authors reflect on the current practice of teaching epigraphy and digital epigraphy. They argue for a teaching model where they are both taught in parallel as there are no substantial differences to justify this separation. It is also worth emphasising how the EpiDoc workshops have attracted students and researchers from audiences outside the echo chamber of Greek and Latin epigraphy, thus contributing to create bridges towards other epigraphies (e.g. Mayan, Egyptian, South-East Asian).

In Chapter IV, Rydberg-Cox describes his open tutorial for absolute beginners of Ancient Greek. The patterns in usage of this tutorial, which was originally aimed at supporting teaching in a classroom, reveal how it engaged users far beyond the boundaries of traditional academic environments. After presenting briefly the main functionalities of this tutorial, the author describes the main design choices he made in creating the tutorial and how they contribute to make this a resource that proved useful for those who want to learn some Ancient Greek wholly online and entirely on their own.

This section is concluded by Chapter V, in which Mambrini examines the implications for teaching of using Treebanking in a classroom setting. Treebanks are a specific kind of linguistic annotations where the syntactic structure of sentences is represented (and visualised) as a tree and is expressed by using a dedicated formalism. Taking as an example the construction of the syntactic tree of an eleven word sentence drawn from Sophocles' *Women of Trachis*, the author shows the wide range of aspects that need to be considered in the process. These aspects range from the literary context of the sentence to its grammar and syntax. The existence of several plausible ways of constructing the syntactic tree of the same sentence constitutes in itself a powerful pedagogical method to let students reflect on the arguments that can be adduced *pro* and *contra* each alternative.

It is worth noting that some of the chapters in this section challenge the thematic organisation of this volume into three distinct sections. Chapter III partly overlaps with the topics covered in the Knowledge Exchange section; in fact, EpiDoc workshops are also about training a generation of scholars to be better at collaborating with colleagues in other disciplines, as they acquire a 'structured way of thinking about and producing data.' Chapter IV could as well have been situated in the Public Engagement section as it shows how a digital tutorial, if properly designed, can engage a wider public well beyond the limits of the classroom for which it was originally created.

Knowledge Exchange

The three chapters in this section consider different aspects of Knowledge Exchange (KE), the bringing together of scholars or practitioners from outside of the traditional disciplines classicists and digital humanists work with—often from beyond academia altogether. The first aspect is the challenges and difficulties of making KE work within interdisciplinary research projects. The second is the adoption and application of specific methodologies to disciplinary areas very different from those where they originated. The third is the extent to which some technologies by their own nature are more effective than others in creating a number of potential collaborations with scholars and stakeholders outside the echo chamber.

In Chapter VI, Tarte reflects on her experience of applying image processing techniques to research fields as diverse as papyrology and trauma surgery. Among the strategies experimented with by the author that have proven useful to foster truly collaborative research there is the discussion of what she calls 'T-words': words that ought to *Trigger a Terminology Twitch*. T-words are words like 'feature' or 'model' that have the characteristic of carrying with them a rich and implicit framework of field-specific assumptions. Therefore, discussing and clarifying within a team the meanings of similar words in different fields can facilitate collaboration and exchange by elucidating these implicit frameworks. Another lesson offered by this chapter is that awareness about the differences between disciplines with regards to their respective modes of collaboration, communication and knowledge production is key to facilitate the fruitful collaboration among scholars with very different backgrounds. Finally, the author argues that interdisciplinary research requires, above all, trust between specialists, which can only be built if participants are able to successfully communicate their expert knowledge to non-experts.

Chapter VII presents a highly collaborative research project whose methodology was informed by methods developed in very distant fields, and where the interdisciplinary nature of the team was key to the project's success. In this chapter Campagnolo et al. describe the creation of an open dataset of multispectral images of deteriorated parchment documents. This dataset can then be used to evaluate different methods and algorithms for the recovery of writing from multispectral images of a manuscript. The idea around which this project evolves is taken from medical physics where *phantom tests* are digital models or material objects that allow for testing a new experimental technique in order to assess its potential usefulness. On this model, this image dataset allows for testing how effective image processing techniques are in recovering writing from documents that have undergone various forms of physical deterioration such as mould, fire, smoke etc. Collaboration between experts in book conservation, image processing and colour science was essential in the various phases of the project, from selecting which damage categories should be reproduced to acquiring the parchment materials to setting up the system for image acquisition.

Chapter VIII, which concludes the section, sees a slight change in focus as Vitale does not reflect on aspects of KE emerging from already concluded projects but rather speculates about the avenues for KE that open up as the result of a technological choice. Specifically, she discusses the implications of devising an ontology (in the computer science usage) to document 3D visualisations in cultural heritage. The problem at stake is one of essential importance for the acceptance of 3D reconstructions in an academic context: how can the interpretative choices entailed in creating a virtual model of a historical artefact be documented and made explicit and transparent? Vitale answers this question with the proposal of SCOTCH, the Semantic Collaborative Ontology for Three-dimensional visualisation of Cultural Heritage. A 3D visualisation, once documented by means of this ontology, ceases to be a merely visual artefact to become a small knowledge repository in its own right. In fact, by following a Linked Open Data (LOD) approach Vitale envisages 3D visualisations documented by means of SCOTCH to be linked to other relevant sources of information available online. Although a potential issue with this solution is arguably the time needed to document the visualisation process by means of RDF statements, the advantages in terms of knowledge sharing and exchange are numerous. Indeed, documented 3D objects can become useful resources for several sectors outside academia: museums and archives can build upon them to create exhibitions, be they physical or virtual; curators and restorers could use the 3D models to monitor changes to and degradation of artefacts and historical buildings; finally, annotated scans of archaeological excavation sites could be shared with urban planners of local municipalities who could use them when planning interventions on the territory.

Public Engagement

The chapters in this section reflect on how resources produced within academia can be made more easily accessible to and usable by the more general public, and how these audiences of citizen scientists—namely interested individuals outside of traditional academic environments—can be successfully involved in the creation of high quality content and resources. While the results of research projects tend to be characterised by high quality standards, academics often fail (or sometimes entirely neglect) to communicate the value of their research outputs to those who live and work outside of the academic echo chamber. Since academic research is largely funded by public money, it is arguably incumbent upon us to find ways to engage the public with our findings—even privately funded academics and projects, or those who do not believe public funding instils a duty of openness, need to engage with the reception of humanities among the wider population, at least if we care about the survival of our disciplines.

Moreover, if we succeed in developing strategies to engage the public in the production of new content, so-called 'crowdsourcing,' enterprises will be possible that would otherwise not have been conceivable.

In Chapter IX, Almas and Beaulieu reflect on the wider implications for scholarship of developing Perseids, a collaborative platform that allows virtually anyone to edit, translate and annotate ancient documents, while maintaining the quality standards of classical scholarship. The motivation for their work lies in the fact that the sheer amount of unedited and untranslated texts now available online renders impractical the traditional single-scholar approach. Perseids leads to a democratisation in the production of scholarship as the variety of tools it offers and the range of tasks it supports ensures that participants from different fields and at every level of expertise. At the same time, the scholarly integrity of all contributions made through Perseids is maintained, as they are vetted by an editorial board, constituting a form of peer-review. The provenance of each individual contribution is tracked, making it possible to attribute intellectual responsibility (key to scholarly method) and credit contributors (important to individual careers).

Chapter X contains an account of the challenges faced by the Ancient Lives project, whose main goal was to 'let the world assist in transcribing the seemingly countless papyrus fragments.'[4] The task performed by the participants was at the same time intriguing and designed with simplicity: using a virtual keyboard with Greek characters, users attempt to transcribe the characters they see on the ancient papyrus. The main technical challenge, which Brusuelas discusses in depth in this chapter, arose from the decision to allow multiple users to annotate the same document: how do you make sense of the huge amount of sometimes conflicting and faulty data generated in this way? This problem was solved by borrowing a method for the alignment of protein and DNA sequences from bioinformatics and adapting it to the alignment of characters from multiple transcriptions. This new algorithm allowed the project team to resolve competing transcriptions of the same individual character through recording consensus, and made it possible to create a corpus of transcribed—yet unedited—papyri out of more than nine million single-character classifications.

Finally, in Chapter XI, Orlandi presents the Europeana Network of Ancient Greek and Latin Epigraphy (EAGLE) project with a particular focus on describing the strategies enacted to engage the public with ancient inscriptions. While the primary aim of EAGLE was to create an epigraphic resource for academics, considerable attention was also paid to finding ways to make this resource more accessible to the general public. To this end, two mobile applications were developed as part of the project. The first, the EAGLE mobile application, provides an intuitive way of accessing the contents of the database and targets tourists and museum visitors in particular: while using sophisticated image recognition technology behind the scenes, this application allows users to search for epigraphic information by uploading a picture of an inscription taken with their smartphone. The second, a storytelling application, enables the creation of user-generated stories around inscriptions by facilitating the integration of multimedia resources that can be found online (e.g. pictures of inscriptions from Flickr or articles from Wikipedia, in addition to the contents in the EAGLE database). The simple yet powerful idea behind this application is that such stories, with their vivid multimedia narratives, can be an effective way to communicate and promote the fascinating richness of this aspect of European cultural heritage.

Coda

There are of course recurring themes between the three sections, and as observed above there are chapters that could quite reasonably have been included in more than one section, particularly between public engagement and teaching. The most striking theme that all chapters share is a recognition of the importance of openness: not only Open Access as a means to reach the widest and most diverse audience possible (as exemplified also by this volume), and not only Open Data as a means to make the research as transparent and replicable as possible, but ideally also the use of Open Standards for interoperability, and preferably Open Licensing of content and use of Open Source Software to encourage the direct engagement with, re-use of, and active improvement of both the tools and the outcome of our research. This openness, core to much of digital scholarship, is an important element of the agendas of most of the projects described in this volume.

In common, the chapters in the three sections discuss work in digital classics that addresses and even targets audiences who are not in the first instance our academic peers. These include our students, interdisciplinary collaborators, practitioners of cognate methods in industry or heritage sectors, and the citizen public at large. The importance of looking outward is manifold, and the particular focus in this volume on digital research and methods within classical and ancient historical scholarship is significant.

As scholars, whether academics and educators, heritage professionals, or others who engage with the ancient world, we believe that our research has value to humanity, not just to those like ourselves who are privileged to study it so closely. In fact in the digital humanities, which often considers digital media and publication methods as indivisible from the research tools and approaches we use to create and study data, is uniquely positioned to reach a wider audience by making material available online, via open fora, interdisciplinary venues and social media. Digital research is also about actively widening the questions we ask of our sources, the approaches we take and even the data we can apply to our scholarly activity; it is also possible (and as the contributions to this volume show, often achievable) to leverage this flexibility in and evolution of scholarship to broaden also the questions and the fields of interest in our discipline, addressing the classics from the perspectives of a wider constituency of potential readers.

Through all of these means we can, and we should, take the opportunity to communicate ancient world research to those outside of the academy. Classics is often thought to be niche, recherché, practically irrelevant, even elitist; if anyone is going to prove those assumptions wrong, surely it is digital classicists?

At the same time, we should also be communicating the importance and relevance of digital humanities practice, which includes a great degree of self-reflection and attention to historical developments, outside of the discipline itself. Making it clear that digital classics is at the hub of many collaborations, innovative teaching and research projects, and instrumental in bringing scientists and citizens to contribute to the study of antiquity, should be a great demonstration of this relevance.

Notes

1 Bodard & Mahony 2008, 2010; Dunn & Mahony 2013.
2 E.g. Crane 2004: 47.
3 Almas & Beaulieu 2016 (This volume, Chapter IX, p. 171)
4 Brusuelas 2016 (This volume, Chapter X, p. 188)

References

Almas, B. & Beaulieu, M-C. (2016). The Perseids Platform: Scholarship for all! In G. Bodard & M. Romanello (Eds.) *Digital Classics Outside the Echo-Chamber*, (pp. 171–186). London: Ubiquity Press.

Bodard, G. & Mahony, S. (Eds.) (2008). "Though much is taken, much abides": Recovering antiquity through innovative digital methodologies. *Digital Medievalist 4*. Retrieved from http://digitalmedievalist.org/journal/4/

Bodard, G. & Mahony, S. (Eds.) (2010). *Digital Research in the Study of Classical Antiquity*. Farnham: Ashgate.

Brusuelas, J. (2016). Engaging Greek: Ancient Lives. In G. Bodard & M. Romanello (Eds.) *Digital Classics Outside the Echo-Chamber*, (pp. 187–204). London: Ubiquity Press.

Crane, G. (2004). Classics and the Computer: An End of the History. In S. Schreibman, R. G. Siemens, & J. Unsworth (Eds.) *A Companion to Digital Humanities*, (pp.46–55). Oxford: Blackwell. Retrieved from http://j.mp/BlackwellCrane

Dunn, S. E. & Mahony, S. (Eds.) (2013). *The Digital Classicist 2013*. London: Institute of Classical Studies, School of Advanced Study, University of London.

SECTION I

Teaching

Learning by Doing: Learning to Implement the TEI Guidelines Through Digital Classics Publication

Stella Dee*, Maryam Foradi[†] and Filip Šarić[†]

*Tufts University,
†University of Leipzig

Abstract

This chapter reviews the current online resources available to learn the TEI Guidelines for structured data in the humanities, as well as the theory that drives their construction and continued improvement. It focuses on the Epi-Doc community as a positive example of a specialist community of practitioners who take a flexible approach to TEI instruction that meets both the shared and individual needs of scholars (cf. Bodard and Stoyanova, q.v.). We also address some of the barriers to multilingual contribution to the online digital Classics, and report on a case study in which we discuss the experience of Masters-level students trained in non-digital Classics methods with the translation and transcription of texts via the Perseids platform (cf. Almas and Beaulieu, q.v.). We consider how templates revealing the TEI markup allow students to gain comfort and familiarity with the XML, as well as to enable their own work to serve as a model for future contributors. However, we also note the pedagogical limitations of contribution without direct instruction as seen in this case study, and posit that a mixed model of experiential education combined with interpersonal guidance might better serve students hoping to contribute machine-actionable data in the digital Classics.

How to cite this book chapter:
Dee, S, Foradi, M and Šarić, F. 2016. Learning By Doing: Learning to Implement the TEI Guidelines Through Digital Classics Publication. In: Bodard, G & Romanello, M (eds.) *Digital Classics Outside the Echo-Chamber: Teaching, Knowledge Exchange & Public Engagement*, Pp. 15–32. London: Ubiquity Press. DOI: http://dx.doi.org/10.5334/bat.b. License: CC-BY 4.0.

1 Introduction

Increasingly, texts that manage to find a readership 'outside the echo chamber' do so through open publication online, often as part of a larger repository, digital library, or website. Of those texts that originate from scholarly sources, many are encoded according to the Text Encoding Initiative (TEI) standards for XML markup.[1] The TEI standards and consortium provide guidelines for the machine-actionable markup of texts in the humanities, including the Classics. Since 1994, familiarity and comfort with TEI XML has often been a prerequisite for an ability to navigate, judge, and participate in the various aspects of open-access digital humanities research. However, to those students and researchers with little prior exposure to the data structures that underpin computational work, TEI XML, or even the concept of a markup language, is not self-explanatory.

This chapter will examine the theory and practice of how those with some form of prior academic expertise in the humanities, more specifically in the ancient Greek and Latin languages and literature, can begin to learn to encode TEI XML text in an online environment. We briefly review some of the theory behind online and adult learning, as well as some of the prior resources available to those hoping to learn to encode texts in TEI XML. We also address some of the communities of practice, including EpiDoc, a curated subset of the TEI Guidelines designed for epigraphic markup, and the papyrologists. These communities of practice have successfully taught each other the skills needed to make digital contributions, with this instruction often happening in a digital space. For all resources under discussion, we reflect on parallels between various practices in the history of education and the principles underlying the technical development of the resources.

Above all, we hope to demonstrate that unfamiliarity with TEI XML need not preclude beginning to make real contributions to the scholarship of cultural antiquity. In fact, we will describe the experience of a number of students and researchers with no formal education in the digital humanities as they began contributing new TEI EpiDoc encoded translations of Classical texts through the Perseids platform, an online resource for the collaborative creation and editing of text in the Classics.[2] In the process, these students became more comfortable working in an elementary way with academic markup. While Almas and Beaulieu (q.v.) discuss in detail the way in which use of the Perseids platform changes interpersonal dynamics and learning within a classroom setting, we concentrate here on how the Perseids platform facilitates self-directed, remotely-collaborative and digital learning.

We also review the challenges facing the markup of Classics material that is truly multilingual. This is because the greatest barrier we ourselves have witnessed to contribution and participation in the digital classics is not the difficulties posed by understanding the technologies themselves, but rather the difficulties posed by the linguistic limitations of those technologies. While a full discussion of multilingual interfaces in the digital Classics is outside the scope of this chapter, we will touch on some of the technical linguistic barriers most frequently encountered by our project.

To date, the Perseids platform has supported scholars and students working with TEI EpiDoc in a number of languages, including Italian, French, Georgian, English, Latin, Ancient Greek, Persian, Arabic, and Hebrew. Of these languages, the most significant technical barriers to learning digital methodologies for working with Classical texts exist for those users whose preferred spoken language is Persian, Arabic, or Hebrew, most particularly those who work with conjoined scripts such as Persian or Arabic.[3] As a consequence, we will focus our user experience section on the issues encountered while working with textual markup and right-to-left script, in particular those of one of the authors, who has been writing and marking-up an original Persian translation of Thucydides' *History of the Peloponnesian War.* We believe that improving the technical infrastructure for working with multilingual TEI XML is critical to opening up teaching, knowledge exchange, and public engagement in the digital Classics.

2 Learning to Read, Learning to Edit, Learning Markup

We focus our attention here on a learner audience at the undergraduate level or above, who are studying or have studied subjects within the humanities, particularly Classics. For this audience, textual markup can be a new means of communicating knowledge that they already possess. Since nearly all students and scholars of the humanities require skills of textual criticism, and textual markup can be understood as a means of encoding textual criticism and interpretation, basic structural and critical markup can be relatively easier for these learners to comprehend. However, Peter Shillingsburg points out that markup can do many things which are not part of a traditional Western education in the humanities; 'scholarly editors are first and foremost textual critics. They are also bibliographers and they know how to conduct literary and historical research. But they are usually not also librarians, typesetters, printers, publishers, book designers, programmers, web-masters, or systems analysts.'[4] One advantage of the TEI is that it can serve as a channel of communication between one area of expertise—that of textual criticism, including familiarity with the material, philological, and bibliographic record—into another, that of production and representation. It allows the publisher, designers and programmers to extract the information they need, and for scholars to retain the analytical record in post-production. The tendency of those projects adhering to the TEI to be collaborative in nature is no less true of the TEI itself, which suggests a community of practice in its very name.

How much of this workflow students of the TEI, or aspiring digital Classicists need to master is an open question, the answer to which varies by individual. However, a significant proportion of learners hope to be directly involved in the publication and visual interface of their markup. A respondent to a recent survey on Learning the TEI requested '...instruction on file publication, rather than only TEI encoding. It is easier to learn the TEI in a self-taught manner using the Guidelines than it is to learn the workflow around TEI, from encoding and transforming and visualizing to publishing in a self-taught way, because that involves a lot more technologies and tools.'[5] Of the various learning resources for the TEI mentioned below, different resources enable exposure to different stages of this workflow, and include different degrees of collaboration with both humans and machines. Of the resources mentioned in this paper, we find the community of papyrologists and the Perseids community to have achieved particular success in involving their users in the publication of their own material. In fact, Perseids and the papyrology environment effectively minimize the need for users to deeply understand markup at all, serving the call of another survey respondent, who declared that 'it's time to make the TEI actually useful to individual Humanists with no digital background, and no support from DH centres.'[6] Through these platforms, students and scholars can create meaningful markup without deep familiarity with the TEI. In effect, learning to read and learning to edit can be enough to begin marking-up. Yet there will always be students who want to learn to make more full use of the technologies upon which these platforms rely; therefore, the next sections will examine the theory behind digital learning, as well as some of the resources currently in place for learning the TEI in a digital environment.

3 Digital Pedagogy

Most students who learn both the theory and practice of the academic Classics and the academic digital humanities currently do so primarily in a physical classroom.[7] However, digital tools and resources often serve as a supplement, and, for a significant minority, a replacement for classroom education. This has sparked a growing field of digital pedagogy—teachers, researchers, and students experimenting with effective strategies for online learning. The next section will provide an illustrative selection of relevant literature from the perspective of the digital Classics, with the intention of defining relevant terms for the resource reviews and case study later in the chapter.

3.1 Growth out of Prior Pedagogical Thought

A brief review of some terminology commonly used in Anglo-American academic discourse on pedagogy serves as a useful introduction to the discussion of resources later in the chapter. Frontal teaching, also known as 'chalk-and-talk' or teacher-centered instruction, refers to the practice in which a teacher stands in front of a class, often with a textbook, doing most of the talking in an effort to impart knowledge to the student. By contrast, in the various forms of student-centered instruction, 'knowledge is "discovered" by the learner.'[8] We consider constructivist, problem-based, and experiential learning to all be forms of student-centered instruction—in other words, learning by doing. Kirschner, Sweller and Clark describe the common elements of these different methodologies: 'first they challenge students to solve "authentic" problems or acquire complex knowledge in information-rich settings based on the assumption that having learners construct their own solutions leads to the most effective learning experience. Second, they appear to assume that knowledge can best be acquired through experience based on the procedures of the discipline.'[9] They go on to critique these forms of instruction, which they describe as using 'minimal guidance.' Part of their criticism is the idea that a student scientist will never draw the same conclusions from an experiment as a professional scientist, and can be led astray by those that they do draw. While some of the resources described here take a student centered, minimally-guided approach, we suggest that they do not fall into this trap, since those resources cater primarily to scholars who are learning mostly new techniques, rather than new concepts—the idea that one can enclose a paragraph in a <p>, as opposed to idea that one can separate text into paragraphs at all.

Classroom teaching can be described as discursive, adaptive, interactive, collaborative, and reflective.[10] A classroom teacher draws out discussion, a form of discursivity. They adapt their syllabus according to the needs of a particular student or group. They ask their students to reflect, giving critical feedback on an activity or concept. They ask their students to think together, collaboratively, enabling students to learn from one another, but respond with individual answers. They interact with the source text, in the form of a book or manuscript, writing their own translations or commentaries.

In a purely digital environment, the same activities and ways of going about things are reinvented. The environment itself can be designed to foster productive dialogue online, either in real time or not; the interface can be designed to adapt to the needs of a particular user, whether that means enlarging the type for someone with a visual impairment, or flipping the placement of elements on an HTML page for someone who reads in a right-to-left script. Dynamic exercises interact with the user, and the ability of the learner to communicate their feedback to the designer encourages reflection on the success of the environment for learning. We will return to these parallels between traditional and digital instruction in a few pages, when we begin to review some of the resources available for learning markup.

3.2 Adult Learning

Since most of the currently-available resources that introduce Classicists to digital methods and markup are targeted at adults, it seems appropriate to briefly review some of the theoretical tenets of adult education. In this chapter, we define 'adults' as those no longer in obligatory education, whatever the degree of obligatory education in their context may be. This definition considers university students to be adults, as well as professional scholars and researchers. Research suggests that for this cohort, task-based, also called use-directed, curricular organization is critical.[11] In other words, because adults operate under logistical pressures that are often absent from the lives of children, they expect the process of learning to be as compelling and worthwhile as the product.[12] A Classicist learning TEI markup might reasonably expect that they can further their work while still learning the best ways and technical arguments to encode their text. 'The approach to adult education will be via the route of situations, not subjects.'[13]

Online resources for Classicists learning to encode in XML must therefore seek to anticipate those situations in which a Classicist unfamiliar with the digital humanities might turn to XML encoding—whether as a way to work collaboratively with far-flung colleagues, to create a digital edition that sparks the imagination of members in their local community, or to build dynamic exercises to help their students learn a language. Moreover, these resources must support an approach that is self-directed,[14] although not necessarily minimally guided. While in the classroom 'one cannot equally serve both objectives—the generalist as well as the specialist—in [a short time],'[15] a digital learning environment can, and usually should, provide resources for both. Perhaps one of the most important points with respect to the final section of this chapter, which discusses the Perseids platform, is that people can learn without necessarily being *taught*.[16]

3.3 Digital Pedagogy

Much of the recent thought in digital pedagogy discusses how best to take advantage of the increased student autonomy and flexibility granted by the digital environment, as well as how best to cope with the accompanying distraction and possible lack of rigor. Through 'transferring to students the responsibility for accessing, sequencing and deriving meaning from information, hypertext was seen to provide an environment in which discovery learning might flourish.'[17] Moreover, the collaborative yet geographically unbound nature of the digital environment allows expertise to be shared across boundaries of geography and language,[18] although there are technical barriers to this exchange that we will confront in later sections. This enables early, graduated, and supervised participation in the creation of content, provided that designers 'redesign the learning environment so that newcomers can legitimately and peripherally participate in authentic social practice in rich and productive ways, in short, make it possible for learners to 'steal' the knowledge they need.'[19] The flexibility of the digital environment benefits learners by providing resources that are accessible on the learner's own time and that suit the learner's existing familiarities and motivation.[20] Ruell, however, draws on data from the online instruction offered by Harvard University to caution that resources for digital learning must impose external time limits and routine assessment to ensure student progress in the face of constant distraction, the downside of the increased flexibility.[21] Scardamalia and Bereiter discuss the need for resources grounded in pedagogical thought; they call for 'intentional learning environments' that are able to identify 'knowledge lacks,' or student areas of unfamiliarity, as well as to make use of 'multiple pass strategies,' that ask learners not simply to repeat, but to reflectively re-interpret.[22]

Chickering and Ehrmann formulated seven 'good practice' elements in online instruction. We list them here, in the hope that they might serve as initial guide for evaluating resources discussed later. According to these criteria, a pedagogically sound online instructional resource:[23]

1. encourages contact between students and faculty
2. develops reciprocity and cooperation among students
3. encourages active learning
4. gives prompt feedback
5. emphasizes time on task
6. communicates high expectations
7. respects diverse talents and ways of learning.

We would recommend appending at least two more to the original seven:

8. acknowledges and makes every contextually reasonable attempt to accommodate the multilingualism of a global digital space
9. enables learners to contribute as soon and as helpfully as possible to research in the field.

This theory is the lens through which we view and evaluate the resources discussed below. Although terms may shift in meaning or even become metaphors when applied to digital resources—students become 'learners' or 'users,' unresponsive or static lists of facts can be a form of 'frontal instruction'—we find this thinking useful as we evaluate the digital landscape.

The following sections will examine the development of various online resources for learning TEI markup, moving from those that are more static, or frontal, to those that are more collaborative and responsive. We will focus on the EpiDoc and papyrology communities for their particular success in teaching digital humanities methodology in an online environment. Finally, we will address the role of the Perseids project as a platform for collaborative editing that has grown out of these communities, including EpiDoc, the Perseus Digital Library, and the Alpheios Project; in particular, we will recount our experience using the Perseids platform to teach markup 'by doing.'

4 Teaching Resources

The following sites are all explicitly designed for users hoping to learn the TEI online. Unlike the collaborative platforms for editing described later, these sites have the benefit of being open to anyone with the necessary internet connection and linguistic abilities. They are scalable, in that questions or problems do not need to wait on a human being to answer them, largely because there is no opportunity to ask questions or voice problems. The webpages published by universities, as well as the resources published by particular individuals, often share a presentation-oriented approach. They provide information, leaving the user to figure out how best to make use of it. *TEI By Example* is a notable exception, in that it is a site designed explicitly for those hoping to learn the TEI as self-guided individuals, and contains tests, exercises, and pedagogical sequencing. However, *TEI By Example* cannot be considered an example of 'learning by doing' as we intend it, since the user of *TEI By Example* is not necessarily working on something personally productive for the user or scholar.

4.1 University Resource Sites and Individual Initiatives

Several universities host sites with basic resources for learning the TEI. The majority of these sites curate or list materials used in the classroom. As a consequence, while these sites certainly do work towards making markup accessible outside the echo chamber, they typically do not serve as examples of enacted digital pedagogy. Rather, their style of curating resources makes them the digital analogue to an extremely teacher-centered approach to classroom instruction. Two particularly rich examples of these sites are those run by Oxford University and Brown University. Just as a teacher lectures, so do these sites provide resources, sometimes sequentially, without making the process necessarily interactive, reflective, collaborative or user-driven. Similarly, a number of introductions to the TEI created by individuals affiliated with the TEI community serve as an example of frontal instruction in a digital space. While incredibly helpful and necessary for a raw beginner, they cannot be said to actively involve learners in the 'doing' of the TEI.

The *TEI@Oxford Teaching* page publishes a list of links to PDFs, XML, and other material from TEI@Oxford presentations, including many with topics of interest to aspiring digital classicists, such as 'A Very Intensive Introduction to TEI with Manuscript Description,' 'TEI:pas pour les nuls,' and 'Getting to know TEI P5: Everything you wanted to know about TEI P5 (but were afraid to ask)!'[24] Many of these links provide detailed and topical information of enormous use to an independently motivated reader who knows what they are looking for. However, they are not sequenced, searchable, nor explanatory at the most fundamental level, and consequently are most likely unable to meet the needs of a true novice. The *TEI Consortium Experimental Getting Started Guide,* also hosted by Oxford, is similarly static. Perhaps the most helpful aspect of the *Guide* is a clear and extensive explanation of when, why and how to use the TEI.

The Women Writers Project (WWP) at Brown University, in addition to hosting face-to-face seminars and workshops to teach text encoding, publishes a number of resources for learning to use TEI markup.[25] *Resources for Teaching and Learning Text Encoding* curates slides, lecture notes, and other materials developed by the WWP for internal workshops. Most modules published on the site include a source, notes, and slides, although a set of basic templates with a schema and stylesheet are also available, as part of a simple package for the presentation of encoded files. The majority of the material published as *Resources for Teaching and Learning Text Encoding* is simply lecture material generously shared online by professors, but nevertheless divorced from the lecture in which it was presented. Therefore, this area is most likely more useful for teachers seeking classroom resources than students seeking instruction. The *Guide to Scholarly Editing* stands alone as an excellent introduction to project workflow, scholarly encoding, and the TEI more specifically. However, the digital textbook lacks the examples, tutorials, and community interaction that some learners find useful. The *Training Materials* include reading, tutorials, how-tos, and references. While the most comprehensive of the WWP resources from a pedagogical standpoint, they also seem to be curated for the primary purpose of supporting in-house instruction and not online drop-ins.

The three individual initiatives described below are all authored by people belonging to the wider TEI community. The Slideshare PowerPoint developed by Laura Mandell is titled 'Introduction to Digital Textual Editing: An UNOFFICIAL Guide to the Value of TEI.'[26] Covering TEI as well as XSLT, Mandell's presentation is coupled with a twenty-minute lecture, and provides a convincing explanation of and justification for the use of both TEI and XSLT. Also accessible from a large, well-known commercial database is the instructional YouTube video titled 'TEI: an overview' published by Amanda Chesley, a current graduate student in the digital humanities.[27] Slightly less accessible to a non-academic community, but perhaps more useful for classicists who are already familiar with the basic concepts of textual markup, are the domain-specific 'Cheatsheets' assembled by Marjorie Burghart. These sheets answer encoding questions that re-occur frequently in various sub-disciplines, and are published on Burghart's personal site as well as the TEI Wiki. Helpful and easy to re-use, these sheets are an excellent resource for any classicist who needs quick answers to questions that arise during their process of encoding.[28]

We hope to be clear that applying the descriptor 'teacher centered' to the resources above is by no means meant to be a value judgment. In particular, the resources developed by individual scholars include some of the most concise, clear, and accessible resources encouraging scholars within the humanities to overcome a lack of technical comfort in order to make use of the TEI. These multimedia resources make an active case for use of the TEI through arguments that assume no prior knowledge of textual encoding. Although the direct impact has not been assessed, these resources are likely to go a long way towards breaking out of the markup community that can sometimes be an echo chamber. However, other resources are required for those beginners who then hope to begin participating directly in encoding work.

4.2 Inter-institutional Resources

With an increased scholarly focus on pedagogy in the digital humanities, as well as rising interest from scholars outside the field, came a number of inter-institutional resources designed to provide a more guided learning experience to advanced students and academics hoping to learn the TEI. These tutorials are often more interactive than the resource directories mentioned above, but users are still in an artificial environment, marking up examples that are often from outside their area of expertise. Therefore, while some of these resources, particularly *TEI By Example*, could be called 'learning by doing,' there is a distinct difference between the kind of 'doing' for *TEI By Example* and the kind of 'doing' required by participation in the EpiDoc or Perseids community.

 Teach Yourself TEI is run by the TEI Consortium and serves as a catalogue for tutorial materials concerning the TEI.[29] Divided into 'Generic tutorials,' 'Guides to Local Practice,' and 'Materials from Workshops and Presentations,' the site states no ambition to be a comprehensive survey of available resources, but does provide a brief description of each listed tutorial. Also run by the TEI Consortium, the TEI Wiki is a publicly available forum for the TEI community. Although not explicitly pedagogical, it does provide an area for discussion, sample files, and various how-tos that users claim to be quite useful.[30]

 TEI By Example is one of the first formal initiatives designed to meet the need for online support for learners of TEI XML. A collaborative work between a number of institutions, including King's College London, University College London, and the Royal Academy of Dutch Language and Literature, *TEI By Example* is a collection of tutorials written for novices as well as more experienced users.[31] The creators of *TEI By Example* differ slightly in their description of the target user base. Melissa Terras wrote in a personal blog-post that 'what I needed, really, was some point and click tutorials that I could direct my masters students to after an introductory lecture on TEI ... Where were examples of marked-up texts people could see to learn from?'[32] We re-visit this question of Terras' in the next section, when we discuss the communities that learn markup while contributing to repositories of marked-up texts. Edward Vanhoutte describes the target audience as primarily self-directed learners, although acknowledges their possible utility for classrooms teachers, saying, 'The tutorials are designed for self-directed learning but can also be used by TEI instructors in classroom and workshop situations.'[33] The *TEI By Example* tutorials demonstrate the encoding of different kinds of document by style or genre, including poetry, drama, and prose. Of all the resources discussed up to this point, *TEI By Example* comes closest to being a standalone pedagogically-sensitive resource for learning the TEI.

5 Communities of Practice

Other models raise the questions: who even needs to learn markup? And how much comfort with markup is necessary in order to do meaningful digital work, and for whom? Two communities discussed below, the community of papyrologists and the Perseids community, provide their users with graduated exposure to XML markup, specifically markup compliant with the EpiDoc subset of the TEI Guidelines.

That tools for digital scholarly editing could serve as a pedagogical tool for learning markup may not be obvious. However, in the words of Siemens and Tittenberger, 'content is generally viewed as something that learners need to cognitively consume in order to learn. But learning is like opening a door, not filling a container. Content can be created through the process of learning, not only in advance of learning.'[34] While the idea of student learning through research contribution has become standard practice in the sciences, it has yet to become standard in most introductory Classics classrooms.[35] The tools available to papyrologists and the Perseids platform gently introduce students and scholars of the Classics to the markup techniques of the Digital Classics, even as these students and scholars continue to conduct the kinds of scholarly annotation with which they may be more familiar.

This approach to learning markup is not nearly as inclusive nor scalable as the frontal resources described above. As of fall 2014, these resources rely on human beings, accessible via email, to answer questions. In this way, while the resources may be minimally human guided, they are still guided, to the benefit of their users. However, this lack of scalability leads to the risk of creating ever more new echo chambers instead of communities, unless concerted effort is made to keep communities in conversation, contributing to a world republic of digital humanities.[36] Moreover, learners require pre-existing expertise in domain-specific methodology. While this requirement allows these resources to avoid the problems caused by 'the improper use of inquiry as a paradigm on which to base instructional strategy,'[37] since users are already proficient in their domain and are likely to choose appropriately among methods of inquiry, it also limits the audience that these resources are able to serve.

Both the papyrologists and the Perseids project rely upon the EpiDoc standards for the TEI guidelines. EpiDoc was originally developed for use encoding epigraphy, and like the TEI itself, EpiDoc is a community, as well as a set of guidelines. Gabriel Bodard, one of the lead authors of the EpiDoc guidelines, is very clear about this joint mission; 'it is a central goal of the EpiDoc Collaborative to create freely available tools, well-documented advice, and a lively community of training and assistance for EpiDoc projects.'[38] While this includes in-person training, like the TEI Community, EpiDoc also publishes online learning materials designed to help scholars through the process of beginning to encode their materials, including those involved in the projects below.[39]

5.1 The Papyrologists

The papyrological community shares a community-based approach to teaching digital methods. Roger Bagnall, a core member of this community, explains that 'Joshua D. Sosin, Duke University, who is the principal project leader, [sees] this nexus of papyrological resources as ceasing to be "projects" and turning instead into a community ... the central feature of the second phase of IDP is the creation of an online editing system that will allow entry of texts ... by any authorized participant.'[40] Gregory Crane, editor-in-chief of the Perseus Digital Library, points out that this is facilitated by a Papyrological Editor which is able to 'shield the raw TEI XML from editors, allowing them to encode very complex textual data in a more traditional format as they publish new and revise existing editions.'[41] In other words, the papyrological community is able to teach digital methods, with XML encoded data, without require the user to fully understand EpiDoc-compliant TEI XML.

5.2 Perseids

The Perseids platform also provides a space for students and scholars to gain comfort working with TEI EpiDoc markup through the process of digital scholarly editing. The Perseids platform grew out of the Perseus Digital Library and Alpheios Project; continued collaboration with these projects, as well as the Open Philology Project, provide Perseids with connections to massive repositories of openly-available scholarly text, as well as a critical focus on pedagogy (cf. Almas and Beaulieu, q.v.). All editions and translations accessible and creatable through the Perseids platform must be encoded in CTS-compliant TEI EpiDoc, creating ever more communities and guidelines which the humanities student must familiarize themselves with.[42] However, Perseids provides a gentle introduction to TEI XML by allowing scholars to complete linguistic annotations without necessarily seeing the underlying XML, to write translations into pre-prepared TEI XML templates, and by providing feedback when XML is invalid.

    Both Perseids and the Papyrology Editor integrate publication, or doing, into the process of learning TEI XML. A number of ongoing projects appear to be heading in a similar direction, either by supporting collaborative editing, or by lowering the barrier to publication of TEI files, or both. These include TAPAS, for publication, TEICHI, for display and download, CWRC-Writer, for in-browser collaborative editing and standoff markup in a 'close-to-WYSIWYG' environment, and TEI Boilerplate, for easier display of TEI texts.[43]

6 Case Studies: Benefits and Challenges of Learning Markup through Community-based Digital Scholarly Editing

The next pages focus on user experience with the Perseids platform, particularly the lessons this experience holds for learning markup in a digital environment through participation in communities of practice. We rely on specific case studies of Masters-level Classics students who 'learned by doing,' who without prior knowledge of digital methods or classroom instruction were able to work with Perseids and TEI/EpiDoc-compliant XML markup. We also address the issue of localization and multilingualism in online pedagogical resources, including Perseids, by discussing the experience of a professional translator and research scholar of translation studies working to create a TEI EpiDoc-encoded Farsi translation, direct from ancient Greek, of a section of Thucydides *History of the Peloponnesian War*. This will include a summary of some of the technical challenges posed by working in the digital Classics with right-to-left scripts.

6.1 Beginning to Work with TEI Markup through Scholarly Editing

In the spring of 2014, the Open Philology Project at the University of Leipzig Department of Digital Humanities hosted four postgraduate-level students of classics, two specialists in ancient Greek and two in Latin, all of whom had attended university in Zagreb, Croatia. None had prior experience working with digital resources. All began working with the Alpheios treebank and alignment editors for completing annotations, as accessible through the Perseids platform, which also allows for the storage and later editing of these annotations.

While the students received brief instruction on how to use the Perseids platform and Alpheios editors, they were given little to no direct instruction on TEI XML. During their time in Leipzig, they completed a number of original translations of Ancient Greek and Latin text into English. Although a research assistant conducted the initial markup of their translations for upload to Perseids, the students were responsible for completing minor XML edits afterwards. They proved themselves able to complete such edits as adding the appropriate EpiDoc markup for co-translators, splitting and renumbering words to mark Latin enclitics, and renumbering sentences in translation alignment XML.

At the end of their stay, however, the students did not feel as if they understood XML at a theoretical or practical level, despite the fact that they were able to recognize and work with it at an elementary level. This does support the limits of 'learning by doing'; ultimately, they would have required direct instruction beyond the guidance built in to the software and the occasional questions they asked to be able to independently work with TEI XML in the future.

6.2 *Technical Barriers to Learning TEI Markup*
through Scholarly Editing

Perseids has also taken steps to move outside the echo chamber of Euro-American academia, by actively engaging participation from scholars working with ancient Greek and Latin texts and translations in Georgian, Farsi, Arabic and Hebrew. However, this effort confronts a number of technical issues with effectively working with TEI markup in certain scripts. We believe these issues bear repeating here, as they serve as a very real barrier to entry to the Digital Classics and TEI EpiDoc encoding for scholars working in right-to-left (RTL) scripts.

The problems that arise include technical difficulties with both digital editing and digital publication. Most of the text editors most commonly used by scholars in the digital humanities have either no or inadequate support for RTL text. Some editors, such as Sublime, display RTL text as LTR, while others, such as Notepad++, display words correctly but shift them unpredictably while the user is working.[44] Oxygen, perhaps the most commonly used editor for working with LTR TEI XML in the digital humanities, poses similar problems. While scholars working with RTL text have come up with work-arounds for nearly all of these issues, the work-arounds tend to be time consuming, frustrating and imperfect, particularly with such situations as the placement of punctuation.

As mentioned above, students are more highly motivated to learn TEI XML when they can see a visible display of their encoding, particularly in the browser. However, the browser poses no fewer challenges for those working RTL text. Meeting this challenge requires commitment on the part of the front-end developer, author of the stylesheet, or teaching materials for XSLT to understanding directionality, mirroring, and the relevant unicode encoding for RTL numbers.

Of course, supporting multilingual participation in the TEI, EpiDoc, and Perseids communities neither begins nor ends with technical support for RTL text. By choosing to write from experience, we have left out addressing issues of internationalization, localization, and vertical scripts, to name just a few. However, we believe that facing these issues is critical to the future not only of humanities markup, but humanities scholarship and its students.

7 Lessons Learned

Emerging evidence suggests that the most efficient path to becoming adept with academic XML markup in the digital Classics requires a combination of online resources and interpersonal support. This support can take the form of message boards, the frontal resources mentioned in this paper, or mailing lists; a recent survey found that of respondents who asked a question via the TEI mailing list, 81% received a satisfactory answer, and of those who reached out to a member of the TEI community for mentorship or guidance, 93% had found their contact information via the mailing list.[45] Mailing lists serve the additional purpose of crowd sourcing the support, so that one teacher is never expected to be the sole resource. However, we do believe that the future will see more platforms of the kind represented by Perseids and the Papyrological Editor. These platforms foster a positive feedback loop, in which scholars learn TEI XML through following examples set by eithers, even as they create examples for those who will follow them. The major challenge lies in making this model scalable, linguistically inclusive, and meaningful across the different fields of the humanities; until it is, each community will continue to be something of an echo chamber.

Notes

[1] TEI: Text Encoding Initiative: <http://www.tei-c.org/index.xml> (last accessed October 2015).

[2] Perseids Project: <http://sosol.perseids.org/> (last accessed October 2015).

[3] Romanov, pers. Comm.

[4] Quoted in Rehbein & Fritze, 2012: 48.

[5] Dee 2014.

[6] *Loc. cit.*

[7] Pierazzo, pers. comm.

[8] Cuben 1990: 4.

[9] Kirschner, Sweller & Clark 2006: 76.

[10] Rehbein & Fritze 2012: 62.

[11] Lindeman 1926.

[12] Dewey 2008: 98.

[13] Lindeman 1926: 6.

[14] Merriam 2001.

[15] Rehbein & Fritze 2012: 73.

[16] Knowles 1972; Adler 1952.

[17] Snyder 2008: 2.

[18] Thorne 2012.

[19] Hansman 2001: 49.

[20] Mahony & Pierazzo 2012: 224.

[21] Ruell 2013.

[22] Scardamalia & Bereiter 1989.

[23] Chickering & Ehrmann 1996.

[24] University of Oxford (n.d.).

[25] Bauman & Flanders (n.d.).

[26] Mandell 2013.

[27] Chesley 2012.

[28] Burghart 2013.

[29] Text Encoding Initiative, n.d., 'Teach Yourself TEI.'

[30] Text Encoding Initiative, n.d., 'TEI Wiki'; Dee 2014.
[31] Van den Branden et al. 2010.
[32] Terras 2011.
[33] Vanhoutte 2011.
[34] Siemens & Tittenberger 2009: 3.
[35] Crane et al. 2012.
[36] Casanova 2004.
[37] Kirschner, Sweller & Clark 2006: 79.
[38] Bodard 2010.
[39] Elliott et al. 2006–2016.
[40] Bagnall 2010.
[41] Crane 2014: 4.
[42] Canonical Text Services at SourceForge [Online] <http://cite-architecture.github.io/> (last accessed October 2015).
[43] TAPAS Project: <http://tapasproject.org/>; TEICHI <http://www.teichi.org/>; CWRC-Writer <http://www.cwrc.ca/projects/infrastructure-projects/technical-projects/cwrc-writer/>; TEI Boilerplate <http://dcl.ils.indiana.edu/teibp/> (all links last accessed September 2014).
[44] Sublime: <http://www.sublimetext.com/>; Notepad++: <http://notepad-plus-plus.org/>.
[45] Dee 2014.

References

Alpheios (n.d.). Retrieved from http://alpheios.net/content/alpheios-texts

Bagnall, R. (2010). Integrating Digital Papyrology. *In* Online Humanities Scholarship: The Shape of Things to Come. Retrieved from https://archive.nyu.edu/handle/2451/29592

Bodard, G. (2010). EpiDoc: Epigraphic documents in XML for publication and interchange. *In* F. Feraudi-Gruénais (Ed.) *Latin on Stone: Epigraphic Research and Electronic Archives.* Lanham, MD: Lexington Books.

Brown University Women Writers Project (n.d.). Resources for Teaching and Learning Text Encoding. *Journal of the Text Encoding Initiative.* Retrieved from http://www.wwp.brown.edu/outreach/resources.html

Brown University (n.d.). TEI-L Home Page. Retrieved from http://listserv.brown.edu/archives/cgi-bin/wa?A0=TEI-L

Burghart, M. (2013). TEI Cheatsheets. *TEI Wiki.* Retrieved from http://wiki.tei-c.org/index.php/TEI_Cheatsheets

Casanova, P. (2004). *The World Republic of Letters.* Boston, USA: Harvard University Press.

Chesley, A. (2013). TEI: an overview. Retrieved from http://www.youtube.com/watch?v=R6iiIFrWvmU

Chickering, A.W. & Ehrmann, S.C. (1996). Implementing the seven principles: Technology as a lever. Retrieved from http://www.tltgroup.org/programs/seven.html

Crane, G. (2010). Give us editors! Re-inventing the edition and re-thinking the humanities. *Connexions*. Retrieved from http://cnx.org/content/m34316/latest/

Crane, G. (2014). The Digital Loeb Classical Library — a view from Europe. *Perseus Digital Library Updates: News and Announcements from the Perseus Digital Library*. Retrieved from http://sites.tufts.edu/perseus updates/2014/09/22/the-digital-loeb-classical-library-a-view-from-europe/

Crane, G., Almas, B., Babeu, A., Cerrato, L., Harrington, M., Bamman, D. & Diakoff H. (2012). Student Researchers, Citizen Scholars and the Trillion Word Library. Retrieved from http://www.humanities.ufl.edu/pdf/Crane-%20Student%20Researchers,%20Citizen%20Scholars,%20and%20the%20Trillion%20Word%20Library.pdf

Cuban, L. (1990). Reforming Again, Again, and Again. *Educational Researcher* 19(3–13).

Dee, S. (2014). Learning the TEI In a Digital Environment. *Journal of the Text Encoding Initiative* 7. Retrieved from http://jtei.revues.org/968

Dewey, J. (2008). *Democracy and Education*. Radford, VA: Wilder Publications.

Elliott, T., Bodard, G., Cayless, H. et al. (2006–2016). *EpiDoc: Epigraphic Documents in TEI XML*. Retrieved from http://epidoc.sf.net/

Hansman, C. A. (2001). Context-Based Adult Learning. *In* S.B. Merriam (Ed.), *The new update on adult learning theory* (pp. 43–113). New Directions for Adult and Continuing Education, No. 89. San Francisco: Jossey-Base.

Kirschner, P. A., Sweller, J. & Clark, R. (2006). Why Minimal Guidance During Instruction Does Not Work: An Analysis of the Failure of Constructivist, Discovery, Problem-Based, Experiential, and Inquiry-Based Teaching. *Educational Psychologist,* 41(2): 75–86.

Knoll, M. (2011). Von Aristoteles zu Dewey. Zum Ursprung der Maxime "learning by doing". *Originalbeitrag. Überarbeitete Fassung von* Dewey, Kilpatrick und "progressive" Erziehung. Kritische Studien zur Projektpädagogik. Bad Heilbrunn: Klinkhardt. pp. 287–298. Retrieved from http://www.mi-knoll.de/128401.html

Knowles, M. (1972). Innovations in Teaching Styles and Approaches Based Upon Adult Learning. *Journal of Education for Social Work,* 8(2): 32–39.

Lindemann, E. (1926). *The Meaning of Adult Education*. New York, NY: New Republic.

Mahony, S. & Pierazzo, E. (2012). Teaching Skills or Teaching Methodology? *In* Hirsch, B.D. (2012) *Digital Humanities Pedagogy*. Open Book Publishers Retrieved from http://www.openbookpublishers.com

Mandell, L. (2013). Introduction to Digital Textual Editing: An UNOFFICIAL Guide to the Value of TEI. Retrieved from http://www.slideshare.net/mandellc/tei-and-xslt-23711832

Perseids (n.d.). Perseids Editing Environment. Retrieved from http://sosol.perseids.org/sosol/

Rehbein, M. & Fritze, F. (2012). Hands-On Teaching Digital Humanities: A Didactic Analysis of a Summer School Course on Digital Editing. *In* B. D. Hirsch (Ed.), *Digital Humanities Pedagogy*. Open Book Publishers. Retrieved from http://www.openbookpublishers.com

Reuell, P. (2013). Online learning: It's different. *HarvardScience: Science and Engineering at Harvard University*. Retrieved from http://news.harvard.edu/gazette/story/2013/04/online-learning-its-different/

Siemens, G. & Tittenberger, P. (2009). *Handbook of Emerging Technologies for Learning*. Retrieved from http://elearnspace.org/Articles/HETL.pdf

Snyder, I. (2008). Research Approaches to the Study of Literacy, Technology and Learning. *In* K. A. King & N. H. Hornberger (Eds.), *Encyclopedia of Language and Education, 2nd Edition, Volume 10: Research Methods in Language and Education:* Kluwer 299–308. New York, NY: Springer Science+Business Media, LLC.

Terras, M. (2011). Birth of TEI by Example. Retrieved from http://melissaterras.blogspot.de/2011/11/birth-of-tei-by-example.html

Text Encoding Initiative Consortium (n.d.). Teach Yourself TEI. Retrieved from http://www.tei-c.org/Support/Learn/tutorials.xml

Text Encoding Initiative Consortium (n.d.). TEI Wiki. Retrieved from http://wiki.tei-c.org/index.php/Main_Page

Thorne, S. L., Fischer, I. & Lu, X. (2012). The semiotic ecology and linguistic complexity of an online game world. *ReCALL*, 24: 279–301.

Terras, M., Van den Branden, R. & Vanhoutte, E. (2009). The need for TEI By Example. *Literary and Linguistic Computing* 24(3): 297–306.

University of Oxford (n.d.). *Getting started using TEI*. Retrieved from http://tei.oucs.ox.ac.uk/GettingStarted/html

Vanhoutte, E. (2011). So You Think You Can Edit? The Masterchef Edition. Retieved from http://edwardvanhoutte.blogspot.de/2011/10/so-you-think-you-can-edit-masterchef.html

CHAPTER 2

Open Education and Open Educational Resources for the Teaching of Classics in the UK

Simon Mahony

University College London

Abstract

New technologies have always introduced new possibilities but these invariably bring fresh problems with them. The expansion and wider availability of digitised teaching content is no exception and there are now new affordances but as a result new questions need to be asked about our teaching practice. Academics within the same departments have always shared teaching materials but a cultural change is taking place in universities, with academics using the internet to share their research (Open Access) and teaching and learning resources (OER: Open Educational Resources) more widely. This chapter draws on the experience of completed Jisc and the Higher Education Academy funded projects for the creation, use, and importantly reuse of OERs. These themes are developed, drawing on the experiences of the Digital Classicist, the Stoa Consortium and other open initiatives in Classical Studies, such as OpenLearn at the Open University, and so situating these ideas within the sphere of the teaching of Classics. As part of this research a systematic search for Classics teaching material was conducted in the major UK repositories and beyond, revealing a paucity in discrete classroom based learning objects, hence raising more questions. This chapter also makes suggestions for best practice in the production of OERs and calls for the establishment of recognised standards.

How to cite this book chapter:
Mahony, S. 2016. Open Education and Open Educational Resources for the Teaching of Classics in the UK. In: Bodard, G & Romanello, M (eds.) *Digital Classics Outside the Echo-Chamber: Teaching, Knowledge Exchange & Public Engagement*, Pp. 33–50. London: Ubiquity Press. DOI: http://dx.doi.org/10.5334/ bat.c. License: CC-BY 4.0.

1 Introduction

New technologies have always introduced new possibilities but these invariably bring fresh problems with them. The expansion and wider availability of digitised teaching content is no exception in that there are now new affordances but as a result new questions that need to be asked about our practice as educators. It is true that academics within university departments have always shared teaching materials; a new staff member will generally take over existing established and perhaps core modules as well as developing new ones based on their research interests. However, over the last decade, a cultural change appears to have been taking place enabled by the internet and digital content whereby academics now share their research (Open Access) and teaching and learning resources (Open Educational Resources: OERs) much more widely. This spirit of collaborative working appears to be increasing, and, it is argued here, has the potential to open up higher education, giving both students and teachers greater access and flexibility and at the same time help to break down the institutional barriers between research and teaching.

This chapter draws on the experience and outputs of completed Jisc and the Higher Education Academy (HEA)[1] funded projects for the creation, use, and importantly reuse of OERs. Firstly, VirtualDutch (www.dutch.ac.uk), part of the Open Learning Environment for Early Modern Low Countries History where a lesser taught language subject community have collaborated in joint teaching projects and developed a wide range of resources.[2] The second is Digital Humanities Open Educational Resources which was set up to create and release a comprehensive range of introductory materials on approaches, topics and methods in the Digital Humanities.[3] A third project, CPD4HE: Open Resources on HE Teaching and Learning, is also included as it has direct relevance to the argument presented here. These themes are developed, drawing on the experiences of the Digital Classicist, the Stoa Consortium and other open initiatives in Classical Studies, such as OpenLearn at the Open University (OU) and so situating these ideas within the sphere of the teaching of Classics.[4]

This chapter does not argue for the transformative possibilities of Open Education or OERs and how they might shift the balance between teaching and learning at a time when educators are stretched by ever mounting demands.[5] Rather, my direct involvement in the OER movement and pedagogy combined with a background in Classics prompted a survey of the open teaching materials available for Classics in the Anglophone world. Following this, the major question that arises is that although there are many exemplary resources within the field of Classics (and Digital Classics in particular) that are suitable to support teaching and also that Classicists have always been at the forefront of new technological developments, why is there a lack of fine grained classroom based 'learning objects' for the teaching of Classics?[6] The argument presented here is that to become used more extensively these resources need to become part of the routine tool kit of educators and that before they can be successfully used they first need to be found. Suggestions for best practice are offered based on the experience of the OER projects mentioned above and a call is made for the establishment of recognised standards and metadata.

2 Open Education and Open Educational Resources at UCL

2010 saw the launch of the UCL Centre for Digital Humanities (UCLDH) and in the following year the new Master's programme enrolled its first cohort of students. UCLDH is a research centre and as such has output in the form of projects and publications but the Master's programme also allows for the integration of research and teaching and thus facilitating research and publishing on teaching itself.[7] Becoming involved in the OER movement has allowed all three of these activities to be pursued.[8]

The projects named in the introductory section consider that the true rationale of openness to be one of reclaiming original academic practice and collaboration.

> Open access stands for unrestricted access and unrestricted reuse. Paying for access to content makes sense in the world of print publishing, where providing content to each new reader requires the production of an additional copy, but online it makes much less sense to charge for content when it is possible to provide access to all readers anywhere in the world (Public Library of Science).[9]

We can trace the origins of the global OER movement back to the UNESCO Conference of 2000 where it is important to remember what the initials stand for in the well-used and perhaps over-familiar acronym (the United Nations *Educational*, Scientific and Cultural Organization).

> Open Educational Resources are teaching, learning or research materials that are in the public domain or released with an intellectual property license that allows for free use, adaptation, and distribution.[10]

The movement gained momentum with the launch of MIT OpenCourse-Ware in 2001 and the founding of Creative Commons with their first licences released in the following year. However, this chapter is not going to give a history of the OA or OER movements as that is widely available elsewhere, nor is it going to argue for their importance but take it as a given.[11] The point here is that in essence the move towards openness has been with us for some time but our approach within education and the development of educational resources should always be new and changing to remain innovative and be part of an increase in the overall culture of Open Access moving away from paywalls and subscription sites.

At the simplest level, and in the context of this chapter, an OER may be just a lecture presentation, a reading list, some class-based task or exercise, topics for seminar discussions or even exam questions. On a broader level they may also include 'full courses, course materials, modules, textbooks, streaming videos, tests, software, and any other tools, materials, or techniques used to support access to knowledge.'[12]

One issue that is currently unresolved and stimulating debate within the movement is that OERs still continue to be relatively unused in most education programmes. There may be many reasons for this: a general lack of awareness of OERs, especially at the more traditional higher education institutions; an unwillingness to use other people's material for teaching; a belief that by releasing the material and making it freely available there is, in some way, a loss of ownership; or it may simply be a reluctance to give away ones precious teaching material for free. There also may be institutional issues; for example the 'employer' (i.e. university) may claim copyright on the employees work and will not allow it to be freely distributed and hence effectively banning the release of OERs. This relative lack of use is an important issue but not one that will be explored in the context of this chapter other than as far as it concerns discoverability; although freely and openly available, it seems clear that OERs will only be used if they are easily findable and also if their use has become part of the standard workflow of the educators. Overall, producing resources and releasing them as OERs is not enough; it is necessary for us to develop communities of practice around the use of re-usable learning objects and materials. In addition, and to facilitate this, the ongoing practice of developing Open Resources for teaching, needs to become part of the training (and professional development) of teachers at all levels; this is the importance of the following project and how it fits into the overall argument presented here.

2.1 Open Resources on HE Teaching and Learning

CPD4HE (Continuing Professional Development for Higher Education), funded by the UK Higher Education Academy and Jisc,[13] was developed to release educational resources to support the professional development of lecturers and teaching staff at UCL (and being released as OERs, to do so more widely). In all UK higher education institutions, probationary teachers and lecturers are required to attend and participate in training programmes (it is also recommended for the continuing professional development of all teaching staff). This is where the creation, release, use and re-use of teaching materials can be instilled in up-and-coming educators. When these methodologies become commonplace in the teaching of educators and the development of their research practice, they will similarly become more commonplace in the arsenal of teaching tools employed by course and module tutors. This is important for building a community of practice around OER release and re-use at an institutional level. Moreover, following the completion of this and the two projects that follow, discussions have been held in consultation with UCL Libraries about the feasibility of setting up an institutional repository for OERs. This is not because we need another OER repository as we already have, *inter alia*, Jorum and HumBox,[14] but rather to make the creation and release of OERs part of normal institutional practice and the workflow of teaching staff just as institutional repositories are now mandated for staff research output. These discussions are, at the time of writing, still ongoing but the move towards such a repository is now acknowledged on the institutional domain.[15] The two other relevant projects are briefly outlined here.

2.2 Open Learning Environment for Early Modern Low Countries History

This was a joint project to bring together teaching materials to support a lesser taught subject community: Dutch studies.[16] Modern foreign languages are recognised by the Higher Education Funding Council for England (HEFCE) as being a 'strategically important and vulnerable subject' area.[17] Dutch is a minority subject despite, arguably, being the European language closest to English and widely taught across the continent. The general decline in teaching modern languages affects all language programmes but is particularly pertinent for those not widely taught.[18] This project resulted in the collaboration between the four institutions in England that teach Dutch at university level (UCL, Sheffield, Cambridge and Nottingham) to develop and release open teaching materials. This allowed cooperation and the sharing of resources to bring more breadth to the curriculum which has been of direct benefit to students and staff at the participating partner institutions.[19] The relevance here is that the decline in learning languages is not restricted to modern ones but to ancient ones too; in addition, combining resources freely, strengthens rather than weakens the subject area. This is a model that could be adopted for strengthening the teaching of Classical languages and particularly by developing and sharing classroom based resources.

2.3 Digital Humanities Open Educational Resources (DHOER)[20]

DHOER created sharable teaching resources taken from the Digital Humanities Master's programme at UCLs Department of Information Studies and made them freely and widely available via HumBox and Jorum. Importantly, these resources go beyond the Digital Humanities sphere and are intended to support many cognate disciplines, including the whole spectrum of the arts and humanities (potentially Classics too), cultural heritage, information studies and library studies. At an early stage the decision was taken (based on the experience of VirtualDutch) that to facilitate the use and re-use of these resources they must not only be open to use in other disciplinary areas but also be released in an open format that allows for their use, adaption and re-use. The standard format for text or graphic based OERs seems to be PDF as these can be opened simply in a browser and handled by almost every platform and end user (including those not comfortable with technology); however, these are of course not 'open' and as such contradict the earlier statements on openness. To resolve this, as well as being released as individual PDFs, resources from this project were also bundled together by module together with the original source files in Open Document Format (ODF) to facilitate reuse, editing and extending the original material. Importantly, these are made available together with instructions and links to Open Source office suites; metadata and licensing details are included as well as how the folders might be unpacked and ODF made use of. Particularly important are details about the assumed level and how and where individual OERs might fit within a programme. Rather than a single large resource, the focus of this project shifted towards the creation of smaller units of learning objects which might be used strategically where needed. This together with the open format, metadata for context, level and discovery should be essential parts of any OER output.

3 Open Educational Resources for Classics in the UK and beyond

The resources released by the projects briefly outlined above, as well as being archived institutionally, have been uploaded to the two main UK repositories for OERs, Jorum and HumBox. As part of the research for this chapter a systematic search was conducted for teaching material for Classics in both these (and other) repositories.

A keyword search for 'classics' in Jorum (all the results that follow are at the time of writing) returns 67 hits; the top ones offer resources on 'information management' and 'essay writing' with some further down the list on Greek drama followed by World War I. By far the most hits are to resources for English grammar which is laudable but they are not 'classics'.[21] Searching 'classical studies' returns 14 hits with little relevance for us here except 'Podcasting the Ancient World' which offers a broken link to that resource. Searching using 'Latin' as keyword brings nothing relevant and 'Greek' returns, amongst many irrelevant hits, 'Greek Drama' and again the broken link to 'Podcasting the Ancient World.'

A similar search for 'classics' on HumBox returns 66 different results but not until hit 29 do we find anything relevant: a collection titled 'Views in Greece from drawings by Edward Dodwell. A collection of drawings of views in Greece by the English traveller and archaeologist Edward Dodwell (1776/7–1832).'[22] 'Classical studies' returns 12 hits; the results of this search are rather curious as the first one is a presentation on 'Open Source and Open Access' (by one of the editors of this volume) which forms part of the DHOER collection and the second by a former colleague who at the time worked at the English Language Subject Centre and both resources were part of the Jisc/HEA OER Phase 2. This is particularly interesting as neither are tagged 'classical studies', 'classics' or 'studies' nor do they contain that as a character string anywhere in the document content.[23] This does raise pertinent questions about the search algorithms used by this resource. When uploading content, authors are asked to select an appropriate Creative Commons licence, and add keyword 'tags' and a brief description; this is supplemented with automatically generated upload metadata such as 'creators' and 'date added'. There is no clear reason why those two resources should come at the top of the list for a search using 'Classical studies' as a search term.[24] Searching 'Latin' and 'Ancient Greek' have similar disappointing results. It is notable then that there is clearly a paucity of OERs for Classics in the two major national repositories of classroom based teaching and learning materials.

It is important to remember that the granular approach of the individual learning object is, of course, not the only methodology for open education as can be seen with the broad based approach of MIT and the increasing number of MOOCs.[25] There is of course a fundamental difference between the two: MIT OpenCourseWare (MIT OCW) offers 'off the shelf' courses for delivery whereas, for example, a Coursera MOOC asks students to sign up and follow a specified programme of study.[26] Both are very different from each other and from the discrete learning objects anticipated by an OER.

Conducting similar keyword searches on MIT OCW ('a web-based publication of virtually all MIT course content') and Coursera ('Take the world's best courses, online, for free') give interesting results.[27] Using 'classics' as a search term in the former returns 63 results which are mainly courses on 'Classics' of Chinese and American literature; in Coursera it returns 3: a course on 'Historical Fiction' and two hits for the same course on the 'Chinese Humanities'.[28] 'Classical Studies' returns no results on Coursera and 58 on MIT OCW: the first being 'Classical Literature: The Golden Age of Augustan Rome' followed by (classical) Music, Engineering and Physics (classical mechanics). As might be anticipated 'Latin' returns hits on both (42 on MIT OCW and 4 on Coursera) with almost all being concerned with 'Latin American' studies.[29] 'Ancient Greek' returns 13 hits on MIT OCW and 2 on Coursera.[30]

For completeness, it needs to be clear that the above are not the only platforms for the discovery of Open Education materials. Udacity ('Advance your career') focuses on technical courses, mainly programming and Computer Science, and seems to be designed to enhance users' skills portfolio; hence nothing for classics there.[31] edX ('great online courses from the world's best universities'), founded by Harvard & MITx (now includes Berkeley and other partners) and unlike Coursera claim to be a collaborative, non-profit organisation, operating on an Open Source platform.[32] Course selection here is by a subject specific dropdown menu with no text-box search interface. Scrolling through 'History' in 'all schools' (39 results) finds 'The Ancient Greek Hero in 24 Hours (Hours 1–5): Epic and Lyric' (a cut down taster for what follows), 'The Ancient Greek Hero' (a 17 week course with no pre-requisites) and 'Was Alexander Great? The Life, Leadership, and Legacies of History's Greatest Warrior' (a 13 week course with no pre-requisites). Again, these necessitate enrolling and following a prescribed course.

A UK based MOOC platform owned by the Open University, FutureLearn ('Connecting people and ideas. The best free online courses in the world'), has a long list of partner institutions, mostly in the UK.[33] Again there is no global search function and courses are available in a list with an image, strapline, start date and duration together with the number of hours per week that are expected from students. For our purposes, the only relevant course in 'New & upcoming' seems to be 'Hadrian's Wall: Life on the Roman Frontier' offered by the University of Newcastle (6 weeks at 4 hours per week). One of the partner institutions is the University of Southampton and looking though their 'past' courses finds: 'Archaeology of Portus: exploring the lost harbour of ancient Rome' (duration: 6 weeks, 2 hours per week). All these courses clearly display their start date, duration, hours per week and whether a certificate is available, together with an image; importantly, this information is displayed in the list itself without having to open the course page to find the necessary details. Once registered, a simple click enrols you on the course with email alerts to prompt progress and discussion in the appropriate fora. It is clear from the lack of a search box in both these platforms that, rather than relying on natural language searching for content discovery, they use an index of keyword metadata system to allow faceted browsing.

4 Widening the search

It seems then that although there are many well known and high profile online digital resources for Classics (and many support teaching), there is little, if anything, in the way of discrete learning based objects that would match the OER criteria. Following this survey and to address this overall lack of granular teaching resources, a new page on the Digital Classicist wiki was launched in late 2013 to gather together Digital Humanities type educational resources and OERs for Classics and further research was undertaken by this author.[34] Adopting a community approach, the various Classics-related Jiscmail lists were circulated as well as popular social media channels such as Classics International (on Facebook) and Twitter with a request for any relevant material.

Close to home, the head of the Classics department at the Open University (OU) responded to the email looking for open teaching resources which prompted further investigation of OpenLearn ('The home of free learning from the Open University').[35] Searching for 'Classics' required scrolling to the second page of hits (default of 10 per page) to discover relevant courses such as Greek tragedy ('A reader's guide to Medea' and 'Oedipus: The message in the myth') and Classical Latin. 'Classical Studies' returns more results with links to Classical Latin, reception studies, and history on the first page. Employing a different search strategy and using the menu with drop down options (to allow a faceted rather than a natural language search), 'History & The Arts' > 'History' > 'Classical Studies' gives more fruitful results: 'Most popular from Classical Studies' from where you can scroll down to a more visually appealing and informative selection with images, brief description of each course and the essential metadata. Included in the metadata for many is the 'Duration' from which the user can clearly determine if this is a taster course ('Getting started on Classical Latin': Introductory level, Duration 10 hours) or something more substantial ('Certificate of Higher Education Open': Duration 1200 hours) and importantly, where appropriate, the level (introductory, intermediate etc.). Again, although these courses are free, vary in duration and level, they are still ones that you sign up for and follow as a student.

What are less easy to find at the OU are the many excellent resources not on OpenLearn but offered by the Classics department itself, particularly taster materials for 'Classical Studies' and the 'Ancient Olympics', and those for language learning more generally, which are freely available under Creative Commons licences. Following the thread: 'Open University' > 'Department of Classical Studies' > 'Taster Material' takes you to 'Taster Materials for Classical Studies' that include podcasts, videos, short essays and sample course materials.[36] For example, links to 'Getting Started on Classical Latin' and 'Continuing Classical Latin' both with Creative Commons BY-NC-SA[37] licences attached with a link to a page clearly defining and making clear what may be done with this material. Having rights and permissions clearly stipulated and spelled out in clear sight is an essential part in getting materials used and re-purposed.

There are of course other alternatives for finding Open Educational Resources. Xpert (Xerte Public E-learning ReposiTory), hosted at the University of Nottingham, is a Jisc funded search engine specifically built to 'to explore the potential of delivering and supporting a distributed repository of e-learning resources.'[38] This project aims to allow a search interface to specifically identify and retrieve OERs. Using 'Classics' as a search term retrieves 366 results with reassuringly some coming from the OU on the first page. However, the results are not universal as testing with searches for DHOER (and other topic related tags used on the DHOER project) return no results.[39] The author contacted the technical developers at Xpert who could not account for this anomaly as their search metadata is allegedly harvested directly from Jorum and the other repositories. What it does return (again on the first page) are links to the Oxford University Podcasts.[40] These feature video recordings of various talks on a variety of topics such as Classics, Roman Comedy, and Classical Literature; most are from the Jisc/HEA OER phase 1 strand and almost all have Creative Commons licences clearly and prominently attached.

The results of the desk-top survey conducted as part of this research show that the availability of class-based teaching OERs in the area of Classics are very limited; those found using anticipated search methods, at present, consist of classical subject paintings in HumBox, podcasts from the University of Oxford (both these developed as part of the HEA/Jisc funding initiatives) and resources that can be extracted (licence allowing) from materials made available by the Classics Department at the Open University.

Some other resources that are important to mention can be found on the Stoa Consortium pages. The Stoa serves as the official blog of the Digital Classicist community but also hosts a wide range of resources with a continuing commitment to Open Access and networked scholarship being fundamental principles.[41] Many of these are legacy sites but others such as 'Suda on line'[42] and 'EpiDoc guidelines'[43] are very much current.

Various open image collections are also available online to support teaching and research in Classics. As well as those on the Stoa, the Ancient World Image Bank, started at the Institute for the Study of the Ancient World, 'is a collaborative effort to distribute and encourage the sharing of free digital imagery'.[44] All images there are freely downloadable from their Flickr account and released with a simple Creative Commons Attribution (CC-BY) licence and so also meet the OER criteria.[45]

It is also important to remember that new resources are coming online all the time such as *Perseids* ('a collaborative editing platform for source documents in Classics');[46] *Iliados* ('grammatical and syntactical searches on the Perseus Treebank');[47] *Alpheios* ('reading tools for Latin, ancient Greek and Arabic').[48] These, along with other high profile resources for Classics, such as the *Perseus Digital Library, Thesaurus Linguae Graecae, Duke Databank of Documentary Papyri, Inscriptions of Aphrodisias, Roman Tripolitania and Cyrenaica* are all in their way excellent resources and serve to support teaching and research in a variety of different ways. However, they do not provide immediately usable and suitably packaged material to be incorporated in the lecture hall, seminar room or computer lab; that is not their purpose and it should not be expected of them. What is missing generally within this broad disciplinary area, are dedicated open teaching resources suitable for the teaching room, collections of copyright free teaching materials that the over-stretched and time-starved lecture or module tutor can turn to when putting together their teaching plan(s).

5 Open Education in Context

With regards to OERs more generally, it is essential to remember that making them accessible, free and online does not necessarily make them available to the people who would benefit from them the most. Once released online, they are indeed open to the world, but only to the 'well connected' world, which is expansive, but not universal. What are needed are not resources that look good on the latest smartphone or tablet device, but ones that display effectively on low-cost mobile phones and incorporate simple, widely used technologies. The most successful online teaching resources are not those that utilise technologies with the highest pedagogical qualities but rather those that make use of 'technologies which are generally available.'[49] Materials should be optimised for the lowest reasonably employable technology, rather than the highest, and producers should not assume that their users will necessarily have access to the same resources that they do.

Further, issues about context and ownership need to be addressed. As we have seen, MIT OpenCourseWare, for example, delivers complete courses and modules pre-packaged, off the shelf and ready to go. However, the user of Jorum or HumBox is generally looking for a task, exercise or learning object to complement a class or lecture, something to aid the students' understanding of what is being taught or indeed even for the students themselves to find and make use of themselves as self-learners. Firstly, the resource needs to be found: it must have adequate and relevant discovery metadata attached, rich enough to fully describe the content, but, at the same time, the metadata needs to be sufficiently focused to prevent the user being overwhelmed with irrelevant results. Once found, the individual OER may lack context which needs to be made explicit; where does it fit within a programme, module, teaching session or task-based learning exercise? This information also needs to be included at an object-based level along with the assumed level of the students' competence. What is the learning context? Who is the intended audience? These are essential questions that need to be addressed when producing OERs regardless of the disciplinary area, whether that be Classics or Digital Humanities.

Moreover, if the teaching that uses the OER is credit based, then there will be the need for assessment. This becomes a potential problem area unless the OER package contains sound pedagogical material that is moving towards that assessment. In addition, different cultures have different learning styles, attitudes to change, memory and aesthetic tastes.[50] This goes far more deeply than the need for translation when adapting learning materials for another global area. This is also equally true of areas where English has become the 'lingua franca,' as the localization of content is still needed to compensate for cultural differences, particularly in the area of graphics, symbols, colours, layout and other variants.[51]

Once all this is taken care of, there still remains the often contentious question of ownership and the continuing relationship between the original author and the re-used and, perhaps, adapted OER. Considerable funding has gone into the creation of OERs and this will be in danger of being wasted without efforts being made to ensure their sustainability and this is where developing the community of practice becomes important. Making the creation and release of OERs part of the normal institutional workflow (which is the focus of the CPD4HE project) will help to ensure that sustainability.

We do not yet have reliable metrics for the measurement of the use of OERs; we can gather download statistics simply enough but that is no indication of whether or not they have actually either been used as a teaching resource or re-purposed and adapted in some way. The long term hope of the OER community is that the teaching materials will be taken, used and improved, and then fed back into the repositories and so becoming an iterative cycle contributing to the growth of knowledge and knowledge production. The situation then approaches one that is analogous to peer review; errors, omissions, typos and broken links can be corrected and the resource returned with improvements and acknowledgement (if required by the licence). This methodology facilitates the equal partnership between research and teaching that is so often claimed but less often observed at the Higher Education level.

6 Conclusions

Within the field of Classics digital resources for teaching and (so-called) e-learning have been becoming more prominent on the agenda. Witness two panel sessions on 'New Approaches to eLearning in Classics' at the (UK) Classical Association Annual Conference at the University of Nottingham (2014),[52] the 'iLatin and eGreek - Ancient Languages and New Technology' symposium hosted by the Open University (2014)[53] and Hestia2 on 'Digital Pedagogy: How are new technologies transforming the interface between research and learning?'[54] The focus of each of these was teaching and the use of technology (in various forms) to support teaching; all were based on research conducted by the presenters and form solid exemplars of the synergy between teaching and research in the field of Classics.

The suggestions argued for here are those recommended by this author based on the experience of running an OER project and by extensive research within the area of Open Education and OERs. With Open Education and OERs specifically what is most important is that the resources should be easily found; they need appropriate discovery and relevant focused metadata. Once found, their place and purpose within an educationally robust curriculum needs to be clear along with an intellectual property licence allowing free use, re-use, adaption and distribution with attribution. The intended audience and level should be apparent. These should be (or have a version that is) in an open format with a low technical threshold. In the case of ancient languages, just as with other vulnerable subject areas, much advantage can be gained by joining together and sharing resources, as has been seen with VirtualDutch, to strengthen and develop the curricula of collaborating departments.

It is unfortunate that despite three rounds of research funding within the UK (specifically to promote usage by encouraging the incorporation of OERs into all government sponsored education), extensive government and private funding in the USA, an Annual Open Education Conference, as well as a dedicated annual OER Conference,[55] there are not yet recognised standards for metadata or best practice. Following the end of the funding period the Jisc pages on Open Education appear to have been archived at the end of January 2013.[56] The closest that can (to date) be found is The Open Education Handbook: '[…] a collaboratively written living web document targeting educational practitioners and the education community at large.'[57] This was (and still is) a community effort and part of the European based LinkedUp Project, kick-started by a series of booksprints, the first of which was held in London and participated in by this author.[58] The handbook pulls together much useful information about Open Education and Open Educational Resources along with finding and using Open Data for education but stops short at advocating any specific standards or metadata schemas.

As far as Classics is concerned we have this anomaly of the seeming lack of fine grained openly available teaching resources. Many innovative and high profile online Classics projects are in evidence and many indeed may be used to support teaching. However, there is a clear dearth of classroom based teaching material ('learning objects') and it is unclear why that is the case. This lack may be connected in some way to the general pedagogical concerns within the teaching of Classics, and as such is outside of the scope of this investigation, and would be a useful focus for a follow up study. An alternative possibility is that they are simply very difficult to find as they are missing the appropriate discovery metadata and hence there would be a lack of awareness of their existence; this scenario would be addressed by following the suggestions for best practice put forward in this chapter and the establishment of recognised standards and metadata.

The methodology for the research on which this chapter is based is admittedly limited in that it examines only the English speaking material. The mailing lists used to contact the Classics communities are indeed international but responses to the requests for guidance towards resources only came from within the UK and the USA. This may introduce a bias but all the same in the context of teaching Classics in the Anglophone world such resources are clearly missing. Despite this it would be useful to have other perspectives from the non-Anglo international Classics community; this would allow a useful comparison (i.e. is this lack specific to the English speaking Classics community or a more general one in the teaching of Classics).

Nevertheless whatever the cause, Open Educational Resources are (or should be) pedagogically driven as should all teaching resources. The discussion around this whole area of Open Education, the creation, release, use and re-use of OERs more generally, granular versus a broad based approach, does have one significant spin-off benefit whether within the field of Classics or elsewhere. It encourages us as educators and researchers involved in teaching to talk about and reflect on our teaching practice and how indeed teaching and research are interlinked.

Whether they are used or not, OERs (and Open Education more generally) have stimulated the discussion on, and research into, the learning process and our pedagogical aims. They have become the agents of change and objects to talk about, giving us the opportunity to interrogate what we do as educators. There is not one single solution or approach and we must work across institutional and disciplinary boundaries and continually push these boundaries.

Acknowledgements

Much of the content of this chapter is revised and updated from my keynote talk as part of the Digital Classicist Berlin seminar programme in October 2013.[59] Many thanks to the seminar organisers for the kind invitation and also to the editors of this volume for facilitating this publication. Many thanks also to the various reviewers for their helpful and valuable comments.

Notes

[1] Jisc/HEA Open educational resources programme: phase 1 <http://www.jisc.ac.uk/whatwedo/programmes/elearning/oer.aspx>; phase 2 <http://www.jisc.ac.uk/whatwedo/programmes/elearning/oer2.aspx>; phase 3 <http://www.jisc.ac.uk/whatwedo/programmes/ukoer3.aspx>.

[2] With thanks to my colleague Ulrich Tiedau who was grant holder at UCL for this and the DHOER project and first introduced me to the OER movement.

[3] DHOER: <http://www.ucl.ac.uk/dhoer>.

[4] CPD4HE: <http://www.ucl.ac.uk/calt/support/cpd4he>; Digital Classicist: <http://www.digitalclassicist.org/>; Stoa Consortium: <http://www.stoa.org/>; OpenLearn: <http://www.open.edu/openlearn/>.

[5] For a very insightful view on the potential possibilities for the transformation of established teaching practice opened up by these resources see Neil Butcher's talk at the 2014 OER Conference in Berlin <http://werkstatt.bpb.de/2013/09/they-must-learn-how-to-learn>.

[6] 'Learning object' is a debated term and very much context related; for the purpose here I note the Jisc usage: '[...] digital assets which represent an educationally meaningful stand-alone unit' and take this to be small individual resources (presentation slides, reading lists, exercises, discussion topics) that can be used in a class context. <https://www.jisc.ac.uk/guides/open-educational-resources>.

[7] See for example Mahony & Pierazzo 2013; Mahony & Tiedau 2013.

[8] Mahony, Tiedau & Sirmons 2012; Tiedau & Mahony 2011; Mahony 2014; Bodard & Mahony 2014.

[9] Public Library of Science (PLoS): <www.plos.org/about/open-access>.

[10] UNESCO, Communication and Information <http://www.unesco.org/new/en/communication-and-information/access-to-knowledge/open-educational-resources/>.

[11] 'Open access (OA) literature is digital, online, free of charge, and free of most copyright and licensing restrictions.' Suber 2012. See HEA for details about their involvement with the movement <http://www.heacademy.ac.uk/oer> and more widely the Support Centre for Open Resources in Education (SCORE) <http://www.open.ac.uk/score/publication-type/review-open-educational-resources-oer-movement-achievements-challenges-and-new-oppo>.

[12] The William and Flora Hewlett Foundation are a major funder of OER grants internationally <http://www.hewlett.org/programs/education/open-educational-resources>.

[13] CPD4HE: Open Resources on HE Teaching and Learning, available: <http://www.ucl.ac.uk/calt/support/cpd4he>; Open educational resources programme – phase 2, available: <http://www.jisc.ac.uk/whatwedo/programmes/elearning/oer2.aspx>.

[14] Jorum, the Jisc funded UK repository for OERs: <http://www.jorum.ac.uk>; HumBox, a repository set up as one of the pilot projects of OER phase 1 with a focus on the Humanities: <http://humbox.ac.uk>.

[15] UCL Teaching & Learning Portal: <https://www.ucl.ac.uk/teaching-learning/technology/oer/OER-repositories>.

[16] Open Learning Environment for Early Modern Low Countries History: a VirtualDutch Open Educational Resource funded by Jisc and the Higher Education Academy: <http://www.ucl.ac.uk/alternative-languages/OER>.

[17] HEFCE: Strategically important and vulnerable subjects (SIVS): <http://www.hefce.ac.uk/whatwedo/crosscutting/sivs>.

[18] Worton 2009.

[19] See Mahony, Tiedau & Sirmons 2012: 175–7.

[20] DHOER: Digital Humanities Open Educational Resources: <http://www.ucl.ac.uk/dhoer>.

[21] Note that none of the following search functions are case-sensitive; identical results were obtained when using capitalisation.

[22] This is a collection of 31 images scanned from the holdings of the Roderic Bowen Library at the University of Wales, Trinity Saint David, Lampeter Campus as part of the Jisc/HEA OER Phase 1.

[23] The former does contain 'classical' but not 'studies' and neither appear in the latter. Changing the search term to 'classical' returns different results with the former coming second in the list and no sign of the latter. The same search was tested on a variety of machines using Chrome 'incognito' and Firefox 'private window' while logged out of any Google account to check that any prior search history recorded either by Google or the browser was not skewing the results.

24 By way of comparison, searching 'classical and studies' (in an attempt at a Boolean search) or locking the words 'classical' and 'studies' together as a single 'string' ('classical studies') returns no results.

25 Massive Open Online Course (MOOC): see for example the University of London International Programmes hosted on Coursera <http://www.londoninternational.ac.uk/coursera>. For more on this and the University of London's aim in using them, see their inaugural report (2013) on their MOOCs <http://www.londoninternational.ac.uk/sites/default/files/documents/mooc_report-2013.pdf>.

26 MIT OCW allows you to freely download a full course together with all the teaching material in a zip file (primarily XML and PDF files) which when unpacked replicates what would be found online. All this is accompanied by a Creative Commons Attribution-NonCommercial-ShareAlike U3.0 S licence   <http://creativecommons.org/licenses/by-nc-sa/3.0/us/deed.en_US>. Coursera is also free at point of use but asks that you sign up and follow the particular course of study. They act as a hosting service for partner institutions for which they charge a fee; for example, see the University of London MOOCs report (2013).

27 MIT OCW: <http://ocw.mit.edu/>; Coursera: <http://www.coursera.org/>.

28 This is not too unexpected as MIT does not have a Classics department, although they do have one for History <http://ocw.mit.edu/courses/find-by-department>.

29 Of particular note is that these results are significantly different from those obtained in preparation (September 2013) for the talk in Berlin which gave 3,970 hits for 'Classics' and 6,320 for 'Classical Studies' on MIT OCW. Similarly, at that time there were 3,770 hits on MIT for 'Latin', although again almost entirely Latin American studies. Either the available courses have been revised or more likely that the keyword searching has been adjusted in some way during the interim (see <http://hdl.handle.net/11858/00-1780-0000-0022-D53B-9#slides> for the slides from Berlin which have screenshots showing the figures).

30 Again with significantly different results on MIT OCW compared with September 2013 when there were 417; Coursera had only one.

31 Udacity: <http://www.udacity.com/>.

32 edX – "About us": <https://www.edx.org/about-us>. It is not clear from their documentation what the 'x' denotes other than 'extension' and the forming of the 'xConsortium' made up of the contributing partners.

33 FutureLearn partners <http://www.futurelearn.com/>.

34 Digital Classicist wiki > Tools > Educational Resources <http://wiki.digitalclassicist.org/Educational_Resources>.

35 See n. 4, above. With thanks to James Robson et al. at the Open University for help in pointing me to these and clarifying things.

[36] Open University Classical Studies: <http://www.open.ac.uk/Arts/classical-studies>.

[37] Creative Commons, Attribution- NonCommercial- ShareAlike <https://creativecommons.org/licenses/by-nc-sa/3.0>.

[38] Xpert, about: <http://www.nottingham.ac.uk/xpert/about.php>.

[39] It cannot, therefore, be fully indexing HumBox and Jorum as would be expected; all DHOER material has been uploaded to HumBox and the metadata for that harvested by Jorum.

[40] Oxford University Podcasts: <http://podcasts.ox.ac.uk/units/faculty-classics>.

[41] *The Stoa Consortium* - about this site: <http://www.stoa.org/about>.

[42] Indeed, the *Suda On Line* has just reached a major milestone with a now complete translation of all the entries <http://www.stoa.org/archives/1998>.

[43] EpiDoc update and release new TEI XML guidelines as they become available; version 8.19 was released on 31/07/2014 <http://sourceforge.net/p/epidoc/wiki/LatestRelease>.

[44] Ancient World Image Bank <http://isaw.nyu.edu//ancient-world-image-bank>.

[45] Creative Commons Attribution 2.0 Generic (CC BY 2.0) <http://creativecommons.org/licenses/by/2.0/deed.en>.

[46] Perseids <http://sites.tufts.edu/perseids>.

[47] Iliados <http://iliados.com>.

[48] Alpheios <http://alpheios.net>.

[49] Keegan 2008.

[50] McLoughlin 1999.

[51] Altarriba 2002.

[52] New Approaches to eLearning in Classics 1 & 2: the programme and abstracts are at <http://www.nottingham.ac.uk/classics/documents/classical-association/conference-booklet.pdf>.

[53] iLatin and eGreek - Ancient Languages and New Technology, February 1, 2014 <http://www.open.ac.uk/Arts/classical-studies/ilatin-egreek.shtml>.

[54] Hestia2 – Digital Pedagogies: <http://hestia.open.ac.uk/digital-pedagogy>.

[55] As well as direct government support in the USA, grants for OER development and research have been awarded by the Hewlett, Mellon and Gates Foundations; the 12th Annual Open Educational Conference, Vancouver BC, Canada: <http://openedconference.org/2015/>; OER15 <https://oer15.oerconf.org/>; OER14 <https://oer14.oerconf.org>.

[56] Jisc Open Education <https://www.jisc.ac.uk/rd/projects/open-education>.

[57] Open Education Working Group: Handbook <http://education.okfn.org/handbook>.

[58] LinkedUp Project: Linking Web and Data for Education <http://linkedup-project.eu>; Open Education Handbook Booksprint, London September 2013 <http://education.okfn.org/open-education-handbook-booksprint>.

[59] Video online at <http://hdl.handle.net/11858/00-1780-0000-0022-D53B-9>.

References

Altarriba, J. (2002). Bilingualism: Language, memory, and applied issues. In Lonner, Dinnel, Hayes & Sattler (Eds.), *Online Readings in Psychology and Culture* (Unit 4, Chapter 4), Center for Cross-Cultural Research, Western Washington University.

Bodard, G. & Mahony, S. (2014). Open Educational Resources and the Digital Classicist community. *Hestia2 Digital Pedagogy: transforming the interface between research and teaching*, Open University seminar, London.

Keegan, D. (2008). How Successful Is Mobile Learning? Available from <http://www.ericsson.com/res/thecompany/docs/programs/the_role_of_mobile_learning_in_european_education/eclo_ericsson_keegan.pdf>

Mahony, S. (2014). Open Educational Resources and their place in teaching and research for Classics. *Classical Association Annual Conference*, University of Nottingham.

Mahony, S. & Pierazzo, E. (2013). Teaching Skills or Teaching Methodology? In Hirsch (Ed.), *Digital Humanities Pedagogy: Practices, Principles and Politics*, Open Book Publishers, Cambridge.

Mahony, S. & Tiedau, U. (2013). Should the Digital Humanities be taking a lead in Open Access and Online Teaching Materials? *Digital Humanities 2013: Conference Abstracts*. University of Nebraska-Lincoln. Available from <http://dh2013.unl.edu/abstracts/ab-283.html>.

Mahony, S., Tiedau, U. & Sirmons, I. (2012). Open access and online teaching materials for digital humanities. In Warwick, Terras & Nyhan (Eds.) *Digital Humanities in Practice*. Facet Publishing, London.

McLoughlin, C. (1999). The implications of the research literature on learning styles for the design of instructional material. *Australian Journal of Educational Technology*, 1999, 15(3): 222–241.

Tiedau, U. & Mahony, S. (2011). Open Educational Resources for the Digital Humanities. *OER11*. Open Educational Resources Conference, Manchester.

Suber P. (2012). *Open Access*, MIT Press. Available from <https://mitpress.mit.edu/sites/default/files/9780262517638_Open_Access_PDF_Version.pdf>

Worton, M. (2009). *Review of Modern Foreign Languages provision in higher education in England*, HEFCE report. Available from <http://www.ucl.ac.uk/vice-provost/worton/myimages1/worton_report.pdf>

CHAPTER 3

Epigraphers and Encoders: Strategies for Teaching and Learning Digital Epigraphy

Gabriel Bodard* and Simona Stoyanova[†]

*University of London,
[†]King's College London

Abstract

This chapter will discuss the EpiDoc (TEI markup for epigraphy and papyrology) training workshops that have been run by colleagues from King's College London and elsewhere for the past decade. We shall explore some of the evolving approaches used and strategies taken in the teaching of digital encoding to an audience largely of classicists and historians. Prominent among the assertions of EpiDoc training is that 'encoding' is not alien to, in fact is directly analogous to, what philologists do when creating a formal, structured, arbitrarily expressed edition. We shall share some of the open teaching materials that have been made available, and consider pedagogical lessons learned in the light of EpiDoc practitioners who have progressed from training to running their own projects, as opposed to those who have learned EpiDoc directly from the published Guidelines or via the TEI (*cf. Dee, q.v.*). We shall also compare the teaching of EpiDoc to the teaching of epigraphy to students, and ask what the pedagogical approaches of both practices (which overlap, since many epigraphic modules now include a digital component, and very rarely teachers of epigraphy are treating EpiDoc as the native format for editing inscriptions) can offer to teachers and learners of both traditional and digital epigraphy.

How to cite this book chapter:
Bodard, G and Stoyanova, S. 2016. Epigraphers and Encoders: Strategies for Teaching and Learning Digital Epigraphy. In: Bodard, G & Romanello, M (eds.) *Digital Classics Outside the Echo-Chamber: Teaching, Knowledge Exchange & Public Engagement*, Pp. 51–68. London: Ubiquity Press. DOI: http://dx.doi.org/10.5334/bat.d. License: CC-BY 4.0.

1 Introduction

This chapter discusses training courses in EpiDoc (TEI markup for epigraphy and papyrology), past and present practices and ideas for future development, and the ways in which it intersects and could be better integrated with the teaching of epigraphy at university level. EpiDoc is one of the most important technical standards for the digital encoding of classics materials, and is the leading format for the structuring and publication of ancient text editions and associated object data. The EpiDoc community makes important contributions to the TEI schema and guidelines through collaborations, conference attendance and membership of technical bodies, and is closely linked to other digital classics communities including Pleiades and Pelagios (for ancient geography), and LAWDI (for ancient linked open data). As an example of the value and utility of digital approaches to classical and ancient historical research, EpiDoc is often taken as exemplary, sometimes to the exclusion of other subdisciplines. We feel it is important therefore to consider what workshops introducing students and scholars to EpiDoc do and indeed should focus on, and whether there is value in closer integration between the teaching of digital epigraphy (for example) and epigraphy *tout court*.

We shall first present a history of EpiDoc training, from the origins of the practice in project workshops in the early 2000s, to major developments with the Inscriptions of Aphrodisias and Integrating Digital Papyrology projects, before discussing the assumptions and methods embedded in training as it has been carried out over the last ten years. Student feedback will be drawn on to explore some possible models of either advanced or more focussed training programmes, and finally we shall discuss the impact of technical methods and skills on the teaching of epigraphy: itself a technical and methodological discipline sometimes dismissed as ancillary to the study of classics and ancient history (although its ancillarity is that of any research that creates resources on which other research builds). We shall conclude with some observations on the value of digital methods in teaching text editing and research.

2 History of EpiDoc Training

The EpiDoc Collaborative produces a set of guidelines, schema and related tools for the encoding of epigraphic and other ancient text editions in TEI XML. The first EpiDoc Guidelines, published in 2000, arose jointly from work on Latin inscriptions by scholars at the University of North Carolina, and from work by the EAGLE Commission of the Association Internationale d'Epigraphie Grecque et Latine.[1] Since then, many major online editions of inscriptions have been published using EpiDoc, including the Inscriptions of Aphrodisias, Vindolanda Tablets Online, US Epigraphy Project, Inscriptions of Roman Tripolitania, Pandektis (Upper Macedonia, Aegean Thrace and Achaia), Roman Inscriptions of Britain, and now massive corpora such as the Duke Databank of Documentary Papyri, Datenbank zur jüdischen Grabsteinepigraphik and the EAGLE Europeana Project, make use of EpiDoc in their workflow.[2]

In the meantime there were two major phases in the development of EpiDoc tools and documentation, under the funded Inscriptions of Aphrodisias and Integrating Digital Papyrology projects respectively.

Inscriptions of Aphrodisias was a major AHRC project at King's College London funded for three years from 2004–2007, and preceded by the small pilot project that led the *Aphrodisias in Late Antiquity* digital publication. In the course of this project, ten international workshops were held, which brought together scholars and practitioners to discuss EpiDoc and the intersections between epigraphic scholarship and archaeology, prosopography, lexicography, numismatics, Byzantine materials and other topics.[3] These workshops were also the venue for significant practical work on tools such as the EpiDoc Example XSLT and the EpiDoc Guidelines, which reached a state of stability of usefulness for public consumption during this process.[4]

Integrating Digital Papyrology was a Mellon-funded project involving a consortium of institutions, led by Duke University, between 2008–2011. This project produced several major new tools (especially the open source Papyrological Navigator the SoSOL collaborative editing platform[5]), and also funded several development and training workshops which further enhanced the EpiDoc Guidelines and training schedule.

Today, an average of two to three times per year, a week-long EpiDoc training workshop is held for trained epigraphists and papyrologists with little to no background in digital skills.[6] These workshops, run in London and elsewhere, regularly accommodate 20 or so participants (at all levels from undergraduate students to professionals and professors) and are always over-subscribed, sometimes with 50% or more of the applicants having to be turned away due to lack of space. These week-long events allow time for a basic introduction to XML, detailed discussion of epigraphic features (including text and edition structure) rendered in TEI, plenty of unstructured 'workshop' time and introduction to tools such as the Papyrological Editor and Example Stylesheets for rendering HTML editions.

Although these workshops began in an *ad hoc* context in London in the early 2000s, they were first funded during the Inscriptions of Aphrodisias project, and underwent a significant evolution—including the addition of training in the use of SoSOL—during Integrating Digital Papyrology. These workshops are now held in London, Bologna, Rome, Lyon, Sofia and elsewhere fairly regularly, and are often supplemented by shorter, one- or two-day training events attached to discipline conferences or other project meetings.

3 What is Taught in EpiDoc Training

The usual target audience consists of Classical epigraphers and papyrologists with traditional Classics background and little or no digital skills. We assume the knowledge of either Greek or Latin, if not both, and familiarity with the Leiden conventions; a willingness to learn computing methods and an understanding of the need for digital publication is perhaps implied by attendance at the workshops in the first place. In the last few years there has been a rise of interest in EpiDoc from specialists in other epigraphies: Ogham, Campa, Mayan, Arabic,[7] and so the assumption of familiarity with classical languages should not be restricted to Greek and Latin.

Though the training is chiefly targeted at classical epigraphers, the demographics of the students vary widely. Many of the students are starting work on epigraphic projects which include a digital component, if not a complete digital publication. They tend to have need of immediate and more detailed training. Another distinct group are students and researchers who have more general interest and curiosity about TEI and EpiDoc. Others attend the workshop to acquire basic encoding skills to boost their CVs, which could then help them to find their way into a project. A usually smaller part of the students are technical support specialists and developers, who have also started working on a digital humanities/digital epigraphy project and would like to know what they will be expected to deliver, what technologies and methodologies have been used and are recommended. A fifth group are people from various disciplines with more general interest in TEI and digital humanities.

At the beginning of the training we make clear the limits of the programme: we will show the students how to transform their XML documents into HTML using the generic *EpiDoc Example Stylesheets*, but will not aim to teach any XSLT coding. It would be unrealistic to include an XSLT tutorial in a week-long workshop targeted at people with little or no technical skills. By the end of the week they understand the principles of XML and can encode more or less easily, but XSLT would require more experience with XML and HTML, which we cannot expect and cannot teach in this time frame.

Another subject we cannot teach at any length is project management. Many of our students are involved or just about to be involved in a project; we will give them the principles of encoding and publishing a corpus in EpiDoc, but we cannot devote much discussion to setting up and managing an entire project, any more than we could cover every possible element of a digital epigraphic edition. While it is by no means obvious to all participants that project management is a key requirement for any digital and especially collaborative work, this issue is a reminder that ongoing support and training is sorely needed, far beyond a few days basic training.

We begin with the assertion that the Leiden conventions are as much a markup language—arbitrary, well-defined, unambiguous—as XML, only designed for a human reader. This perhaps counter-intuitive theoretical point is driven home in our introduction to XML, where an example of replacing human-facing with machine-readable markup is shown. The students are then introduced to the *EpiDoc Guidelines* and a pair of 'Cheatsheets', which take the form of concise tables listing the most frequently needed descriptive features and Leiden sigla, respectively, against their TEI equivalents.[8] At this stage the students begin to practise usually on their own material. It proves more useful and stimulating for them to do exercises rather than listen to presentations/lectures. This allows them to familiarise themselves with the Oxygen XML Editor,[9] the XML syntax and the principles of EpiDoc, and to feel more comfortable about encoding, before going into too much detail. After they have done basic encoding on a few texts, they are shown how to perform an XSL transformation to see their texts in human-readable HTML and double-check their encoding—a crucial step in understanding the relationship between digital encoding and multiple outputs.

Until recently the practice was to first introduce the students to the more detailed text markup, and afterwards to the monument description markup, with the presumption that the majority of epigraphers are primarily interested in the text of their inscriptions, and it also logically followed the general introduction and initial exercises. During the 2014 London training workshop the instructors decided to change this sequence and start with an overview of an entire document structure, followed by the monument description part of the publication. The detailed text markup came at the end, after some exercises only on the supporting information. This strategy proved to be clearer and more comprehensible to the students. It shows immediately that the structure of an EpiDoc document is exactly the same as the structure of a traditional epigraphic publication. This gives the students better understanding of the structure of the XML file and makes their work easier and more efficient.

After the students have practiced encoding whole publications with both supporting information and text, they are then introduced to the principles of lemmatizing and indexing in EpiDoc—a crucial point illustrating that the rigorous intellectual effort of indexing in a tradition project is changed in the digital process, but not replaced by an automated process. This part of the training usually comes at the end, because it requires some understanding of certain elements and their application. Also, this structure follows the workflow of an epigraphic project, where the indices, tables of contents, lists of lemmata etc. are produced at the end of the project from the encoded XML files.

In the second half of the training workshop the students are introduced to the *Papyrological Editor* online editing platform, which is used to enter, edit and translate texts from papyrological collections.[10] The *Papyrological Editor* runs on a tags-free editing interface called SoSOL, in which users enter the punctuation and Leiden sigla largely in the form they are used to from traditional editing, with a few innovative sigla (dubbed 'Leiden+') to represent more features in the underlying XML. While SoSOL effectively allows the editing of EpiDoc

XML via an interface in which tags are invisible, the platform also allows editing directly in XML, and it is worth mentioning that some students claim to prefer working in the XML view of SoSOL, as it allows them more control and flexibility over the encoding, and they find it more transparent than Leiden+.

Other models of EpiDoc training in which we have been involved include: (i) short, one- or two-day workshops attached to conferences, (ii) specific training of students, interns and research assistants and (iii) EpiDoc training re-cast for students as part of digital humanities or other courses. These programmes have been useful in developing methods and materials for the more thorough workshops, and we shall mention some of the significant points here.

(i) Preconference workshops on EpiDoc have been held most recently at the TEI annual conference in Rome in 2013, and the Digital Humanities conference in Lausanne in 2014. These provide a combination of very basic introduction to XML and the EpiDoc mapping of Leiden and conventional editions to TEI, an opportunity to discuss a range of other issues around digital publication of epigraphy and papyrology, such as conversion tools or linked open data, and feedback from the students and users in general on what training, tools or other materials are most wanted from the EpiDoc community. These sessions have been a very useful exercise in giving accelerated introductions to both practical and theoretical concepts, and have been an especially valuable sounding-board for how EpiDoc can be useful outside of the circle of the most active users and developers.

(ii) Student interns and research assistants on EpiDoc-based projects (especially many of those at King's College London) have often been offered an intensive XML and EpiDoc training session over the course of an hour or two. Students are then immediately given the opportunity to put their training into practice, and they familiarise themselves with different aspects of the use of EpiDoc on the job. The fact that they are working under supervision, on already existing projects with access to sample files and documentation, facilitates a rather quick induction and good progress in XML and other skills. The importance of hands-on experience with real materials, and preferably involving texts and records that the student will continue to work on, is highlighted by the success of these events. We have regularly asked students at workshops to bring texts with them so we can try to build on this advantage.

(iii) One of the formats we have taught was a 90-minute class within an MA course on Digital Scholarly Editing and Textual Criticism at the University of Leipzig. The majority of the students were master students in Computer Science, and the humanists were non-epigraphers from different disciplines: Classics, Egyptology, Byzantine Studies, Near-Eastern Studies, Translation and Reception Studies and Linguistics. In this case the class had to be balanced between the very different skills and needs of the students. The computer scientists required as much humanities understanding as the humanists XML training. The goal of the class was to demonstrate the dire need of efficient communication between humanists and computer scientists, without which a successful DH project is impossible. After a general introduction to EpiDoc and a live demonstration of encoding an inscription, the instructor drew upon the strengths of each group and specialty represented in the class, which resulted in achieving the desired dialogue and subsequent collaboration between the representatives of these disciplines.

The interdisciplinarity and wide range of interests at these shorter events have added to the richness of the EpiDoc environment, and in particular provided valuable feedback not only on the training itself, but on EpiDoc tools and other materials themselves.

At most training workshops, whether a full week or the half-day introduction, we try to make time for a feedback session where we ask all participants to consider:

1. what they came here expecting to learn, and whether their expectations were satisfied;
2. to what extent EpiDoc is applicable to the material or project they are working on (particularly important in the case of those studying non-classical epigraphies or other texts);
3. what more they would like to have learned, either in the current workshop or, more speculatively, in a more advanced training event in the future.

These prompts generally lead to in-depth discussion among the students, as well as questions directed at the trainers, and as such helps to bring out a general sense of the attendees' satisfaction with the workshop as a whole. The fruitfulness of these discussions, along with many students' professed need for further feedback on their markup exercises, led the London trainers to set up an EpiDoc Workshop blog at which students can continue these discussions or ask for feedback on XML examples in a more convivial and less-public environment than the Markup discussion list.[11]

Feedback on the current workshop varies from suggestions about the content of training materials, to requests for more exercises, more in-class demonstrations or more structured presentations. These vary from group to group, but are generally very useful in helping to improve the workshops. Comments on both structure and content of the training, on balance between lectures and practice highlight not only the strengths of a current workshop, but also provide coverage of needs, some of which, inevitably, were not met. Responses to the second question have led to some discussion of the value of a workshop directed specifically at epigraphers of non-alphabetic languages (Mayan, Egyptian, Linear A/B, Chinese) and non-linear scripts; such a workshop would be extremely interesting, as the consensus has suggested that while EpiDoc handles such epigraphies reasonably well, some customization is needed in the areas of palaeography, linking of glyphs to transcriptions, rendering of languages for which Leiden is not appropriate, and handling of dialects and non-Unicode scripts.

The most interesting question is invariably the third, to which there is regularly a strongly expressed desire for more advanced training in the future. Participants often request further introduction to XSLT, the scripting language used to transform EpiDoc XML to web or print editions, which they encounter, but are not required to understand, in the form of the EpiDoc Example Stylesheets[12] used to render in HTML, and therefore to some extent sanity test their markup exercises. Other suggestions include: more advanced XML training, such as the encoding of authority lists, bibliographical concordances, prosopographies, and using them to link between texts and editions; more introduction to Linked Open Data for the ancient world, and ways in which EpiDoc editions can link into the LAWD[13] network; hands-on 'hackfest' events, at which participants take on some task, such as converting a legacy dataset to standards-compliant EpiDoc, building something from an open access EpiDoc corpus, or making and exploiting connections between multiple epigraphic or papyrological datasets; project management information, how to set up, build, run and publish an EpiDoc corpus from the top level: who to hire, who to collaborate with, and what skills to acquire.

4 Possible Future Models for Teaching EpiDoc

Participant feedback at the end of EpiDoc workshops is one source of ideas for future models of more advanced or more specialized training events. We also have our own ambitions for the development of EpiDoc, tooling and guidance, and ways in which training workshops fit into the workflows of our own projects, both as testing grounds for methods and as a form of essential public engagement and community benefit from often publicly funded work. (These are the grounds on which both the Aphrodisias and IDP projects, and now the EAGLE Europeana Network, contributed to the EpiDoc community, after all.) We shall discuss now some of the ways in which we would like to see EpiDoc training develop in the future. Some of these might require further (funded) development work before becoming possible, but are worth considering in any case.

At present most projects handle authority lists and controlled vocabularies (e.g. names for types of stone or places of archaeological finding) in idiosyncratic ways, either linking to existing typologies and ontologies or, more often, minting their own. Discussion is ongoing whether to include more guidance on specific vocabularies within the EpiDoc Guidelines, but there is no consistency or consensus on how to achieve it. One step in this direction might be to encourage newcomers to EpiDoc, in the form of attendees at training workshops, to follow the examples of existing practice in generating and handling of controlled vocabularies, bibliographies, person- and place-lists, and the indices, concordances, prosopographies and gazetteers that are built upon them. A workshop in this area might focus on a deeper discussion of the principles and implications, recommended encoding and authorities, and give examples from existing projects, both as good practice and as cases where previous usage could be improved.

There has been enthusiasm for a more in-depth introduction to Linked Open Data (LOD) in the context of digital epigraphic training. Especially in the context of the EAGLE Europeana Network, one could well imagine a workshop that introduced both EpiDoc and LOD in tandem; in fact a side effect of this sort of event might be further work on integrating LOD advice and recommendations in the EpiDoc Guidelines themselves. Since one use case of LOD is normalizing to authority lists via RDF, a brief introduction to the topic as part of the above-mentioned vocabularies and authorities workshop is also a possibility, albeit less depth would be possible in that context.

Another technique that would be valuable to address in the process of discussing authority lists, and especially prosopographical and geographical information, is Named Entity Recognition (NER), the process of identifying (perhaps with computer assistance) names of people or places. In a corpus of any size, this is normally a part of the process of linking from instances of names to the authority list that serves to disambiguate and index them. There are some useful techniques involving relatively accessible tools, pioneered for example by the Trismegistos Project, and open source tools such as Recogito, coming out of the Pelagios project and related work.[14] We have yet to fully integrate any of this activity into the workflow of the epigrapher or papyrologist, however, and further training in this area would doubtless result in better integration with EpiDoc guidance, and quite possibly new project collaborations.

Since the workshops offer basic XML training, a common request for a possible follow-up workshop is further training in XSLT and XPath, tools for the transformation of semantic XML data into online and other publications. After a demonstration of transformations with the EpiDoc example stylesheets, many students have suggested that this would be a more useful next step, whereas they could study more advanced XML and acquire further EpiDoc skills independently.

One key reason we have not implemented this in past training is that XSLT is not an EpiDoc- or even TEI-specific skill. We are unlikely to fit any significant XSLT component into a four-day EpiDoc workshop, and even a dedicated, week-long XSLT course would only scratch the surface, it might be more efficient for those students with a need or desire to study XSLT (which will by no means be all epigraphers), to find a more generic XSLT training programme, perhaps closer to their home institution or even online, or self-study using a book.[15] The knowledge of XML they acquire is usually enough to give them a good start in an XSLT course.

One more suggested topic of advanced training was discussion of project management issues and the combination of technical and administrative questions around how to assemble all of the components of a digital corpus into a polished and dynamic online publication. It might be useful to discuss the range of technical and other skills required for a project of this scale, advice on costing the funding bid realistically, identifying user needs and modelling outcomes, and other issues of collaboration. Most of these questions are not specific to an epigraphic or papyrological project, of course, although the answers will be specific to any individual project.

One way to incorporate both programming and project management training into an EpiDoc training context is under development with a project to build an EpiDoc-specific form of the Kiln XML publishing infrastructure, under the title EpiDoc Front-End Services (EFES).[16] This tool is envisioned as a delivery, search and browse platform that can be set up and customized for an individual EpiDoc XML-based project with only minimal training and technical skill on the part of a project team. The authors of EFES plan to offer advanced, follow-up training workshops for students already familiar with EpiDoc, but lacking further technical skills, with a view to empowering them to create and manage all stages of their digital publication, from modelling to indexing to publishing online. It remains to be seen how successful this training will be.

5 Teaching EpiDoc/Teaching Epigraphy

EpiDoc has mostly been taught to students or scholars who already have a background in epigraphy or papyrology (or at least in classical languages and the rudiments of text editing). There have been students at EpiDoc workshops who come from a technical discipline, or a different branch of the digital humanities, and need to gain some understanding of epigraphy as they go along, but this is less usual. As a result, EpiDoc training has tended to focus on how digitally to express and exploit those intellectual distinctions that we already understand from our grounding in the classics.

Conversely, when epigraphy is taught at university level, usually as a postgraduate module or doctoral methods seminar in ancient history, the vast majority of both lecturers and students lack any knowledge of or even interest in digital humanities methods or principles—even if they have not been actively dissuaded by sceptical mentors. With the possible exception of the use of invaluable online databases for search purposes, epigraphy is often taught today in a way that would not have surprised or dismayed a student of one hundred years ago: texts are read (from autopsy or photographs, or even paper impressions known as 'squeezes'), a preliminary transcription may well be made by hand, editorial conventions, apparatus criticus and commentary are created with a view to printing for reading by scholars knowledgeable in the same conventions, and little thought is given to any afterlife of the publication, since paper publications after all have rather predictable destinations.

By way of analogy, epigraphy and the texts of inscriptions are sometimes also used as a supplementary topic in the teaching of other subjects; most obviously in an advanced graduate history programme, but also in elementary language teaching. Because of the relatively simple language and formulaic nature of many inscriptions, instructors sometimes use inscriptions (with or without introducing the texts as objects or giving the added challenge of deciphering original letters and scripta continua) to give students the sense of connection to the surviving writings of ancient scribes themselves.[17] As with the occasional references to technology as an ancillary topic in epigraphy classes, we do not know of any cases in which ancient languages are taught entirely or primarily from epigraphic sources, or in which epigraphic methods are intrinsic to the language course.

Although there have been some experiments in teaching an introduction to epigraphy and digital editing methods in tandem, these are as yet a rarity, and so while they are worth briefly mentioning here, for this section we shall discuss the more common situation which is that digital skills and epigraphic practice are taught in separate circumstances, to distinct audiences, and by lecturers who seldom overlap.

One of the first experiments for integrating digital epigraphy training in a traditional epigraphy class was conducted by Monica Berti in 2010 and 2013 at Tufts University.[18] At the end of her Latin epigraphy module, four classes were devoted to introducing the principles and best practices of digital epigraphy. Students were given a brief training in EpiDoc and practised with texts from the Epigraphic Database Roma.[19] Another project she was involved with was the 2011 epigraphy and archaeology programme 'The Stones of Ancient Latium',[20] held in Italy, which provided students with EpiDoc training alongside the teaching of epigraphy in museums and in the field.

As discussed above, the Digital Philology masters module at Leipzig has recently begun bringing together students with backgrounds in the humanities and informatics with a view to teaching traditional and digital encoding of ancient texts as a single skill-set, fostering the levels of collaboration and interdisciplinarity necessary for work in this area, and bringing the technical and disciplinary values of both communities to bear on a single problem.[21] In a separate exercise, colleagues in Classics and the university library at Duke University in 2015 began teaching an epigraphy seminar to graduate students in Classics there, in which the principles of digital editing, EpiDoc encoding and the SoSOL interface are presented not as a new, special or unusual way to encode epigraphic editions, but simply as an integral part of the epigrapher's toolkit, much as paper and ink, or a word processor and Greek font are presented in most traditional epigraphy classes.[22]

Professors of ancient history at Bologna University, where EpiDoc workshops have been taught regularly for several years, regularly involve students of epigraphy in encoding EpiDoc editions both of project texts and their own coursework.[23] Similarly, the 2015 Roman epigraphy graduate seminar at Brown University for the first time did not include separate training in and preparation of Leiden editions, but students were taught EpiDoc editing from scratch, using the homegrown US Epigraphy Project[24] XML template with the basic metadata filled in according to the USEP supporting information structure. In addition to the EpiDoc training provided in class, there were also several lab open sessions, as well as more general discussion of EpiDoc and digital epigraphy issues during the seminar.[25] Personal sources inform us that Oxford is planning a similar introduction to EpiDoc as part of Greek and Latin epigraphy training in the near future, but there is no public record of this programme as yet.

In practice, however, EpiDoc training and the teaching of epigraphy are usually distinct operations, and for the remainder of this chapter we shall describe the world in which there is seldom significant overlap between the two. The parallels in the way they are taught are nevertheless striking, albeit unsurprising when we consider the technical, arguably ancillary, nature of the epigraphic discipline itself.

As we lay out in Table 1 below, the introductory sessions in a typical epigraphic seminar follow a very similar structure to the content of an EpiDoc workshop. The epigraphy lecturer assumes that students come to their class with advanced knowledge of Greek and Latin, but is prepared to teach the technicalities and disciplinary habits of epigraphic practice from the very beginning. Students are provided with reference materials in the form of standard epigraphic handbooks, and usually customized summaries of important conventions such as the Leiden sigla and other explanations of the form and appearance of an edition. The core of the teaching of epigraphy is then via practice; students read as many texts as possible in the time available, produce their own transcriptions and commentaries, exercising the skills acquired under the supervision of the tutor.

Typically in an epigraphy course as taught in a classics or ancient history department, there may be one class devoted to introducing the students to digital resources. They are shown various online databases of texts and images, search and reference tools, concordances. They are likely to learn how to use these resources from a user's point of view, with little or no attention paid to the underlying infrastructures, limiting the understanding and insight into

Teaching EpiDoc	Teaching epigraphy
Assume epigraphic/classical knowledge	Assume Greek and Latin
Introduce technology	Introduce epigraphic practice
Give reference materials (Guidelines) and customized summary of reference (Cheatsheets)	Give reference materials (handbooks) and customized summary of reference (Leiden conventions)
Give lots of exercises and practice	Give lots of exercises and practice

Table 1: Comparison of Teaching EpiDoc with Teaching Epigraphy.

the process of creating a digital resource (which insight, it should not need explaining, would be very valuable to students and indeed scholars who need to know how to assess the unique value and shortcomings of the tools of their trade).

Often a guest lecturer from outside the classics department may be invited to give such a class at the end of term, further highlighting the impression that this is somehow 'special', outside the curriculum, less academic and worthy of attention from the serious classicist. On the other hand the digital humanities specialist may take the opportunity to use such a class to show the students the process of digital creation and research, in the way that a traditional epigrapher might not, via for example an exercise in deciding which features of an epigraphic transcription and edition are worth encoding digitally and exploiting through transformation, indexing or search.

In a similar way, some epigraphy courses have included one or two classes dedicated to learning EpiDoc encoding, as in the classes at Tufts, described above. The principles and benefits of an electronic publication are explained, as well as a realistic summary of the additional training needed. The focus of such a class is not so much an intensive EpiDoc training, but rather demonstrating that structured markup is nothing more than structured thinking about data. The structure of an XML document reflects the structure of an epigraphic edition. Following the strict hierarchy of XML forces one to better organise one's thoughts, approach towards, and work on an epigraphic document. We have found that it is highly beneficial to be able to process and produce information in a well structured and clearer way, even if the students do not show interest in further DH training.

The introduction to digital editing and electronic publishing also stresses the importance of scientific attribution, credit and responsibility. In a humanities publication more often than not some aspects of the decision making process are left fuzzy and not very visible. Since an electronic publication implies making a text machine actionable, all decisions (or uncertainties about a decision) have to be explicitly expressed, visible, recording the evidence which lead to them and pointing to the person responsible for each decision. In this way, proper attribution and credit can be given, as well as a clear statement of responsibility and degree of certainty.

These principles which are widely applied to digital publications, lead to a more 'scientific' approach to research and publication. Clear, explicit statements and visible attribution have long been features more characteristic of publications in the natural sciences, than in the humanities. In digital humanities, however, they are the norm. Thus, for the traditionally trained epigrapher (classicist, humanist) an EpiDoc or a more general DH training leaves the sense of a distinct change of methodology. This change, however, is usually perceived as an improvement, the 'scientific' methodology adding more detail and nuances to the publication, though sometimes it can leave an uncomfortable feeling of not being allowed any fuzziness.

6 Conclusions and Recommendations

The parallels between the methods and outcomes in the teaching of EpiDoc, as detailed in this chapter, and the teaching of traditional documentary disciplines such as epigraphy, lead to some interesting observations. Both are highly technical sets of skills, but involve deeply interpretive materials, require a balance of precision and flexibility, and engage with a community of practice and reference materials. As we have observed, teaching the two skill sets in parallel would bring tangible benefits to students. And although the uni-disciplinary nature of most university degree modules seems to limit the practicality of such a unified approach at the moment.

There are a number of benefits that come with EpiDoc training, aside from simply being able to do EpiDoc. Even if students do not go on to work on an EpiDoc-based project, they have acquired a set of valuable transferable skills beyond the realm of digital epigraphy: structured way of thinking about and producing data, management of complex sets of information and collaborative project work. One such crucial skill in the realm of research, is approaching one's subject of study (in our case epigraphy) from outside one's comfort zone, being able to look, question and explore it from different perspectives based on different bases, needs and project objectives. For instance, digital encoding of data and semantics often involves the disambiguation of concepts that prose descriptions express in a fuzzy way—this need to disambiguate is not always comfortable: scholars complain of 'spurious exactitude'[26] when asked to express 'early fourth century' as a figure, for example. The attention this forces us to pay to our own writing can only be valuable, however.

Some of the approaches to EpiDoc training, and in particular the use of SoSOL for transcribing and editing papyrological editions in the Duke Databank or annotating photographs and translations in Perseids and the EAGLE Europeana Project, walk the frontier between traditional practice-based teaching and crowdsourcing. Trevor Owens has argued that the leveraging of social information and enthusiasm often known as crowdsourcing is at its best when it benefits the contributors both by imparting research skills and feeding a thirst for discovery.[27] We would go further and suggest that the educational and public engagement benefits of crowdsourcing activities are more significant and important than the content creation or enrichment achieved by the process.

Students of digital epigraphy learn to 'look under the hood' of the digital tools they use and even more importantly, to understand the reasoning behind the construction and design and the functionality, of these tools. This practice in turn encourages them to think about possible methods to apply in their own research, while assessing the suitability and relevance of the digital humanities methodologies to their own field.

Digital epigraphy also provides valuable lessons for the teaching and studying of digital humanities. Practice-based learning, including working with tools in a classroom lab, lies at the base of much digital humanities study; similarly in epigraphy, students create epigraphic editions as part of the learning process. Introducing and practicing the principles and best practices of digital humanities reasoning and publishing gives the students a number of transferable skills applicable above and beyond the field of epigraphy, Classics and the humanities in general. As such, the field of digital humanities is often seen as a bridging discipline or a bridge between disciplines, considering its inherent need for interdisciplinarity.

Our observations in this chapter are offered by way of highlighting the apparent differences between the teaching and learning of two skill sets (digital editing and publication *versus* autopsy-based philology) to argue for bringing the disciplines together. As well as hoping that there are lessons for both groups of educators in the other's area, we believe that just as the philologist learns by applying digital methods to her traditional practice, so students from both areas will gain a deeper understanding of their discipline by studying the traditional and digital methodologies side-by-side, or rather, as a neatly dovetailed unit. We have used the example of epigraphy and digital epigraphy to make this case here, but we believe the conclusions stand across a much larger array of digital classics and even philology as a whole.

Acknowledgements

The authors would like to thank the editors, the publishers' peer reviewers, and also Pietro Liuzzo, Franco Luciani and Jonathan Prag for constructive feedback on the contents of this chapter.

Notes

1. See 'About EpiDoc' at <http://epidoc.sf.net/>; fuller history at Cayless & Roueché 2009 ('1.3 EpiDoc') and Bodard 2010, pp. 101–4; On the EAGLE commission, see Panciera 1999.
2. EpiDoc projects listed and described at <https://wiki.digitalclassicist.org/Category:EpiDoc>.
3. Inscriptions of Aphrodisias: 'Calendar', <http://www.insaph.kcl.ac.uk/project/calendar/index.html>.
4. Bodard 2008, § 4.
5. Esp. Baumann 2013; cf. Sosin 2010. Papyrological Navigator, <http://papyri.info/>; SoSOL ('The Son of Suda-Online'), <http://github.com/papyri/sosol>.
6. 'EpiDoc Summer School', <http://wiki.digitalclassicist.org/EpiDoc_Summer_School>.
7. Ogham in 3D <ogham.celt.dias.ie/>; Corpus of the Inscriptions of Campā <http://isaw.nyu.edu/publications/inscriptions/campa/>;   Textdatenbank und Wörterbuch des Klassischen Maya <http://www.iae.uni-bonn.de/

forschung/forschungsprojekte/laufende-projekte/idiom-dictionary-of-classic-mayan>; Digital Archive for the Study of pre-Islamic Arabian Inscriptions <http://www.dasiproject.eu/>.

[8] Guidelines, see Elliott, Bodard et al. 2007-; Cheatsheets, see Bodard 2006–2015 and Bodard & Stoyanova 2014.

[9] Oxygen XML Editor, <http://oxygenxml.com/>, while a commercial tool, is considered to be so rich in features, including XSLT transformation, and available under a reasonable education license, that it is currently without competitor among the free offerings available. Students often use a free 30-day demo version, and of course free XML tools are available for projects for whom even the modest $99 cost is a barrier.

[10] Papyrological Editor, <http://papyri.info/editor>; on PE and SoSOL, see Baumann 2013.

[11] EpiDoc Workshop Blog: <http://epidocworkshop.blogspot.com/>.

[12] EpiDoc Example Stylesheets, see Elliott, Au et al.

[13] On the Linked Ancient World Data (LAWD) initiative, see <http://lawd.info/> and <http://wiki.digitalclassicist.org/Category:LAWDI>.

[14] On Trismegistos NER, see Depauw & Van Beek 2009; Recogito, see Simon, Barker, et al. 2013–2015.

[15] E.g. Tennison 2005, or W3Schools online XSLT tutorial at <http://w3schools.com/xsl>.

[16] *Kiln*, see Vieira, Norrish, et al. 2011–2015; EFES under development at <https://github.com/EpiDoc/EFES>.

[17] See e.g. LaFleur 2010; similar ideas proposed by Rubenstein 2003; Carpenter 2006; cf. Parisinou & Shipley 2004.

[18] Syllabus, Berti 2010.

[19] Epigraphic Database Roma. <http://www.edr-edr.it/>.

[20] Berti & Harrington 2011.

[21] Syllabus, Berti 2014.

[22] Sosin, Baumann & Cayless 2015.

[23] Bencivenni & Agrimoni 2014.

[24] US Epigraphy Project: <http://usepigraphy.brown.edu/>.

[25] Bodel & Mylonas 2015.

[26] Tarte 2011.

[27] Owens 2012.

References

Baumann, R. (2013). The Son of Suda On-Line. In Dunn & Mahony (Eds.) *The Digital Classicist 2013* (pp. 91–106). Bulletin of the Institute of Classical Studies supplement 122, London: Institute of Classical Studies, University of London.

Bencivenni, A. & Agrimonti, S. (2014). The IGCyr Project: Encoding Codes, Translating Rules, Communicating Stones in Ptolemaic Cyrene and in Contemporary Bologna. In Orlandi et al. (Eds.) *Information Technologies for Epigraphy and Cultural Heritage* (pp. 351–368). Collana Convegni 26, Roma: Sapienza Università Editrice. Retrieved from http://www.eagle-network.eu/wp-content/uploads/2015/01/Paris-Conference-Proceedings.pdf

Berti, M. (2010). Latin Epigraphy, Syllabus, Fall 2010. Tufts University. Retrieved from http://www.monicaberti.com/wp-content/uploads/2015/09/Latin_Epigraphy_Syllabus_2010.pdf

Berti, M. (2014). Module: Digital Scholarly Editing and Textual Criticism 1 (DH.DSE-1). University of Leipzig. Retrieved from http://www.dh.uni-leipzig.de/wo/courses/winter-semester-2014/module-digital-scholarly-editing-and-textual-criticism-winter-semester-20142015/

Berti, M. & Harrington, J.M. (2011). The Stones of Ancient Latium. Inscriptions and Archaeological Remains, and the Geographic Contexts of Latium Vetus. Retrieved from http://sites.tufts.edu/latiumvetus/

Bodard, G. (2006–2015). *EpiDoc/Leiden Cheatsheet*. Retrieved from https://sourceforge.net/p/epidoc/code/HEAD/tree/trunk/guidelines/msword/cheatsheet.doc

Bodard, G. (2008). The Inscriptions of Aphrodisias as electronic publication: A user's perspective and a proposed paradigm. *Digital Medievalist* 4. Retrieved from http://digitalmedievalist.org/journal/4/bodard/

Bodard, G. (2010). EpiDoc: Epigraphic Documents in XML for Publication and Interchange. In F. Feraudi-Gruénais (Ed.), *Latin On Stone: epigraphic research and electronic archives* (pp. 1–118). Plymouth: Lexington Books.

Bodard, G. & Stoyanova, S. (2014). *EpiDoc Structure Cheatsheet*. Retrieved from https://sourceforge.net/p/epidoc/code/HEAD/tree/ trunk/guidelines/msword/structure-cheatsheet.docx

Bodel, J. & Mylonas, E. (2015). Epigraphy Seminar: Syllabus. Brown University. Retrieved from<http://cds.library.brown.edu/projects/usepigraphy/Latin Epigraphy2014/RomEpig2014-Syllabus.pdf>

Carpenter, B. (2006) MAGISTER DISCIPVLIS H F: Using Funerary Epigraphy with Intermediate Students of Latin. *CPL Online* 3.1. Retrieved from http://www.camws.org/cpl/cplonline/files/Carpentercplonline.pdf

Cayless, H., Roueché, C., Bodard, G. & Elliott, T. (2009) Epigraphy in 2017. *Digital Humanities Quarterly* 3.1. Retrieved from http://digitalhumanities.org/dhq/vol/3/1/000030/000030.html

Depauw, M. & Van Beek, B. (2009). People in Greek Documentary Papyri. First Results of a Research Project. *Journal of Juristic Papyrology* 39: 31–47.

Elliott, T., Au, Z., Bodard, G., Cayless, H., Lanz, C., Lawrence, K.F., Vanderbilt, S., Viglianti, R. et al. (2008). *EpiDoc Example Stylesheets* (version 8). Retrieved from https://sourceforge.net/p/epidoc/wiki/Stylesheets/

Elliott, T., Bodard, G., Mylonas, E., Stoyanova, S., Tupman, C., Vanderbilt, S. et al. (2007). *EpiDoc Guidelines: Ancient documents in TEI XML* (Version 8). Retrieved from http://www.stoa.org/epidoc/gl/latest/

Fernando-Luis, Á., García-Barriocanal, E. & Joaquín-L. G. (2010). Sharing Epigraphic Information as Linked Data. In Sanchez-Alonso & Athanasiadis (Eds.), Metadata and semantic research (pp. 222–234) Heidelberg: Springer.

Flanders, J. & Roueché, C. (2005). Introduction for Epigraphers. *EpiDoc Guidelines.* Retrieved from http://www.stoa.org/epidoc/gl/latest/intro-eps.html

LaFleur, R. A. (2010). *Scribblers, Sculptors, and Scribes: A Companion to Wheelock's Latin and Other Introductory Textbooks.* New York: HarperCollins.

Owens, T. (2012). The Crowd and the Library. Series of 4 blog posts. Retrieved from http://www.trevorowens.org/2012/05/the-crowd-and-the-library/

Panciera, S. (1999). Nouvelles de l'AIEGL 1999. *Epigraphica* 61: 311–313. Retrieved from http://www.eagle-eagle.it/Italiano/Documenti/Document2_it.html

Parisinou, E. & Shipley, G. (2004). *Hellenizein: A Flexible Structure for Teaching Greek to Archaeologists and Ancient Historians.* Milton Keynes: Higher Education Academy.

Rubinstein, L. (2003). The use of inscriptions in language teaching. Paper presented at the Classical Association Annual Conference, Warwick. Programme available at http://www.classicalassociation.org/pastconferences/Warwick%202003.pdf

Simon, R., Barker, E. et al. (2013–2015), *Recogito.* Available at https://github.com/pelagios/recogito

Sosin, J. D. (2010). Digital Papyrology. Congress of the International Association of Papyrologists, 19 August 2010, Geneva. Available at http://www.stoa.org/archives/1263

Sosin, J. S., Baumann, R. F. & Cayless, H. A. (2015). GRK582s Epigraphy: syllabus s15. Duke University. Available at http://people.duke.edu/~jds15/grk-582s/syllabus-s2015.html

Tarte, S. (2011). Digitizing the act of papyrological interpretation: negotiating spurious exactitude and genuine uncertainty. *Literary and Linguistic Computing* 26(3): 349–358. Available at http://llc.oxfordjournals.org/content/26/3/349

Tennison, J. (2005). *Beginning XSLT 2.0.* Berkeley: APress.

Vieira, J.-M., Norrish, J., Giacometti, A. et al. (2011–2015). *Kiln.* Available at https://github.com/kcl-ddh/kiln/

CHAPTER 4

An Open Tutorial for Beginning Ancient Greek

Jeff Rydberg-Cox
University of Missouri-Kansas City

Abstract

For the past three years, I have been developing an open online digital tutorial for Ancient Greek designed for beginners with no previous knowledge of the language. This tutorial is available online at http://daedalus.umkc.edu/FirstGreekBook. The drill and practice exercises in this tutorial are designed to engage a broad public audience both inside and outside traditional university classroom settings. The techniques and approaches used for syntactic annotation and translation alignment that are discussed in the articles about the Perseids Platform and the Treebanking environment elsewhere in this volume have informed the pedagogical approach of this tutorial.

In calendar year 2014, there were 15,178 unique visitors who viewed tutorial pages some 58,137 times. This chapter will explore patterns of data usage and describe the audiences that have been using the tutorial.

Digital tutorial programs for other languages such as Duolingo or Rosetta Stone successfully engage large audiences outside of traditional academic environments while most resources for the study of Ancient Greek are designed for use within traditional classrooms. An understanding of the usage patterns for this one digital tutorial will help illuminate ways that pedagogical materials can be crafted in order to engage with broader audiences.

How to cite this book chapter:
Rydberg-Cox, J. 2016. An Open Tutorial for Beginning Ancient Greek. In: Bodard, G & Romanello, M (eds.) *Digital Classics Outside the Echo-Chamber: Teaching, Knowledge Exchange & Public Engagement*, Pp. 69–82. London: Ubiquity Press. DOI: http://dx.doi.org/10.5334/bat.e. License: CC-BY 4.0.

1 Introduction

Being a professor of Classics is often a paradoxical position. Enrollments in Classics courses are often not large enough to justify offering courses in Greek and Latin and many programs have faced closure due to low student numbers. The Modern Language Association's 2015 report on enrollments in language courses reports a 35% decline in the number of students enrolled in Ancient Greek and a 16% drop in the number of students enrolled in Latin in the since 2009.[1] A recent article in *Inside Higher Education* describes an enrollment pattern in Greek and Latin courses at Centenary College that will sound familiar to many classicists. 'Enrollments of five to seven students are good for upper division courses and most years there are only a few majors, sometimes just one.'[2]

Despite low enrollments in university classes, the ongoing presence of Ancient Greece and Rome in popular culture generates a steady stream of students who are interested in the study of Greek and Latin and also a population of adults outside the university who are interested in studying these languages for personal interest and enrichment. These two populations who desire to study Greek or Latin live 'outside the echo chamber' because they do not participate in the intellectual life of larger universities that draw a substantial enough student population to justify offering Greek and Latin. There are certainly resources available for these populations such as the independent study guide to the Joint Association of Classics Teachers Ancient Greek curriculum. There are also online resources that are connected to textbooks such as Maurice Balme and Gilbert Lawall's *Athenaze*, Donald Mastronarde's *Introduction to Attic Greek*, Cecila' Lusching's *An Introduction to Ancient Greek: A Literary Approach* and Anne Groton's *Ancient Greek: A Literary Approach*.[3] While these online resources are all connected to textbooks that are designed to be used within a traditional university classroom, there are fewer resources that will allow these groups to study Ancient Greek entirely online and entirely on their own.

A great deal of my digital work for the past three years has been devoted to developing this sort of online tutorial. With 15,178 unique visitors who viewed tutorial pages some 58,137 times in 2014, the tutorial has reached a broader audience than I ever expected and proven to be an effective mechanism for those students and lifelong learners who live outside the echo chamber to study Ancient Greek.

2 A Brief Overview of the Tutorial

In its current instantiation, the tutorial consists of an interactive version of John William White's *First Greek Book* that reimagines a late 19th-century textbook as a digital workbook.[4] White's original book contains eighty chapters with each introducing an element of syntax and morphology alongside vocabulary and guided readings that are designed to lead students to the ability to independently read Xenophon's *Anabasis*. The digital tutorial is available online at http://daedalus.umkc.edu/FirstGreekBook.

The tutorial consists of 84 static HTML pages that preserve the original textbook's basic structure. The HTML pages also include multiple-choice quizzes that allow students to memorize vocabulary, declensions and conjugations. The vocabulary and grammatical paradigms from each chapter are also available for download as tab delimited UTF8 files so that users can import the data into flashcard programs or use the data for other purposes. The tutorial is open access in two senses; first it is freely available for use online by any interested individual and—as of the summer of 2015—all of the material is also available for download, extension, and reuse under a Creative Commons Non-Commercial-By Attribution-Share Alike license.

The tutorial also includes two types of translation exercise built around the sample readings in White's original tutorial. As illustrated in Figure 1, the first translation exercise asks users to match words or phrases from the Greek with the corresponding word or phrase in an English translation. The second translation exercise shown to the left asks students to identify the grammatical role of each word in the sample sentences. Both of these translation practice exercises were inspired by the work of the Alpheios project and the Perseids Platform that are described elsewhere in this volume.[5] The approach of matching words with their correct translation is an extremely simplified version of the Alpheos translation alignment tool that allows readers to match words and phrases in a passage with their equivalents in a translation.[6] The exercises that ask students to identify the grammatical role for each word in a sentence is inspired by the Perseids treebanking project that is also described elsewhere in this volume. The inspiration for the tutorial itself, in fact, came out of a class in

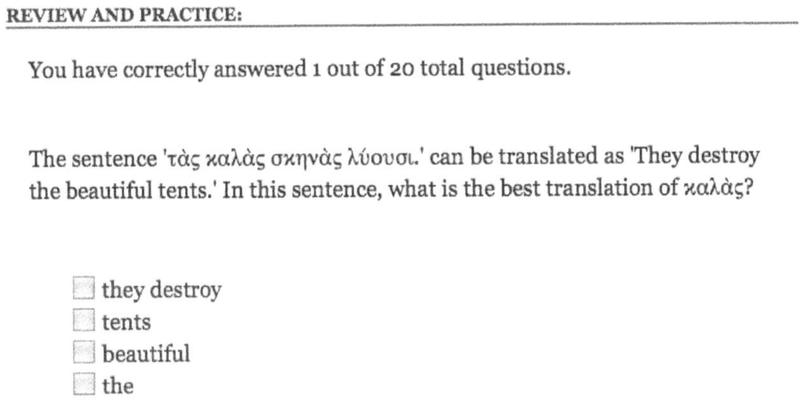

REVIEW AND PRACTICE:

You have correctly answered 1 out of 20 total questions.

The sentence 'τὰς καλὰς σκηνὰς λύουσι.' can be translated as 'They destroy the beautiful tents.' In this sentence, what is the best translation of καλὰς?

- they destroy
- tents
- beautiful
- the

Figure 1: Sample translation exercise.

which I was asking beginning students to work on treebanks and realized the need for an approach that would lead learners with absolutely no knowledge of Ancient Greek to a point where they could reasonably begin to create treebanks for existing texts.

These exercises are supplemented by a gamified system that helps readers track the material that they have learned and what material is ready for review.[7] In this system, users can earn virtual drachmas as they work through the exercises. These drachmas serve as markers of progress rather than a virtual currency that can be used to purchase add-ons or additional exercises as one can with Duolingo's lingots. There are ten drachmas available in each chapter and users earn one drachma every time they correctly answer ten percent of the questions in that unit. The tutorial employs local storage in the users' browser to keep track of the questions that have been answered correctly and to prompt users to review material on a spaced repetition schedule. If a user answers a question correctly on day 1, he or she is prompted to review that question on day 2. If it is answered correctly, they are then prompted to review it again on day 4, day 8, day 16, etc. If at any point, they answer the question incorrectly, the period until its next review returns to one day. The number of drachmas that are shown for each chapter corresponds to the number of questions that are ready for review. If users do not see the full complement of drachmas for a chapter that they have already studied, they know that they need to review the material in this chapter.

The tutorial is designed to work on mobile browsers with a minimal responsive design (see Figure 2). By default, the tutorial is designed to fit into a width of 768 pixels, so that it displays the same way in both desktop browsers and on tablets such as the iPad or Kindle Fire. In smaller form factors, the font size shrinks but the interface remains fundamentally the same. While this design means that the tutorial does not take advantage of the possibilities of different types of pedagogical exercises that would be possible on a larger screen with a physical keyboard, it does respond to the necessities of small shop digital humanities, where software development time is balanced between teaching, service and other research duties. Design simplicity ensures that the tutorial can function without the need for any additional server software, security updates, or reconfigurations as new tablet form factors are introduced.

The drachma system is implemented using the local storage function of HTML5 and so it is limited to a single browser on a single device. If a user wants to use the tutorial from both a mobile device and a desktop, the drachma system does not carry over. While the ability for a user to track their progress on more than one device would perhaps be the most useful enhancement to the tutorial, the considerations of design simplicity and small shop digital humanities have led to this decision at the current time. Tracking user activity across devices would require the creation of user accounts and passwords that must be stored and maintained on a server. Once again, my focus on design simplicity and the lack of a full time system administrator who can ensure security

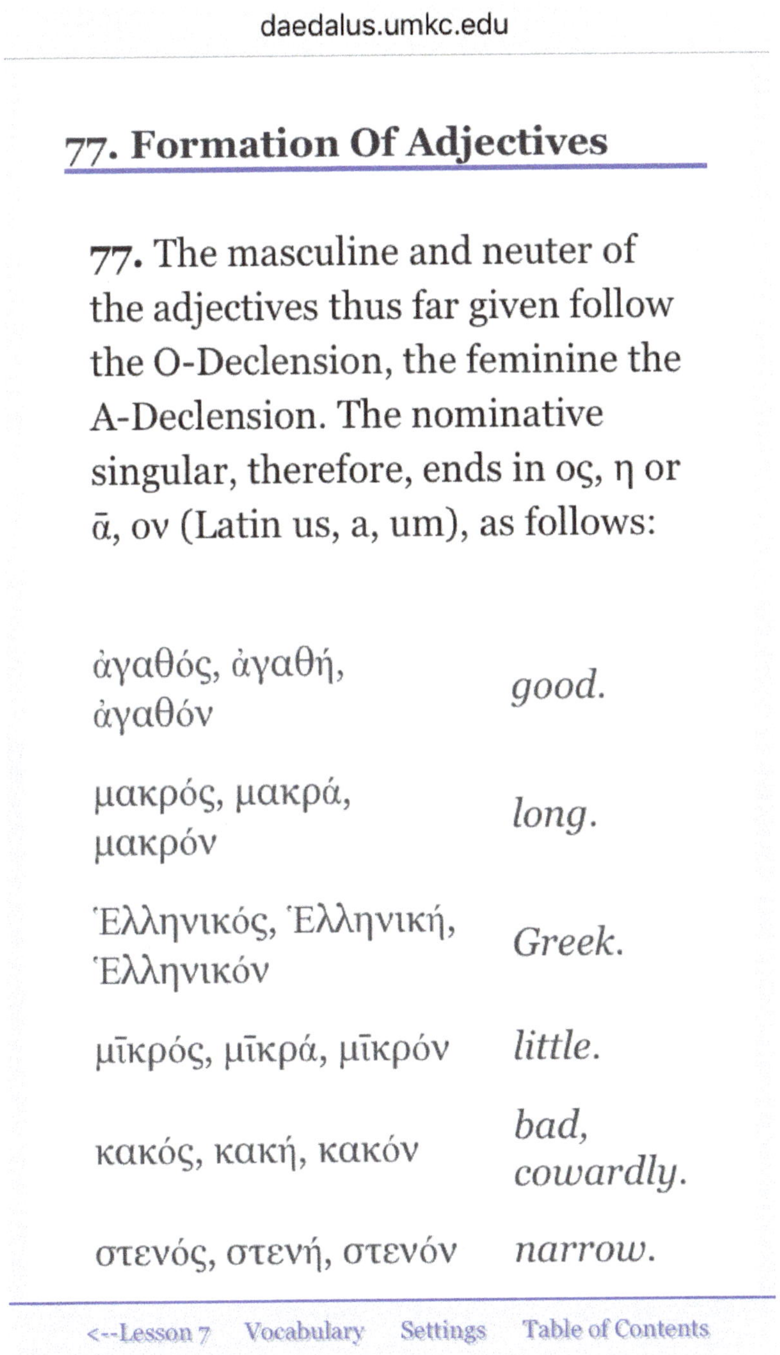

daedalus.umkc.edu

77. Formation Of Adjectives

77. The masculine and neuter of the adjectives thus far given follow the O-Declension, the feminine the A-Declension. The nominative singular, therefore, ends in ος, η or ᾱ, ον (Latin us, a, um), as follows:

ἀγαθός, ἀγαθή, ἀγαθόν	*good.*
μακρός, μακρά, μακρόν	*long.*
Ἑλληνικός, Ἑλληνική, Ἑλληνικόν	*Greek.*
μῑκρός, μῑκρά, μῑκρόν	*little.*
κακός, κακή, κακόν	*bad, cowardly.*
στενός, στενή, στενόν	*narrow.*

<--Lesson 7   Vocabulary   Settings   Table of Contents

Figure 2: Tutorial lesson on a mobile device.

and constant uptime has led to the decision rely solely on local storage for the tracking system.

3 Who Uses the Tutorial

While I do use this tutorial as part of my traditional university classroom, as an open-access resource it has also reached many more people than I could reach in my classroom. The decision not to require user accounts makes it more difficult to understand how people are using the tutorial. I do not have direct access to information about how often specific individuals access the tutorial, how long they use it once they begin, how far they are able to progress through the tutorial before they lose interest, etc. Despite the lack of individual user data, information provided by Google Analytics provides some insight into the nature of the audience for this tutorial.

In calendar year 2014, some 15,178 unique individuals viewed 58,137 pages in the tutorial. As shown in Figure 3, tutorial users primarily reside in the United States (57.75%) with other users in the United Kingdom (7.8%), Australia (4.4%), Canada (3.7%), Brazil (2%), Germany (1.7%), Greece (1.4%), India (1.3%), Italy (1.2%) and Spain (1%).

While there is no easy way to determine how many of these users are traditional students, data about internet service providers might provide a proxy. According to Google Analytics, the top internet service provider for non-mobile traffic with 6% of the traffic is 'not set.' The next seven most common service providers that account for twenty two percent of the tutorial sessions are major American internet service providers such as Time Warner Cable, AT&T, Verizon and Comcast indicating that a good percentage of the users are accessing the tutorial outside the confines of a traditional educational institution. Of course, one cannot tell whether these are students doing homework away from campus or learners outside of the echo chamber, but it certainly does suggest that there are not large clusters of university students using the tutorial from their dormitories. The first identifiable educational institution does not appear on the list of most common service providers until number forty and this institution accounted for only .29% of the traffic for the calendar year 2014. In the list of the top one hundred of most common service providers, there are only eleven identifiable educational institutions and these taken together account for just 2% of the total traffic in the same period.

Further, while 98% of the tutorial users are using computers that are not connected to the internet on a traditional campus, their usage pattern over time only partially reflects the ebb and flow of the academic year. There are noticeable peaks in July and at the end of the year, months when one might expect a decline due to holiday schedules if the primary audiences for the tutorial were located within traditional academic institutions (see Figure 4).

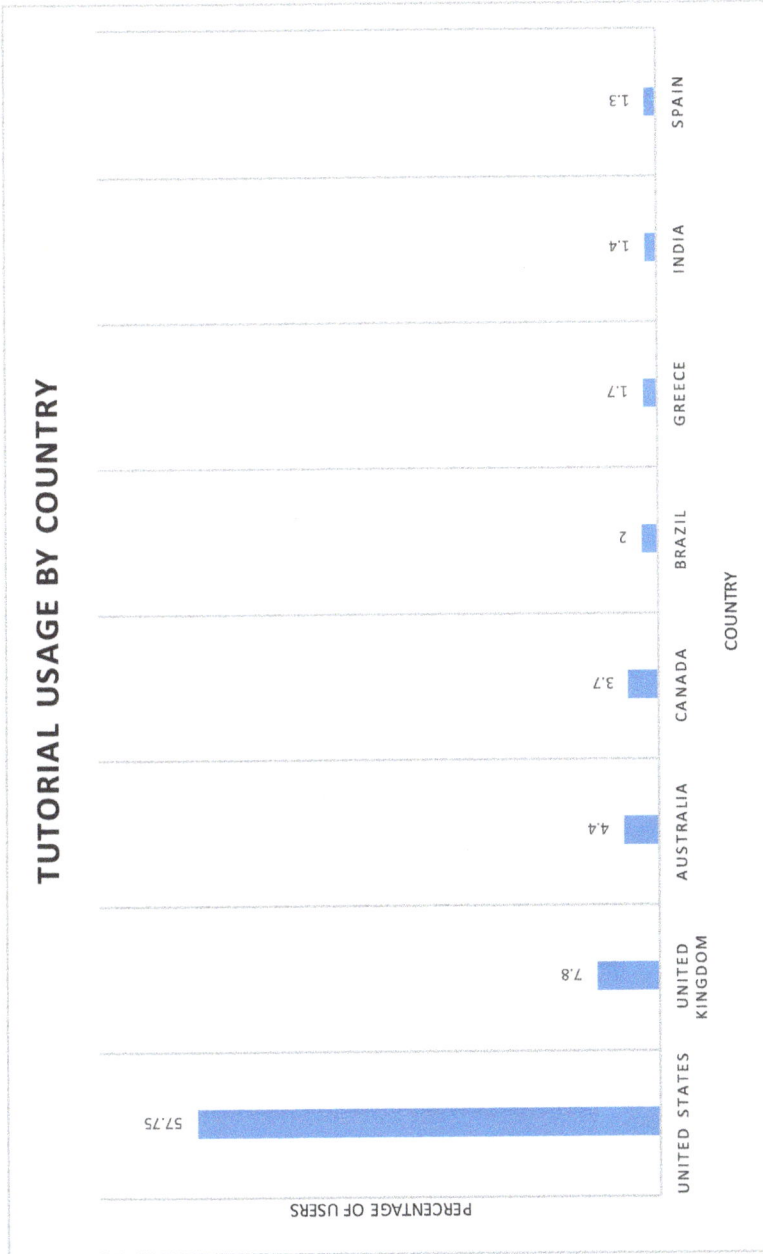

Figure 3: Tutorial usage by country.

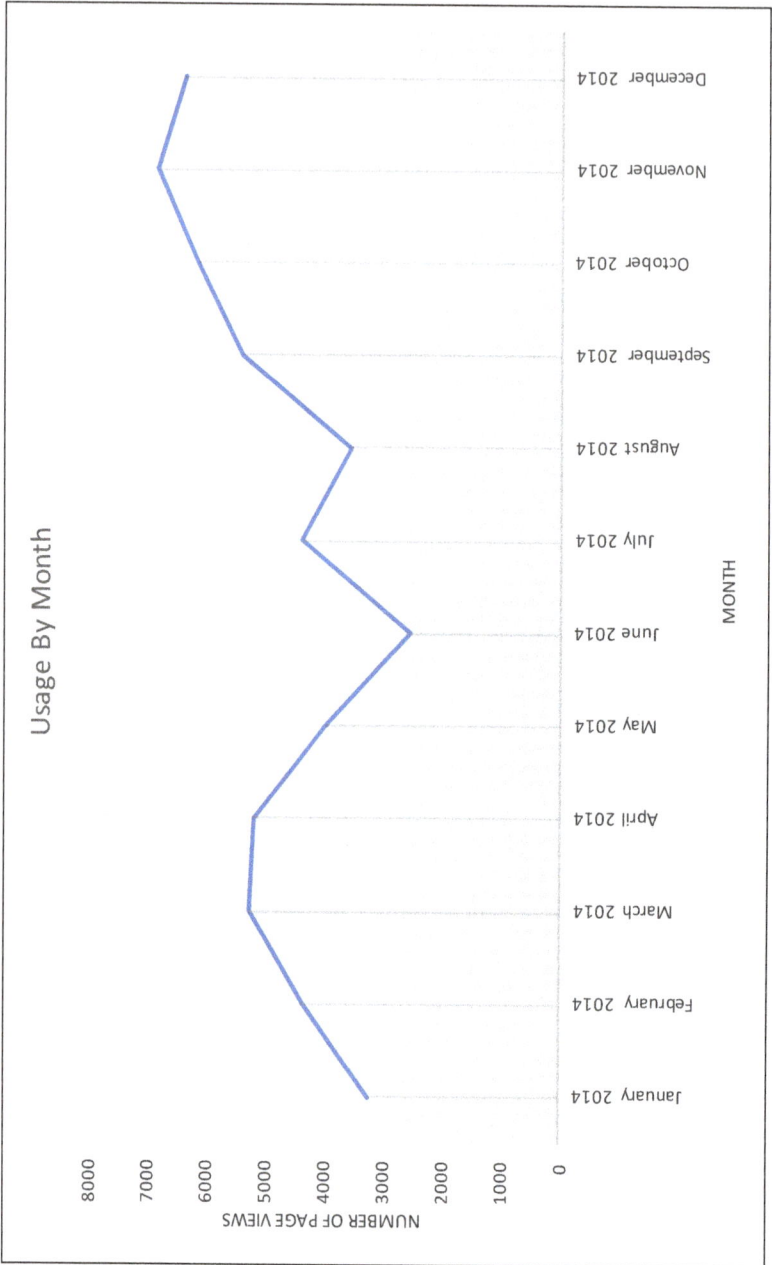

Figure 4: Tutorial usage by month.

25 MOST FREQUENTLY USED CHAPTERS

PERCENTAGE OF TOTAL VIEWS

CHAPTER

Chapter	Percentage
CHAPTER 1	12.00%
CHAPTER 12	4.56%
CHAPTER 3	3.88%
CHAPTER 2	3.32%
CHAPTER 5	3.26%
CHAPTER 10	2.65%
CHAPTER 4	2.57%
CHAPTER 7	2.21%
CHAPTER 17	1.90%
CHAPTER 6	1.78%
CHAPTER 18	1.59%
CHAPTER 8	1.58%
CHAPTER 11	1.53%
CHAPTER 49	1.46%
CHAPTER 13	1.45%
CHAPTER 23	1.45%
CHAPTER 15	1.44%
CHAPTER 9	1.39%
CHAPTER 43	1.37%
CHAPTER 20	1.34%
CHAPTER 14	1.33%
VOCABULARY	1.30%
CHAPTER 32	1.26%
CHAPTER 16	1.22%
CHAPTER 19	1.21%

Figure 5: Most frequently used chapters.

The pattern of usage for the individual chapters shows that more users start the book than complete it with a noticeable drop off somewhere around the 10th chapter (Figure 5). The earlier chapters are used more frequently than the later ones, but the decline is not linear in relation to the chapter numbers. The data show that many people browse only the first chapter. Chapters two through fifteen all appear in the list of the top 25 most frequently visited chapters alongside an assortment of chapters from the first half of the book.

Table 1 shows that the spread among chapter usage after the first few chapters is very small; this suggests that there are four types of users: users who browse the first chapter and decide not to use the tutorial further, a larger cohort who get through approximately 15 chapters and then trails off, a middle group of users who get about halfway through the tutorial and a smaller group of users who complete the entire tutorial.

This distribution also suggests that the tutorial is reaching an audience outside of traditional classrooms because there are no clear break points at the chapters where one might expect them if the tutorial were being used in a two or three semester Ancient Greek sequence.

One of the design goals for this tutorial was to make it usable from mobile devices in addition to computer web browsers. As I was engaged in the initial planning of this project, I noticed that many e-learning content management systems offered only minimal functionality to mobile users even it seemed that progressively more of my students were wanting to access them using mobile devices. The usage data bear this out but not perhaps to the extent that I might have expected; roughly one third of the users access the tutorial using a mobile operating system. More interesting, however, is the apparent equal division between phone-sized platforms and tablets in the usage data. Roughly half

Percent of Page Views	Number of Chapters in Range	Chapters in Range (in descending order)
12%	1	1
2%–5%	7	12, 3, 2, 5, 4, 7
1%–1.99%	19	17, 6, 18, 8, 11, 49, 13, 23, 15, 9, 43, 20, 14, Vocabulary, 32, 16, 19, 21, 24
<1%	59	Flashcards, 28, 22, 30, 25, 40, 31, 38, 48, Appendix, 26, 34, 29, 27, 37, 33, 79, 52, 50, 44, 39, 80, 41, 57, 47, 53, 35, 36, 56, 75, 65, 42, 45, 74, Settings, 46, 55, 76, 71, 51, 58, 60, 78, 66, 73, 77, 59, 70, 54, 61, 63, 67, Contract Rules, 62, Contract Nouns, 72, 64, 68, 69

Table 1: Distribution of chapter usage throughout the Greek tutorial.

of the mobile operating system sessions with the tutorial were initiated using devices with phone-sized screen resolutions and the other half were initiated using tablets.

4 Conclusions

The usage data for this tutorial shows that there is a sizable population of readers who are not affiliated with universities who are interested in studying ancient languages. This follows a pattern of use that also appears for other online scholarly resources. Gregory Crane more than fifteen years ago pointed out that the Perseus Digital Library saw a spike in users outside of educational institutions at lunch hours and in the evenings.[8] More broadly this reflects the pattern of usage for online materials that Chris Anderson described in 2004 as the 'Long Tail.' Anderson describes how physical media such as books or DVDs could only be stocked in a brick-and-mortar store if it could 'generate sufficient demand to earn its keep.'[9] Further, since an item had to generate this demand from a limited geographic area, a film or a book could only be available in areas with a high concentration of interested consumers. Those who lived outside these echo chambers that lacked a sufficient population who shared their interests had difficulties gaining access to these items. The long tail describes the phenomenon whereby online access allows geographically dispersed communities of users to emerge in sufficient numbers to support the development of material that might not be viable in an environment that depends on physical access.

It is not at all difficult to imagine the traditional university as one of Anderson's brick-and-mortar stores. The physical university has served the function of concentrating people who are interested in a specific topic into a physical location in sufficient numbers to support the creation of courses, books, articles, etc. about these areas of interest. Textbooks, monographs and other research publications were largely designed based on the assumption that they would be consumed within such a geographically concentrated community. This is still the case today; many fine textbooks are still being written in such a way that they would only be useful to a student who is using them in a traditional classroom setting in consultation with a trained professional. Other resources for learning modern languages such as Babbel, Duolingo, Lang-8, etc. have provided clear models for self-directed language pedagogy and large geographically dispersed communities of interest have formed around these resources. In a time when the university is no longer serving to gather people interested in the study of the ancient world together in sufficient numbers to support classes, should we begin to wonder if the paradoxically positioned Classics professor might be best served by turning their attention towards developing resources and programs that leverage the long tail of people who are interested in the study of the ancient world?

Further, a tutorial such as this one can also serve as a building block for a program of broader participation in Classical research on the citizen science model. The Ancient Greek and Latin Dependency Treebank and the Perseids project described elsewhere in this volume provide a robust environment for citizen philologists to make concrete and real contributions to the study and understanding of Ancient Greek and Latin. While Perseids and the Treebank project have developed programs for students and citizen philologists to gain the basic skills required to participate in these projects, wholly independent tutorials such as this one provide another avenue for students and scholars who work outside of the echo chamber of traditional universities to gain the baseline skills required to contribute to projects such as these.

Notes

[1] Goldberg, Looney & Lusin 2015. See also Flaherty 2015.

[2] Jaschik 2015. Beard 2012 offers an insightful discussion of the 'End of Classics'.

[3] Joint Association of Classical Teachers 2008, Blama, Lawall & Morwood 2014; Groton 2013; Luschnig & Mitchell 2007; Mastronarde 2013. Rebecca Frost Davis offers a discussion of available resources at <https://rebecca frostdavis.wordpress.com/2013/05/24/challenges-of-blended-learning-in-the-humanities-ancient-greek/> and <https://rebeccafrostdavis.wordpress. com/2013/05/28/challenges-of-blended-learning-in-ancient-greek-follow-up/> while Toon Van Hall offers a directory of resources at <http://greek grammar.wikidot.com/introductory-courses>.

[4] This tutorial has been described in more detail in Rydberg-Cox 2013.

[5] For more details on the treebanking and Alpheos projects, see Bamman and Crane 2007; Bamman and Crane 2006; Bamman et al. 2009.

[6] Available at <http://alpheios.net> under 'Apheios Alignment Editor'.

[7] For conversations about gamification and pedagogy, see Kapp 2012; Landers a & Callan 2011; and Renaud & Wagoner 2011.

[8] Crane 1998.

[9] Anderson 2004, This article was expanded into the book Anderson 2006. For a discussion of the long tail and pedagogy, see Brown and Adler 2008.

References

Anderson, C. (2004, October). The Long Tail. *Wired Magazine* 12(10).

Anderson, C. (2006) *The Long Tail: Why the Future of Business Is Selling Less of More* (Hachette Digital, Inc.).

Balme, M., Lawall, G. & Morwood, J. (2014). *Athenaze, Book I: An Introduction to Ancient Greek*. 3rd Edition. Oxford: Oxford University Press.

Bamman, D. & Crane, G. (2006). The Design and Use of a Latin Dependency Treebank. In *Proceedings of the Fifth Workshop on Treebanks and Linguistic Theories (TLT2006)*, pp. 67–78.

Beard, M. (2012, January 12) Do the Classics Have a Future? *The New York Review of Books*. Retrieved from http://www.nybooks.com/articles/archives/2012/jan/12/do-classics-have-future/

Brown, J. S. & Adler, R. P. (2008). Open Education, the Long Tail, and Learning 2.0. *Educause Review* 43(1): 16–20.

Crane, G. (1998). New Technologies for Reading: The Lexicon and the Digital Library. *The Classical World* 91(6): 471–501.

David, B. & Crane, G. (2007). The Latin Dependency Treebank in a Cultural Heritage Digital Library. *ACL*, 33.

David, B., Mambrini, F. & Crane, G. (2009). *An Ownership Model of Annotation: The Ancient Greek Dependency Treebank*. In Proceedings of the Eighth International Workshop on Treebanks and Linguistic Theories (TLT8). Milan, Italy: EDUCatt, pp. 5–15.

Flaherty, C. (2015, February 11). MLA Report Shows Declines in Enrollment in Most Foreign Languages. *Inside Higher Ed*. Retrieved from https://www.insidehighered.com/news/2015/02/11/mla-report-shows-declines-enrollment-most-foreign-languages.

Goldberg, D., Looney, D. & Lusin, N. (2015). Enrollments in Languages Other Than English in United States Institutions of Higher Education, Fall 2013. Retrieved from http://www.mla.org/pdf/2013_enrollment_survey.pdf

Groton, A. H. (2013). *From Alpha to Omega: A Beginning Course in Classical Greek*. 4th Edition. Newburyport, MA: Focus.

Jaschik, S. (2015). Turning Off the Lights. *Inside Higher Ed*. Retrieved from https://www.insidehighered.com/news/2010/03/04/clark

Joint Association of Classical Teachers. (2008). *An Independent Study Guide to Reading Greek*. 2nd Edition. New York: Cambridge University Press.

Kapp, K. M. (2012). *The Gamification of Learning and Instruction: Game-Based Methods and Strategies for Training and Education*. Hoboken, NJ: John Wiley & Sons.

Landers, R. N. & Callan, R. C. (2011). Casual Social Games as Serious Games: The Psychology of Gamification in Undergraduate Education and Employee Training. In *Serious Games and Edutainment Applications* (pp. 399–423). New York: Springer. Retrieved from http://link.springer.com/chapter/10.1007/978-1-4471-2161-9_20

Luschnig, C. A. E. & Mitchell. D. (2007). *An Introduction to Ancient Greek: A Literary Approach*. 2nd Edition. Indianapolis: Hackett Publishing Company, Inc.

Mastronarde, D. J. (2013). *Introduction to Attic Greek*. Second Edition. Berkeley: University of California Press.

Renaud, C. & and Wagoner, B. (2011). The Gamification of Learning. *Principal Leadership* 12(1): 56–59.

Rydberg-Cox, J. (2013). A Digital Tutorial for Ancient Greek Based on John Williams White's First Greek Book. *Classical World* 107(1): 111–17.

CHAPTER 5

The Ancient Greek Dependency Treebank: Linguistic Annotation in a Teaching Environment

Francesco Mambrini
German Archaeological Institute

Abstract

This chapter argues that manual linguistic annotation of Ancient Greek texts can be effectively employed to teach of Greek literature and languages. Under the supervision of a teacher, students can be engaged into the ongoing creation of the Ancient Greek Dependency Treebank. With the help of one example from Sophocles (*Tr.* 962–3), we will illustrate how the collective work of treebanking in a class environment provides an ideal occasion to discuss the methods of Classical Philology and the history of interpretation of a given passage; more importantly, while producing a treebank annotation, students can learn how to read a complex text in its literary and communicative context following the methods of textual criticism. New and old research questions emerge from the work; at the same time, through the final annotation the students will produce a tangible contribution to a crucial initiative that is likely to change the way Greek grammar will be studied in the future.

1 Introduction

In the fall of 2009, the Perseus Project published the first edition of the *Ancient Greek Dependency Treebank* (AGDT),[1] a digital corpus of Greek literary texts that include a word-by-word morphological and syntactic annotation. At the

---

How to cite this book chapter:
Mambrini, F. 2016. The Ancient Greek Dependency Treebank: Linguistic Annotation in a Teaching Environment. In: Bodard, G & Romanello, M (eds.) *Digital Classics Outside the Echo-Chamber: Teaching, Knowledge Exchange & Public Engagement*, Pp. 83–99. London: Ubiquity Press. DOI: http://dx.doi.org/10.5334/bat.f. License: CC-BY 4.0.

moment, the last published version of the treebank (AGDT 1.6) include the complete extant opus of Homer, Hesiod, Aeschylus, five of the seven surviving plays of Sophocles, and smaller selections of Plato (the *Euthyphro*) and Athenaeus (Book 12 of the *Deipnosophistae*).[2]

Treebanks are a powerful resource for data-driven linguistic research which are likely to have a great impact on the way the grammar of the ancient languages is studied. Traditional grammars have often limited themselves to register the existence of certain linguistic facts, providing at best a detailed classification of the constructions and a number of examples from the ancient texts. For example, we learn from grammar that in Greek coordinated subjects can trigger either plural and singular agreement with the verb, and that singular verbs occur more often with or-coordinates than with subjects joined by 'and';[3] we do not find any indication, though, of how frequent each of these constructions is, how the two agreement patterns are distributed among the authors and texts, and what the different meaning of these constructions (if any) might be. A large digitized repertoire of texts that can be searched for specific syntactic constructions will make these information easily retrievable to students and scholars alike.[4] Moreover, the treebank formalism, which allows to represent the sentence as a tree-shaped graph as in Fig. 1, provide a formidable tool to visualize the sentence structure.

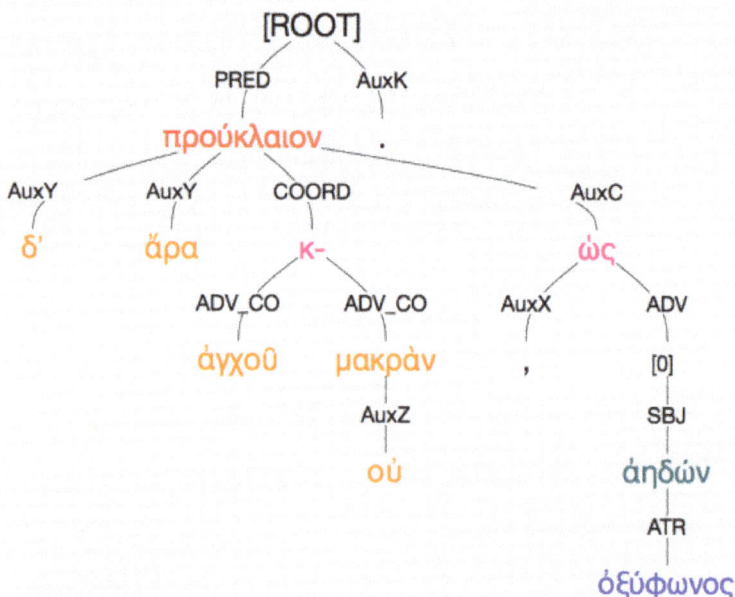

Figure 1: Sophocles, *Trach.*, 962–3.

1.1 Treebank annotation

Although some experiments on (semi-)automatic parsing of Latin and Greek have already been carried out,[5] so far, all the information, including part of speech, morphological features (tense, mood, person etc.), and the syntactic relations between each word in the texts, have been entered manually by human annotators. This process of word-by-word enrichment can be facilitated with the help of graphical interfaces and online tools, such as Arethusa (see Section 1.2).

Some of the texts, and the poems of Homer and Hesiod in particular, were annotated by students in the context of graduate programs in Classics.[6] The pedagogical value of such an exercise of close reading cannot be overestimated.[7] In fact, by using the formalism of the AGDT to enrich an ancient text with morpho-syntactic information, students can both practice their language skills and contribute to the advancement of the available resources to an extent that is scarcely matched elsewhere in the Classics. Not only will it be possible for students to 'learn by doing', but the publication in the AGDT corpus can also offer an immediate gratification to their efforts.

Along this line, my paper will draw the attention on what contribution the annotation process can bring to the teaching of Greek language, literature, and civilization. We will present the case for engaging the students in the practice of collective treebanking, using the formalism and the guidelines of the AGDT and under the supervision of a teacher.[8] The advantages in terms of grammar and language acquisition that are inherent in the process of a word-by-word morpho-syntactic annotation are immediately evident. However, instead of focusing only on them, my analysis will attempt to show the wide spectrum of methodological and historical problems that a formalized linguistic annotation entails. Reading even a simple sentence at the level of detail that treebanking requires is a process that goes far beyond grammar and can be leveraged to teach Greek civilization *tous azimuts*.

Methodological questions on how to reconstruct, interrogate, and interpret an ancient text are, as we shall see, especially prominent in treebank annotation. Moreover, we will stress that students must be encouraged to question the meanings and interpretations of a text that each of the possible reconstructions of a sentence imply. Finally, by searching the collection of the already annotated texts, students can also be asked to reflect on the relation of the text they are reading in the larger context of the ancient Greek literature.

1.2 Reading through treebanking: Sophocles, Trachiniae, 962–3

In what follows, we try to articulate this program with one example, limited to a short sentence from Sophocles. The discussion will touch only a minimal part of the potential benefits of treebanking in a classroom environment.

Others application (e.g. interdisciplinary projects involving students in computer science and linguistics in cooperation to improve the efficiency of the research tools) will be left out of the present work. The use of corpora to generate drills and exercises, that can also be applied to measure each student's familiarity with single grammatical aspects and assess personalized training sessions on the weakest point, is also a potentially crucial use that we will have to leave aside.[9]

We will consider one sentence taken from the fourth choral ode (*stasimon*) of Sophocles' *Women of Trachis*.[10] Fig. 1 shows how the sentence is annotated in 'Arethusa', the new annotation framework that has been recently made available as part of the Perseids editing environment and can be freely accessed on the Internet.[11] The Greek text of Sophocles, along with a minimal paraphrase, is reported below; this starting point should mirror the situation in a class: students should be confronted immediately with the original, and no translation (except for the basic meaning of some of the most unusual words) should be provided. A more articulate translation will emerge while we progress in the annotation:

ἀγχοῦ δ᾽ ἄρα κοὐ μακρὰν προύκλαιον,
ὀξύφωνος ὡς ἀηδών
near and not far off then [I was?] weeping beforehand, like the shrill-voiced nightingale.

The *Women of Trachis* is probably not one of the most popular tragedies in school curricula. Moreover, the short passage that we selected does not belong to the most memorable passages of the play; these words are likely to be overlooked as a moment of transition between two important scenes. Yet precisely these reasons convey interest to our choice: one of the aim of the paper is to illustrate how even a short and apparently uninteresting sentence can in fact, when considered through the lenses of treebank annotation, raise complex literary and historical questions to engage students in fruitful discussions.

2 The Sentence in its Context

It is often customary to remind beginners in Greek and Latin that every fresh analysis of a sentence should start by the identification of the main verb. This approach is certainly sound; since the prototypical dependency tree is generally rooted to the main predicate, which in turns governs a bunch of satellites (as in Fig. 1), the indication to start there is also well suited to the theoretical frame our treebank is built upon.[12]

Yet one of the first lessons that can be learned while reading a sentence like this is that knowledge about the context constitutes an even more fundamental premise. Context (intended both as the 'intra-textual' net of references and presuppositions to other passages of the work, and as the communicative situation a text is inserted in) is a primary linguistic element, which is often crucial in disambiguating syntactic and semantic problems. As we will see, our sentence offers a good illustration of this point.

The *Women of Trachis* dramatizes the agony and death of Herakles, which is involuntarily caused by the gift sent by the hero's wife Deianeira on the occasion of his return to Greece. After the narrative of the lines 899–946, where the Nurse told how Deianeira killed herself after she discovered the real effects of her actions, the Chorus awaits the second and final evil; the agonizing Herakles will be eventually brought to the scene and displayed to the audience.

As it is typical of Greek tragedy, it is a song by the Chorus, which in the play impersonates a group of young maidens from the town of Trachis, which builds the dramatic tension and bridges the two sections. Our fourth song is dominated by the opening questions: 'which evil shall we bewail first, which of the two is more grievous' (947–9)? The sight of the escort that brings the bier of Herakles reveals that the evil that the Chorus has already anticipated is almost at hand.

It is typical of choral odes, and of Sophocles in particular, that the first strophes of a *stasimon* are concerned with general questions or with mythical paradigms, while the last stanzas bring the focus back to the stage events and introduces the scene to come.[13] Our sentence operates precisely this shift. The meaning of the words (with an emphasis of 'near' and 'to mourn in advance'[14]) points to the dramatical function of introducing the new characters that are about to enter the scene and the theme of the episode; if the general meaning is clear, the exact grammatical interpretation of the words proves to be more challenging.

3 Morphology

Identifying the main verb of the sentence requires students to define the part of speech of each of the words and then to concentrate on the full morphological analysis (mood, tense, person) of the verbs. Often, students will meet ambiguous words, where more than one analysis is possible. In such cases, disambiguation will have to rely on the syntax or on the general knowledge of meaning and context.

In our sentence, only one word is liable to two different interpretations, as it is shown in the interface for morphological annotation of Arethusa (Fig. 2).[15] The main verb προὐκλαιον can be interpreted as:

1. indicative imperfect 1st person singular of προκλαίω (*we mourned/were mourning*);
2. indicative imperfect 3rd person plural of προκλαίω (*they mourned/were mourning*).

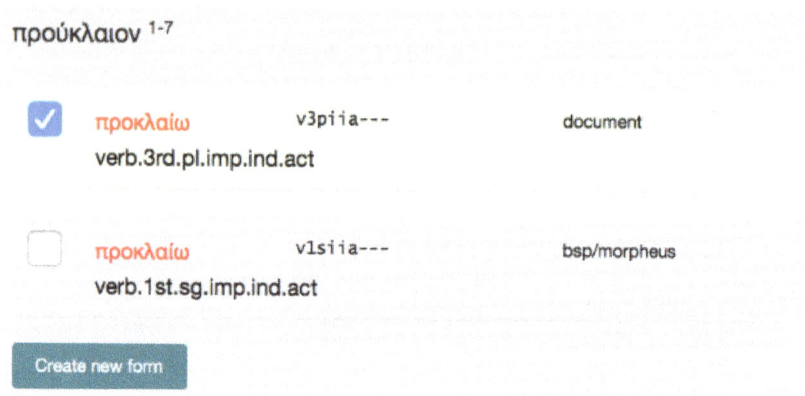

προύκλαιον [1-7]

☑ προκλαίω   v3piia---   document
  verb.3rd.pl.imp.ind.act

☐ προκλαίω   v1siia---   bsp/morpheus
  verb.1st.sg.imp.ind.act

[Create new form]

Figure 2: Arethusa: annotation interface for morphology.

Since the sentence lacks an explicit subject, both are theoretically possible. With n.1 the implied subject is the Chorus, who can, as usual, shift between *I* and *we* for self-reference.[16] With n.2, the subjects are the men who carry Herakles on the litter.

Advanced readers of Greek will be in no doubt about the correct answer, but it is interesting to note that both interpretations are attested in the history of scholarship. N.2 is adopted by an ancient commentator whose opinion is preserved in the medieval manuscripts, in a marginal note (*scholium*) to the line:

ἀντὶ τοῦ προκλαίουσιν· ὁ χορὸς αἰσθάνεται τοῦ Ἡρακλέους πλησίον φερομένου καὶ πλήθους θρηνούντων ἐπακολουθούντων αὐτῷ

[*they were lamenting*] instead of *they lament*: the Chorus perceives that Herakles is brought near and [perceives] the crowd of mourners that is escorting him.[17]

At this point, students should be encouraged to discuss: are the two interpretations equally admissible? Do we have arguments to choose between them? The context that we described above provides several strong arguments to reject the interpretation of the scholium. The closing of the stanza, in which the Chorus asks why the escort is advancing in such an ominous silence (cf. 965–7), speaks strongly against it, as it was already noted by an eminent scholar.[18] Another argument is grounded in grammar: the equivalence between imperfect and present that the scholiast invokes cannot be seriously considered.

On the contrary, the imperfect makes a perfect sense if it is referred, as it is, to the laments that the Chorus was uttering in the preceding stanzas. The meaning that we chose for the verb ('lament in advance', 'weep beforehand') is perfectly at home in reference to the first part of the ode where maidens were lamenting the sort of Herakles even before seeing it. Now, with the approach of the litter, the time of foreboding is over.

4 Syntax

4.1 ὀξύφωνος ὡς ἀηδών

The easiest syntactic structure of the sentence is that formed by the last three words. This phrase introduces a simile in which the lament of the Chorus is compared with the wailing of the nightingale. 'Nightingale' (ἀηδών) and 'shrill-voiced' (ὀξύφωνος) thus make a noun–epithet pair, and the similitude has to be connected with the main verb (προύκλαιον). In the case of comparisons introduced by 'like', the guidelines of the AGDT require annotators to take the term of comparison (ἀηδών) as the argument of an implied circumstantial of the compared verb (as shown in Fig. 3); the phrase is therefore annotated as if it were: '[we mourned] (Predicate) as (Conjunction) a shrill-voiced nightingale (Subject, SBJ) [does/mourns] (Implied circumstantial, ADV)'.

Instead of mechanically applying those rules to similar easily identifiable constructions, students should be encouraged to reflect about the meanings that each of the elements in the graphs introduces. The edges that connect the verb of mourning to the noun and the noun to the adjective are both laden

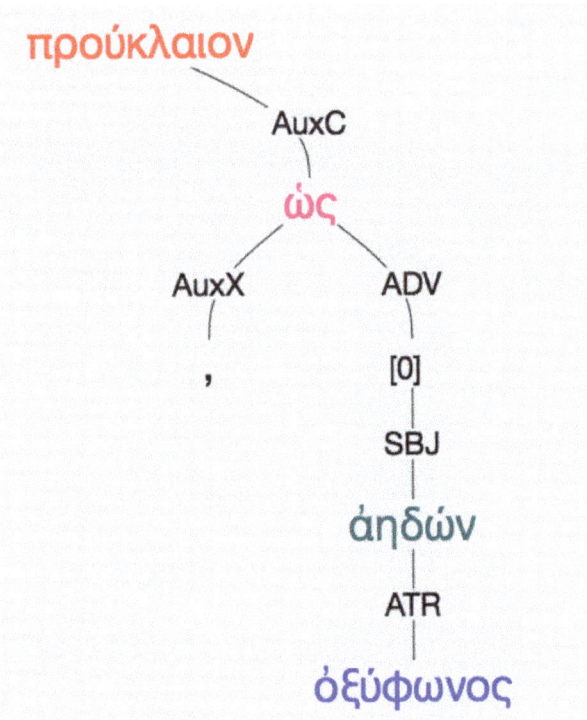

Figure 3: Like the shrill-voiced nightingale.

with a rich cultural history. The piercing voice of the wailing bird is one of the most traditional images of Greek literature, and so is the connection of the nightingale with the poetical representation of mourners. The adjective ὀξύς ('sharp', 'shrill') and derived, whether they point to the high pitch of the sound or to his piercing emotional effects, are often used for the characterization of sounds.[19] The nightingale, via the mythical paradigm of Procne, is the model for the everlasting mourn of a woman (Penelope) already in the *Odyssey*.[20] And especially in Attic tragedy, the bird is often invoked as a paradigm for the performers of dirges.[21]

The value of a treebank goes also beyond the process of annotation, even in a discussion about such questions of literary history. The AGDT includes the whole text of the *Iliad* and *Odyssey*, which notoriously provided a vast cultural repertoire of models for similes. Using the same formalism as in our passage (ὡς + implied ADV + noun), students may interrogate the treebank to extract, classify and discuss the similes in a given text.

4.2 A Polar Expression

One of the clearest features of this sentence is the coordination of a positive affirmation with the negation of its contrary ('near and not far'). This kind of antithesis is generally referred to as *polar expression*; it is typically a solemn way for a speaker to stress the reality of his utterance.[22]

Once again, a treebank provides a formalism to describe the syntax of the construction (visualized in Fig. 4), and a general corpus where comparable phrases can be searched. A polar expression, however, requires a supplementary semantic level (the two terms must have opposite meaning) which is not captured by the

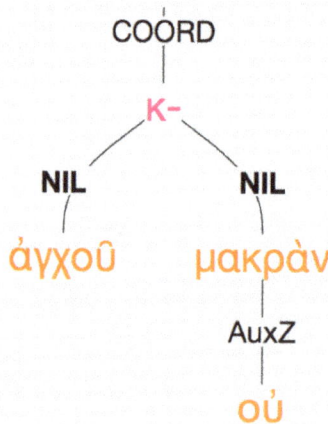

Figure 4: The polar expression.

current annotation. A query on the treebank for a coordinated phrase where one of the term in negated will probably return pertinent results along with a number of false positives. Students may be asked to search for relevant construction and identify and discuss the authentic polar expressions in their context.

4.3 How to Mourn Near and Far

If it is clear that the two adverbs are coordinated in a polar expression, it remains to be seen what their construction and exact meaning is in this particular sentence. Many readers have noted the conciseness, if not the oddity, of the expression 'to mourn near and not far off'; not surprisingly, a majority of them have tried to explain the syntax by looking for a word that is left implied and would, if supplied mentally, clarify the syntax.

The object of προκλαίω is left unexpressed: unless we suppose that the verb is used absolutely ('lament in advance'), we have to reconstruct it from the context. Logically, it is precisely the object of the Chorus' lamentation that is drawing near to the scene. Thus, some commentators take the two adverbs to refer to the (implied) object, thinking either of Herakles or of a more generic evil of the woeful situation. The former solution is argued by Hermann (1848), the latter by Jebb (1892). This reconstruction (which is reflected in the tree of Fig. 5) is by far the most widely accepted interpretation of the sentence and is

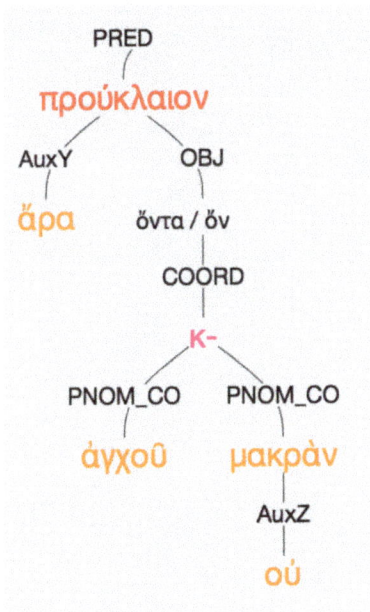

Figure 5: Hermann's interpretation.

reflected in most of the translations of the play.[23] The construction, however, is rather bold. The two passages from Sophocles that are brought as parallels by the commentators seem, as noted by Jebb, easier to understand.[24]

The plainest alternative to Hermann's construction is to attach the adverbs directly to the verb, as complements that specify the location where the main action is performed.[25] The sentence can be then paraphrased as: '(being) near and not far off (to the object of my lamentations), I mourned in advanced' and can be annotated as in Fig. 6.

Both interpretations, as phrased in most of the modern commentaries, have one point in common: they try to identify a precise lexical word that is left implied and should be supplied to govern the adverbs. Yet according to the guidelines of the AGDT this step is not mandatory. Even in case of ellipsis, all that annotators are requested to do is to mark that a word performing a certain syntactic function is missing in the text, without any obligation to explicitly identify the lexical element that is left out. Rather than being a limitation, this simpler notation can even be thought to carry a more radical interpretation of our sentence. In its turn, this interpretation has interesting implications on the way we reconstruct the communication between the actors and the audience of the play. In the original design of the Prague Dependency Treebank, from which the guidelines of the AGDT were derived, the tag for elements governed by elided words (ExD) is used as a signpost that marks the absence of an explicitly realized construction.[26] It can be liable to two different readings:

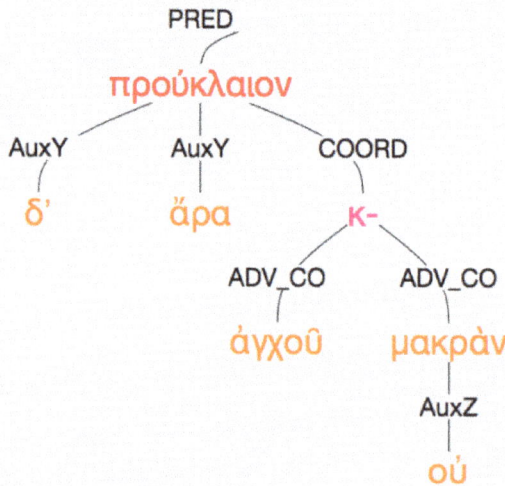

Figure 6: Circumstantials with the verb.

1. the governing element is implied from the context;
2. the element is lacking any proper construction; for example, its construction is suspended as the sentence, which started according to a certain pattern, moves abruptly toward a different organization.

Read from the standpoint of interpretation n.2, the annotation represented in Fig. 7 implies that ἀγχοῦ is left hanging, because with the addition of οὐ μακράν προύκλαιον the sentence shifts to a different structure where the first adverb has no proper place.

As a matter of fact, even this reading has already been anticipated in the critical literature. Some commentators (especially Campbell 1881) have noted that the two adverbs are not quite as well coordinated as they appear at first sight. μακράν ('for a long stretch') constructed with a verb of speaking points normally to duration in time, rather than to distance in space; so κοὐ μακράν προύκλαιον could mean: 'not for long did we mourn in anticipation'. According to Longo (1968), this passage should be seen as an example of 'blurring' of different constructions, where competing tendencies operate in the same sentence. Two ideas are fused together, namely: 1. that Herakles is nearer than it was imagined 2. that 'lamentation in forebode' is over and did not last for long; the transition is reached in the polar expression. The adverb 'near' brings about the formulation of the former idea. At the same time the adverb μακράν places

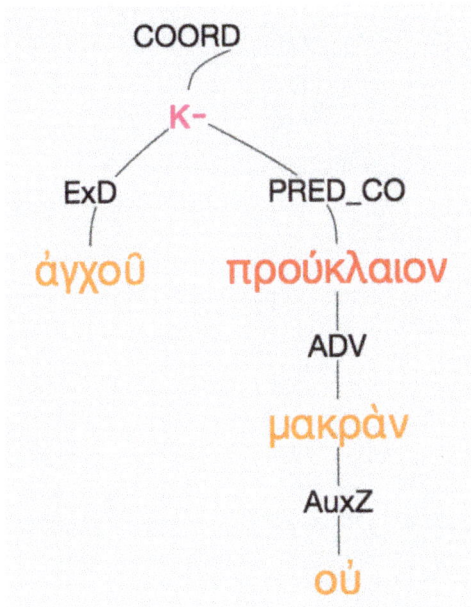

Figure 7: A broken edge?

the main accent on the latter. As a result, the first adverb is loosely attached to the main verb, to which only the second properly belongs.

Such a progressive restructuring of the syntax is often observed in spoken language, since there is no other way in which uttered sentences or sentence fragments can be corrected.[27] Yet this phenomenon is by no means exclusively a mark of hesitation or error. It can also be a strategy to unfold the meaning of a performed utterance progressively. We should certainly not forget that tragedy was a performance-oriented genre; some of the phenomena which are more typical of the spoken rather than written language should not surprise us even in the carefully polished poetical language of the Athenian dramatists. Other cases of sentences whose syntax is structured progressively, and yet very carefully, are indeed often found in Sophocles.[28] This interpretation points to a tension between the syntax of the coordination and the semantics of the two adverbs that is certainly operative in the sentence. And yet it is equally undeniable that, however 'perturbed' by competing structures and in spite of any 'false start' that the first adverb suggests, the words do reach a coherent syntactic construction centred around the coordination of ἀγχοῦ and μακράν. This is a crucial difference with the model of sentence restructuring typical of oral conversation (and diagrammed in the tree of Fig. 7), where the starting elements are obliterated or left unrealized. We would certainly go too far if we posited that ἀγχοῦ is left without a construction. My personal preference, therefore, goes to the interpretation of Fig. 6, even if the sort of zeugma that can be seen in the construction of the verb with the two adverbs cannot be properly captured in it.[29]

1.1 Complex Syntax in a Class Environment

The previous discussion involves a level of complexity and subtlety that might be suitable only for advanced students in Classical philology. However, two crucial points must be stressed.

Firstly, annotators must be encouraged to notice how even the smallest change in the collocation of the words within the sentence tree or in the use of the AGDT labels for the syntactic relations is going to affect dramatically the general interpretation of the sentence.

Secondly, students can be fruitfully reminded that most of the different reconstructions that they can obtain by moving around words in Arethusa and attaching them to different parts of the trees are likely to be already attested in the history of the interpretation of the text they are annotating. Students should be always invited to investigate the commentaries in search to alternative ways of structuring a sentence, and of different arguments to argue either for or against some of the possible reconstructions.

These two steps can be attempted in both direction: starting from the original interpretations of the students to find the precursors in the previous criticism, or from the history of criticism to an original reading. Yet they both form the indispensable steps toward a fully informed critical annotation.

5 Conclusions

Soph. *Trach*. 962–3 has confronted us with simple linguistic tasks (such as identifying the correct morphological interpretation of προὔκλαιον) and more complex interpretative problems; in cases as such, and in most cases when reading Greek tragedies, the construction of a syntactic annotation of a sentence should be seen more as an open process than a mere application of a series of grammatical rules. Interpretations like those reflected in the trees of Figs. 5, 6, and 7 can be (and in fact, as we saw, have been) defended with good arguments. This situation, which is certainly peculiar of treebanks of ancient literary texts, seems to defy the notion itself of a reference treebank: how could a corpus that allows so much space for conflictual interpretation be used as a research tool to investigate linguistic phenomena?

Several answers can be addressed to these sceptical remarks. On the one hand, we can observe that, for one very controversial point in the reading of the sentence, our treebank annotation records several indisputable facts that contribute positively to the advancement of the resources available for the study of Greek. Such facts include the morphology of the words, the lemmatization, or the syntactic annotation of certain syntactic structures, like the similitude introduced by ὡς; other sentences, no matter how controversial in decisive details they might be, would also include subjects, direct objects or other words whose construction would not pose the minimal problem to readers. If similar pieces of information seem trivial within an eleven word sentence, at the scale of the whole corpus of Sophoclean tragedy (let alone the 5th-century poetry or the whole Greek literature) the impact increases exponentially. Thanks to the students that have annotated every words in the Greek texts they were reading, the AGDT already provides enough evidence to conduct comprehensive studies on e.g. the usage of the nominative in Aeschylus, Sophocles, and Homer.[30]

But in parallel to the 'distant reading' that the massive quantitative evidence of the treebank allows, I hope that my discussion has shown that linguistic annotation encourages the work of critical 'close reading' of ancient texts in their original language.[31] The problems that the annotators will face are indeed the same that Gottfried Hermann or even the ancient *scholia* speculated about. The application of treebank annotation in the class is a crucial opportunity to discuss the methods that constitute the most vital legacy of Classical Philology. Linguistic annotation challenges us to find a solution for passages that are often problematic and then to encode it in a well-defined formalism that can be read, compared, and criticized by all that are familiar with the same annotation schema, across every barrier of language or culture.

Notes

[1] AGDT: <http://nlp.perseus.tufts.edu/syntax/treebank/>.

[2] A version 2.0, with some revisions and new features, has been announced. More annotated texts are constantly published in the GitHub repository of the Perseus Digital Library: <https://github.com/PerseusDL/treebank_data>.

[3] See e.g. Smyth 1920: 265; Kühner, Raphael & Bernard Gerth 1898: 77–82.

[4] On the subject, see now the treebank-based analysis of Mambrini & Passarotti 2016.

[5] Mambrini & Passarotti 2012.

[6] Bamman et al. 2009: 7.

[7] For a discussion of a case study on the use of treebank annotation in language and linguistics classes see Gerdes 2013.

[8] The guidelines for syntactic annotation of the AGDT can be accessed online at: <http://nlp.perseus.tufts.edu/syntax/treebank/agdt/1.7/docs/guidelines.pdf>.

[9] See Gerdes 2013 and the paper of Rydberg-Cox in this volume for a remarkable example of similar applications.

[10] The work of annotation starts from the digital text published in the Perseus Digital Library. In this format, the seven extant tragedies of Sophocles consist of 5,973 sentences, which is 71,690 words. Thanks to the integration of Perseus' annotation framework within the Perseids editing environment (see the paper by Beaulieu and Almas in this volume), annotators are free to make modification to the Greek texts they are working with.

[11] Perseids: <http://sosol.perseids.org/tools/arethusa/app/#>.

[12] A fundamental point of departure for the dependency grammar is the work of Tesnière 1959. In particular, the AGDT is closely inspired by the analytic annotation of the *Prague Dependency Grammar* of Czech, whose theoretical foundations are laid in Sgall et al. 1986.

[13] Burton 1980.

[14] Others (e.g. Ellendt 1872 *s.v.*) take προκλαίω to mean 'mourn openly, publicly'. This translation is indeed entirely possible; the other interpretation of the pre-verb πρό, however, fits much better in the dramatic context that we are highlighting.

[15] In Fig. 2, the data from the morphological analyser Morpheus (Crane 1991) are preloaded in the editor for the annotators to choose. If one prefers, this configuration of Arethusa can be deactivated, so that the identification of all the admissible morphological interpretations can be entirely left to the students. In a class, students that are already familiar with the conjugation of the Greek imperfect will eventually come to (or be guided to) the same conclusions that are output here by Morpheus.

[16] Kaminio 1970.

[17] Cf. Xenis 2010: 214; note that πλήθους is Nauck's easy correction for πλῆθος transmitted by the manuscripts.

[18] Hermann 1848.

[19] Kaimio 1977: 174–81, 227–8.

[20] *Od.* 19. 518–23, with full commentary in Nagy 1996: 7–38, 39–58.

[21] See e.g. Soph., *El.* 103–9 and the other examples discussed by Loraux 1999.

[22] See Bruhn 1899, 118–9, and Easterling 1982 *ad S. Tr.* 234–5.

[23] Se e.g. Jebb: 'Ah, he [which implies Herakles as the object] was not far off, but close to us, he for whom I cried in advance"; or Lloyd-Jones 1994: 'So when I lamented like the shrill-voiced nightingale, it was for what was near, not what was far [which implies the neuter ὄν as object]'. The same interpretation can also be found in Easterling 1982.

[24] In Soph. *Ph.* 26 μακράν is constructed predicatively with the object of the verb: τοὔργον οὐ μακρὰν λέγεις, i.e. 'not far off is the task that you speak of'. This relation is easier to understand precisely on account of the presence of an object. In Soph. *fr.* 210.38–9 (quoted by Davis 1991), the object is not expressed: ἀγχοῦ προσεῖπας (sc. τὸν δαίμονα)· οὐ γὰρ ἐκτὸς ἑστὼς συρεῖ δὴ φύρδαν. But the προσ- in the verb gives in any case a sense of direction: one can easily be said to 'address near', i.e. to the vicinity (cf. also Soph. *fr.* 380: ἀγχοῦ προσῆψεν).

[25] This is construction is fully compatible with the interpretation of Kamerbeek 1970, which suggests to take the adverbs with the implied οὖσαι.

[26] The guidelines of the PDT for syntactic annotation can be read online at: <http://ufal.mff.cuni.cz/pdt2.0/doc/manuals/en/a-layer/html/index. html>.

[27] This phenomenon is expressed by a famous quotation from Hor. *Ars Poetica* 390: *nescit vox missa reverti*, a word once uttered cannot come back.

[28] This kind of interpretation is privileged in the aforementioned commentary of Longo 1968: for examples in the *Trach.*, see his index on p. 418 under 'sovrapposizione (fusione, contaminazione) di costrutto' ('overlapping, or fusion, contamination between constructions'). To these passages, we may add a sentence in the exchange between Athena and Odysseus in the *Ajax* (42–3); to the question τί δῆτα ποίμναις τήνδ᾽ ἐπεμπίπτει βάσιν; ('why did he fall in this assault upon the flocks?'), the goddess answers: δοκῶν ἐν ὑμῖν χεῖρα χραίνεσθαι φόνῳ ('because upon you he thought that he was staining his hands with murder'). As my translation of line 43 suggests, the phrase ἐν ὑμῖν ('upon you') is not easy to construe with the following χεῖρα χραίνεσθαι φόνῳ, which appear concluded in itself. His initial position in the clause suggests rather that it may be influenced by the common construction of πίπτειν + ἐν ('fall upon') and dative, prompted by the ἐπεμπίπτειν in the question.

[29] This is also the interpretation that I have adopted for my annotation of the *Women of Trachis* for the AGDT, which is represented in Fig. 1.

[30] Seminal works on this direction are already being produced: see e.g. Mambrini & Passarotti 2016 on agreement patterns with coordinated subjects.

[31] On the notion of 'distant' and 'close' reading see most recently Jockers 2013.

References

Bamman, D., Mambrini, F. & Crane, G. (2009). An ownership model of annotation: The Ancient Greek Dependency Treebank. In *Proceedings of the Eighth International Workshop on Treebanks and Linguistic Theories (TLT 8)*, Milan: EDUCatt, pp. 5–15.

Bruhn, E. (1899). Anhang. In *Sophokles*, Erklärt von F. W. Schneidewin und A. Nauck. Achter Band: Oedipus auf Kolonus. Berlin: Weidmann.

Burton, R. W. B. (1980). *The Chorus in Sophocles' Tragedies*. Oxford: Clarendon Press.

Campbell, L. (1881). *Sophocles. Edited with English notes and introduction. Vol. II: Ajax. Women of Trachis. Electra. Philoctetes. Fragments.* Oxford: Oxford University Press.

Crane, G. (1991). Generating and parsing classical Greek. *Literary and Linguist Computing* 6(4): 243–245.

Davis, M. (1991). *Sophocles. Trachiniae*. Oxford: Oxford University Press.

Easterling, P. E. (1982). *Sophocles. Trachiniae*. Cambridge: Cambridge University Press.

Ellendt, F. (1872). *Lexicon Sophocleum. Editio Altera. Curavit Hermannus Genthe*. Berolini: Borntraeger.

Gerdes, K. (2013). Collaborative dependency annotation. In *Proceedings of the Second International Conference on Dependency Linguistics (DepLing 2013)*, Prague: Matfyzpress, pp. 88–97.

Hermann, G. (1848). *Sophoclis Trachiniae* (2nd Edn.). Lipsiae: Apud Ernestum Fleischerum.

Jebb, R. C. (1892). *Sophocles. The Plays and Fragments. Part V. The Trachiniae.* Cambridge: Cambridge University Press.

Jockers, M. L. (2013). *Macroanalysis: Digital Methods and Literary History*. Chicago: University of Illinois Press.

Kaimio, M. (1970). *The Chorus of Greek Drama within the Light of the Person and Number Used*. Helsinki: Societas Scientiarum Fennica.

Kaimio, M. (1977). *Characterization of Sound in Early Greek Litterature*. Helsinki: Societas Scientiarum Fennica.

Kamerbeek, J. C. (1970). *The Plays of Sophocles. Commentaries. Part II: The Trachiniae* (2nd ed.). Leiden: Brill.

Kühner, R. & Gerth, B. (1898). *Ausführliche Grammatik der griechischen Sprache. Zweiter Teil: Satzlehre. Erster Band.* Hannover: Hahnsche Buchhandlung.

Lloyd-Jones, H. (1994, January). *Sophocles, Volume II. Antigone. The Women of Trachis. Philoctetes. Oedipus at Colonus.* Loeb Classical Library. Cambridge, MA: Harvard University Press.

Longo, O. (1968). *Commento linguistico alle Trachinie di Sofocle*. Padova: Antenore.

Loraux, N. (1999). *La voix endeuillée*. Paris: Gallimard.

Mambrini, F. & Passarotti M. (2012). Will a parser overtake Achilles? first experiments on parsing the Ancient Greek Dependency Treebank. In *Proceedings of the 11th Workshop on Treebanks and Linguistic Theories (TLT11)*, Lisbon (pp. 133–144). Lisbon: Colibri.

Mambrini, F. & Passarotti M. (2016). Subject-Verb Agreement with Coordinated Subjects in Ancient Greek. A Treebank-based Study. *Journal of Greek Linguistics* 16, forthcoming.

Nagy, G. (1996). *Poetry as Performance. Homer and beyond*. Cambridge: Cambridge University Press.

Sgall, P., Hajičová, E. & Panevová, J. (1986). *The Meaning of the Sentence and Its Semantic and Pragmatic Aspects*. Dodrech: Academia/Reidel Publishing Company.

Smyth, H. W. (1920). *A Greek Grammar for Colleges*. New York: American Book Company.

Tesnière, L. (1959). *Éléments de syntaxe structurale*. Paris: Klinksieck.

Xenis, G. (2010). *Scholia vetera in Sophoclis "Trachinias"*. Berlin: De Gruyter.

SECTION 2

Knowledge Exchange

CHAPTER 6

Of Features and Models: A Reflexive Account of Interdisciplinarity across Image Processing, Papyrology, and Trauma Surgery

Ségolène M. Tarte

University of Oxford

Abstract

Image processing specialists rarely work on their own, entirely disconnected from the domains of application for which the image processing algorithms are required. In this chapter, I scrutinize my experience of developing image processing approaches for Medicine and for Classics. Through this reflexive take on interdisciplinarity and knowledge exchange and by relating my own experience to the literature on interdisciplinarity, I present observations and strategies that have proven useful in handling the intrinsic difficulties of multidisciplinary collaborative undertakings.

What I call T-words, words that Trigger a Terminology Twitch, are those abstract words that apparently have an obvious meaning, but, within their respective context, are in fact semantic handles that implicitly activate field-specific frameworks. Identifying them and investigating their deep meaning in their field-specific context is therefore an essential first step in establishing a working multi-disciplinary collaboration.

Furthering the knowledge exchange process, it is essential to learn about the epistemological foundations of the domains. These are made as much of

How to cite this book chapter:
Tarte, S M. 2016. Of Features and Models: A Reflexive Account of Interdisciplinarity across Image Processing, Papyrology, and Trauma Surgery. In: Bodard, G & Romanello, M (eds.) *Digital Classics Outside the Echo-Chamber: Teaching, Knowledge Exchange & Public Engagement*, Pp. 103–120. London: Ubiquity Press. DOI: http://dx.doi.org/10.5334/bat.g. License: CC-BY 4.0.

the established conventions of the domain (of collaboration, of publication) as of the actual practices (e.g. familiarity with ways of seeing and looking—in particular when it comes to applying image processing techniques to different fields).

Finally, in response to the black box problem—where algorithms are perceived as producing difficult to interpret output—I contend that experts' minds are black boxes too, and that it is therefore at least as important (if not more) to establish trust between experts as it is to make the black boxes transparent.

1 Introduction

Image processing specialists rarely work on their own, entirely disconnected from the domains of application for which the image processing algorithms are required. In this paper, I scrutinize my personal experience as an image processing expert working for applications in the domains of computer-assisted orthopaedic and trauma surgery, and for applications in papyrology and palaeography. It is therefore a reflexive take on interdisciplinarity and knowledge exchange and how the author has experienced them. The assumption is that, although the thoughts laid bare here are drawn from personal experience, many of the working processes and strategies deployed might be generalizable. The intention is not to crystallise a dualistic vision of the sciences and the humanities (as expressed by C.P. Snow[1]), but rather to unpick the approaches I have adopted in the very specific contexts of image processing applied for computer-assisted surgery and radiotherapy on one hand, and for papyrology and palaeography on the other hand. I will first introduce these domains of application through the identification of polysemic words that proved key to the research endeavour. Having identified the importance of acknowledging the frameworks that such words implicitly carry with them, I will broaden the perspective by relating my experiences and observations to more general considerations on epistemic cultures, in particular: of modes of knowledge creation and of collaborative models. Finally, I will address the question of methodologies, arguing that as a complement to an understanding of field-specific epistemic cultures, an understanding of the cognitive underpinnings of the research process along with tuned narratives can only benefit collaborative research in Digital Classics and in the Digital Humanities.

2 Polysemy of Words Crossing the Wires of Communication

In order to set the scene of interdisciplinary research and the difficulties that can be encountered, I shall first present examples of the use of words in image processing, trauma surgery, papyrology, and palaeography that have, in my experience, lead to confusion. These confusions are interesting because, although they might seem anecdotal at first glance, they are symptomatic of a deeper knowledge exchange challenge. The two following words have proven to be polysemic and to carry with them, as implicit luggage, much more than their apparent meaning; they are: 'feature', and 'model'.

2.1 Where 'Features' are Prominent

The noun 'feature', according to the Oxford English Dictionary online, when not referring directly to the body or face, is defined as:[2]

> [...] (4) A distinctive or characteristic part of a thing; some part which arrests the attention by its conspicuousness or prominence. [...]

In all the academic contexts where I've encountered the word 'feature', the word always takes on this meaning of distinctive or characteristic part, yet each context also appends more to the word and assumes some kind of general, yet field-specific, framework. Within the computer sciences, whilst 'feature' appears both in the image processing expression 'feature detection' and in the pattern recognition and machine learning expression 'feature vector', the features in question do not designate the same abstraction—there can be some overlap, but in general they are rather different objects. In image processing terms, feature detection is the search for specific behaviours of the colours or grey levels in an image (assumed here for simplicity to be a grey scale image), such as sharp changes. These sharp changes can be described quite simply in the pixel-value space as a sudden drop or increase in value when moving from one region to another (steps), but they can also be characterised by a change of behaviour in a transform space, such as the presence of a local maximum in the accumulator space of a Hough transform (used for example to detect lines); in pattern detection, a feature vector is a row of numerical descriptors where each value characterises an aspect of a specific pattern that is searched for, such as Fourier descriptors which have the property of being translation, rotation, and scale invariant, and are therefore quite useful to describe a shape, abstraction made of its position in space (hence a very useful property when one has a template of a shape that is being searched for). After some years working alongside other image processing and pattern recognition experts, this explicit distinction faded, and context naturally and implicitly informed the meaning of the word 'feature'. Further, working specifically in computer-assisted surgery and radiotherapy, the word 'feature' came to mean 'any medically interesting structures' for the surgeons and oncologists I was collaborating with. For example, if the bright white streaks appearing in Computerised Tomography (CT) scans and radiating around metallic elements such as screws and plates are *sensu stricto* features in an image processing context, to medical doctors, those are artefacts, where an artefact is understood as noise that obscures regions of interest and that needs removing. In computer-assisted trauma surgery, the features that surgeons were interested in were all the visual evidence revealing aspects and configurations of the broken bony anatomy; in oncology, the features were all the visual evidence leading to the identification of tumours and their extents. The shift from trauma surgery to oncology meant a readjustment of my understanding of the word 'feature', but only insofar as the structures of interest in the CT images were different structures: in oncology, the specific application was lung cancer; in trauma surgery, it was pelvic and acetabular fractures. Changing the domain of application to work with papyrologists, the word 'feature' was also used, but this time to describe the palaeographical characteristics of the scripts that papyrologists were working on. Whereas in the medical domain, the word 'feature' was a technical word used primarily by image processing experts and adopted by medical doctors to designate the areas of interest in their specific context, in a palaeographical context the word 'feature' is already used routinely to describe a script, its specificities, and the specificities of scribal schools or even hands; what papyrologists and I were facing as collaborators was an encounter of two different pre-existing uses and thus meanings of the word 'feature', not just a sliding of meaning from one domain into another to accommodate needs and work processes. Interestingly, medieval digital palaeographers use the word 'feature' to designate 'A descriptive label which can be applied to a component, idiograph or graph (e.g. "long", "short", "wedged")'.[3] In this endeavour, an explicit effort is made to produce a definition of the word 'feature' that fits both the contexts of palaeography and of image processing.

Other examples of the use of the word 'feature' in different domains range from archaeology to corpus linguistics, and from electron microscopy to human–computer interaction; what all have in common is that although the meaning of the word is at first glance the same and seems to adhere to the OED definition, each usage actually implicitly carries a contextual framework that relies on skilled vision, on a socially and culturally learned way of looking and seeing that is deeply field specific.[4]

2.2 Where 'Models' can Fit

Models and modelling have been of long-standing interest in the Digital Humanities, as demonstrated by a panel discussion at the 2014 Digital Humanities conference,[5] and by a number of extensive threads on the Humanist Discussion Group.[6] The object here is not to discuss what modelling in the Digital Humanities might be, but rather to show how speaking of models and modelling might differ from field to field. The noun 'model', according to the Oxford English Dictionary online is:[7]

> (I) A representation of structure, and related senses.
> [...]
> (I-8-a) A simplified or idealized description or conception of a particular system, situation, or process, often in mathematical terms, that is put forward as a basis for theoretical or empirical understanding, or for calculations, predictions, etc.; a conceptual or mental representation of something. Freq. with modifying word. [...]
> As a verb, 'to model' is defined as:[8]
> [...]
> (5-b) To classify, arrange in a system
> [...]
> (10-a) to devise a (usually mathematical) model or simplified description of (a phenomenon, system, etc.)
> [...]

In all the academic contexts where I've encountered the word 'model', it was used to designate as much the process as the result, and it was used as much to understand a phenomenon or object as to simplify it in order to use it for a specific purpose. In computer-assisted trauma surgery of the pelvis, the noun 'model' was used to designate two distinct objects, one digital, and one physical. The digital object was a 3D virtual model of the broken pelvis, built from CT data of the broken anatomy. This 3D model allowed surgeons to visualize the 3D anatomy directly, rather than to have to mentally extract the 3D information from the stack of 2D images that constitute the CT data. This 3D model extraction, which is now routinely performed, was in its infancy and very much limited by computational power when I was working with surgeons (over 10 years ago). The virtual models of the fragments could further be manipulated independently from one another and abstracted from the soft tissue surrounding them; they allowed surgeons to see the fragments as 3D objects in their entirety ahead of physically manipulating them in the operating room (OR).[9] The producing of the virtual object went through the act of modelling, which in this case meant translating the characterisation of the bony anatomy from visual criteria into mathematical image properties. In cases where the pelvic and acetabular fractures are complex, trauma surgeons often resort to physically manipulating a plastic model of the pelvis. On this physical model, they can trace the fracture lines as they understand them from the CT data and from the 3D virtual model, and even recreate the fragments by breaking the plastic model according to the fracture lines; by further referring to the classifications of pelvic and acetabular fractures,[10] they can decide upon an adapted surgical approach to reduce the fracture.

In complement to the virtual 3D model, the plastic model is a useful tool not only for teaching, but also for researching and understanding how the pieces of the complex 3D jigsaw puzzle that is the fractured anatomy fit together;[11] with this physical model, surgeons already engage with an aspect of the surgical act before stepping into the OR.

In lung cancer radiotherapy the model that we[12] produced was a 4D model,[13] an animated 3D model, informing oncologists of the most probable location of the tumour at any point within the breathing cycle, thereby helping them to establish a radiotherapy plan—unlike bones, whose geometry is fixed, lungs are flexible and change shape during breathing, so that a tumour within the lungs will move during the breathing cycle, thereby requiring the radiotherapy treatment to take tumour movement into account. The process of building the model revealed many aspects of the variability in breathing, and even if the final model did not take all the variations into account, the process itself informed us of these and allowed us to identify some of the shortcomings of the model (breathing is irregular, especially in lung cancer patients, and the model is by essence regular, even if it allows for statistical deviations). Here again, the process of modelling involved the translation of a real-world phenomenon (breathing, as captured by CT images) into a mathematically formalised behaviour (the 4D model).

In papyrology, an example of modelling is the work I conducted to simulate the Artemidorus Papyrus as a roll[14] in order to assess the reordering of the fragments proposed by D'Alessio.[15] Here again, modelling involved simplification and idealisation as it used the equation of a spiral to describe the roll—and that only will describe a perfect roll, not a skewed roll, no looseness in the roll, no folds, which all could have occurred of course. The virtual model was however helpful and showed conclusively that reordering the fragments was reasonable; and, just as with the virtual and plastic pelvis models, the physical model that I produced by printing the reconstructed papyrus based on the new fragments order served to physically convince the papyrologists by letting them manipulate an avatar[16] of the papyrus that let them assess the appositeness of the reordering for themselves.

'Model' was a less contentious word than 'feature', as all collaborators expressly wanted a mathematical model of some sort. The core of the work as an image processing scholar however was always to gather sufficient domain-specific information in order to make the models not only relevant but also useful for the experts. Building a model as a 'simplified or idealized description or conception of a particular system' requires identifying the aspects of the system or phenomenon that need to be encapsulated, represented by the model in order for the domain experts to find some use for the model.

Other examples of words like 'feature' and 'model' would be: 'pattern' (in trauma surgery, in papyrology, in linguistics, in the computer sciences) 'ontology' (in philosophy, in the computer sciences), 'skeleton' (in trauma surgery, in image processing, in palaeography), 'process' (in the cognitive sciences, in the computer sciences, in engineering, in anatomy), and even a word like 'science' takes on a different meaning whether used in English or in Latin languages such as French or Spanish (where its meaning covers all forms of academic knowledge, including the Humanities).[17] It is worth noting further, that whilst researching rigorous definitions of some of the terms above in the respective contexts I have encountered them in, I was often at pains to find a definition; for example, the word 'feature' does not appear in the index of Bischoff's book on Latin palaeography;[18] and in the index of Gonzalez and Wood's book, commonly known as the image processing bible, the term 'feature' appears only in 'feature selection' and refers the reader to the word 'descriptor'.[19] These conceptual terms seem to be general enough to often not warrant a dedicated field-specific definition, and yet their intrinsic meaning shifts subtly away from their general meaning with use in every field.

The intention in pointing out these words is not to unify their use, or to decide normatively of their meaning, but rather to point out a crucial aspect of collaboration. Such words need to be looked out for, discussed, and clarified, so that all involved can grasp what their interlocutors are talking about; in brief, these words ought to *Trigger a Terminology Twitch*, and I have therefore dubbed them *T-words*. T-words often designate abstractions that carry an implicit framework with them, and so discussing them will often open the way to fruitful collaboration. Asking seemingly naive questions of and around T-words has always helped me unveil some of the implicit field-specific assumptions and thus facilitated exchanges. Indeed, T-words act as semantic handles within their varied contexts, implicitly activating field-specific theoretical frameworks within which they take on a specialised meaning, a meaning that relates directly to the mode of knowledge creation of the fields that use them.

3 Modes of Knowledge Creation

It is no surprise that the T-words evoked above all deal with designating abstractions. As abstractions, they can only be deeply connected to the domain that handles them. Questioning their deep meaning therefore inevitably leads to asking epistemological questions about the domain they emanate from. Some aspects of applied epistemological enquiry are therefore always present in my approaches to collaboration. Such enquiry enables to understand how epistemic cultures differ from field to field, where an epistemic culture is defined as 'those amalgams of arrangements and mechanisms—bonded through affinity, necessity, and historical coincidence—which, in a given field, make up *how we know what we know*'.[20] Conducting a field-specific epistemological enquiry when working on a Digital

Humanities research project, and indeed on any interdisciplinary project, serves multiple purposes:

1. to identify the methodologies that are being mobilised by making them explicit, be they traditional or computational. As a result, it becomes easier to understand the various modes of thinking that scholars engage in; it also helps with the identification, design, and implementation of adapted methods, be they digital or not, be they interdisciplinary or not;
2. to identify the interesting research questions for all fields involved. As a result, it becomes easier to align the expectations of all scholars involved, thus helping to avoid the trap by which scholars in one field might become disengaged due to a lack of interesting/challenging/relevant research question for them in the collaborative project;
3. to identify the implicit collaborative models of each of the fields involved, making people explicitly aware of the different conventions of publication and dissemination that need to be accommodated within a collaborative research project.

3.1 Field-specific Epistemologies

According to Becher and Trowler, the nature of knowledge as it is created within academia can be classified as:[21]

- cumulative and atomistic, yielding discovery/explanation, such as mathematics and physics;
- reiterative and holistic, yielding understanding/interpretation, such as anthropology and history;
- purposive and pragmatic, yielding products/techniques, such as software engineering and clinical medicine;
- functional and utilitarian, yielding protocols/procedures, such as law.

This intriguing and potentially controversial classification correlates well however with my limited experience. In computer-assisted surgery and radiotherapy, it became very soon apparent that computer scientists, as well as medical doctors, engage with research questions in a problem-solving mode; the understanding of a given problem might be somewhat different, but scholars approach it indeed in a 'purposive and pragmatic' manner, aiming to yield a product, a technique, a solution. In trauma surgery for example, a research question might be 'How do we assess the accuracy of the reduction of a fracture?'; related questions such as 'what does accuracy mean? In reference to what? To functional rehabilitation? To geometrical congruency?' need to be addressed ahead of the accuracy question, so that each new question can securely build upon the previously established answers. The secure aspect is crucial, even if it is primarily so in the scholars' perception and understanding. This makes this approach a foundationalist approach to knowledge creation.[22] The accent in these fields is on providing answers (and even if identifying research questions is naturally reiterative, the focus remains on the answers, not on how to best formulate the questions). It is even so obvious that answers have to be provided that, in a publication context (e.g. in the computer sciences), a cursory glance at the titles of journal or conference articles will show how it is *the methodology and methods* used to get the answers that are highlighted—as answers are assumed to be provided. This type of approach might be dubbed diagrammatic, and its main characteristic is that it is predominantly linear, each step requiring the previous one to be completed before build upon it.

In papyrology and palaeography, scholars approach their problems iteratively, which means that they have no qualms about continually revisiting, revising, and reformulating a question. This reiterative approach to research questions is at the core of their knowledge creation process. Answers to such questions matter of course, but here, the accent is on the questions. Even if scholars strive for security in their findings, they are always very conscious that new findings might act as modifiers for pre-existing knowledge; in this sense, their approach is more coherentist than foundationalist.[23] This also affects the titles of publications, where titles will tend to highlight *the themes and results* (e.g. in palaeography), leaving the often complicated and multi-layered process to get them for the core narrative of the paper. This type of approach might be dubbed radial or fractal, its main characteristic is that it operates predominantly through indexing and cross-referencing to build the scaffold of an argument.

This difference in epistemic cultures became particularly obvious to me at a computational palaeography seminar where one half of the scholars were palaeographers and the other half were computer scientists.[24] This difference in field-specific modes of knowledge creation manifested itself clearly in a lengthy exchange were computer scientists endeavoured to answer palaeographers' questions by proposing tools and solutions, and upon hearing the answers, palaeographers kept reformulating their questions, refining criteria, evoking exceptions and special cases.

For an image processing expert, it means that in computer-assisted surgery and radiotherapy, the task is to provide medical doctors with definite answers/tools, whereas with papyrologists and palaeographers, it will never be possible to provide a tool that is a definite answer; the best that the tool can be is a useful way to get elements of an answer that will allow scholars to refine their question in order to create new knowledge. An example of such a tool is the work that Campagnolo et al. have conducted, to create a reference tool for the identification of the types of stains and associated damage that can occur in manuscripts.[25]

3.2 Collaborative Models

Drawing further on Becher and Trowler, it becomes evident that the collaborative models I have experienced as well as the publication conventions I have encountered correlate with what they call the urban and rural contexts scenarios:[26]

> **urban context:** characterised by a high people-to-problem ratio, with 'a generally busy—occasionally frenetic—pace of life, high levels of collective activity, close competition for space and resources, and a rapid and heavily used information network'. The areas of study are generally narrow, with discrete and separable problems; there are few salient topics; the changes in the research landscape are fast (fast-paced research); competition is intense; and there is also more funding available in urban-type fields;
>
> **rural context:** characterised by a low people-to-problem ratio, and only displaying the characteristics of urban areas in occasional bursts. The areas of study are wide with open problems that are not sharply delineated; a wide range of themes exists (in contrast to the salient topics of urban contexts); issues are long range, requiring time-demanding research; labour is divided, the lone-scholar model is a frequently found one; and less funding is available in rural-type fields.

When engaging in interdisciplinary research, it is important to know what kind of environment one steps into because the associated collaborative model and publication conventions will reflect elements of the urban/rural context along with elements of the linear/radial thinking and associated epistemologies. There are a number of within-field collaborative models that range from little to no collaboration to huge teams:[27]

- The little-to-no collaboration model is that of the lone scholar, of which a prime example would be St Augustine.
- Small teams will tend to adopt the sports team model, a model where the hierarchy is very flat, and all team members' voices have equal standing.
- Larger teams will tend to adopt an orchestra model, where there is a very clear hierarchical structure and decisions tend to be made from the top.
- The last model, which has recently gained visibility through citizen sciences projects such as those of the Zooniverse suite[28] (and which is not mentioned in Becher and Trowler's 2001 work), is that of huge teams that rely on a (possibly fluctuating) base of volunteers performing simple tasks that have been designed by researchers having adopted a problem reduction approach in order to gather large amounts of data.[29]

For the computer sciences and for medical applications the context is urban, and medium to large teams of researchers work on a project. The teams might however have different kinds of dynamics and ways of organising labour. In the medical domain, the most common model is that of the orchestra. A surgeon for example, habituated to being the decision-maker in the OR, will naturally fall into a conductor role, where all the others in the team (the members of the orchestra) have very precise roles, and the responsibility of coordinating and bringing all the pieces of work together is the conductor/surgeon's. As an image processing expert, stepping into such a collaborative environment means meeting expectations; it does not always allow for being creative and proposing new or different ways of tackling the global problem, so that out-of-the-box thinking is only appreciated if it remains strictly within the confines of one's specific domain of expertise. One possible explanation for this is the amount of pressure and time constraint that surgeons and oncologists are under, which leaves them with little time and patience for what they might perceive as unorthodox thinking. In contrast, the model I've encountered with papyrologists is more one that follows that of a sports team, where all players contribute to an overall task, for example the transcription, edition, and commentary of a papyrus. In my experience, an image processing expert in this context is welcome as an other and different voice.

These organizational differences in how teams operate is clearly reflected in publications, this time through authorship. Single author publications are extremely rare in the computer sciences and in the medical sciences, and when they occur they usually are a sign of seniority. Not only multiple authors are the norm, the order of the authors in the list of authors is meaningful. In the biomedical sciences for instance, the last author is usually the head of department, or senior scholar who received the funding to conduct the work, regardless of the actual amount they have contributed to the work being published. In the Humanities, the norm is more that of single author publications. This poses intriguing questions for Digital Classics, and more generally for the Digital Humanities, whose conventions are still in the process of being developed and might deviate quite significantly from the Humanities tradition of single author publications – as Digital Humanities projects often bring together people from different epistemic cultures.[30]

Having thus reviewed some of the global considerations of interdisciplinary work, tying in my personal experiences and observations with the literature, I now come back to more specific considerations to show how collaborative work has lead me to consider how field-specific narratives of knowledge creation affected my research in computer-assisted trauma surgery and in Digital Classics.

4 Tuning Narratives for Knowledge Exchange & Communication

4.1 Cognition for Epistemology

Citing Becher and Trowler, it is important to attend to 'cognitive as well as social factors in any attempt to make sense of academic interaction'.[31] In trauma surgery, as well is in papyrology, I have found it not only useful but also inspiring to attempt to understand the processes in which experts engage. I have therefore endeavoured to never shy away from asking the candid questions in an attempt to understand how my image processing work might help experts in their work without replacing them. A rule of thumb has been to attempt to grasp what experts are familiar with, in order to ensure that, whilst proposing a new tool, the new tool retains some elements of familiarity, thereby encouraging the uptake of the tool. One example from trauma surgery would be my attempt to transpose and generalise their criteria for the evaluation of the accuracy of fracture reduction. The mode of visualization that trauma surgeons were the most familiar with (over 10 years ago, but this is most likely still the case) was cross-sections of the anatomy so that when I programmed the piece of software that allowed them to visualize and virtually manipulate 3D virtual models of bone fragments, I made sure to add a functionality that would allow them to see the cross-sectional outlines of the fragments along a plane that they could interactively reposition in space. That was a success, as this cross-sectional visualization chimed with what they were used to looking at when working with CT images. However, drifting away from familiarity, I further attempted to develop a single quantitative measure for the accuracy of the repositioning of the fragments;[32] to the best of my knowledge, although this measure was a mathematical success, it was never really adopted, I believe that the main reason is that it was too remote from the three measurements that they were used to making to evaluate reduction accuracy.

A striking example of familiarity in papyrology involves more than familiarity and points towards one of the characteristics of experts as having internalised so much of their own cognitive processes that they have built shortcuts making them blind to aspects of what they are actually doing (integration of cognitive units[33]). I was asked to remove the horizontal striae of the woodgrain from an image of a ancient Roman tablet, as they were perceived as a distraction, as noise in the data, which I did.[34] And although the papyrologists were thankful, I noticed that they made little use of these woodgrain-free images, reverting to using the images with the visible woodgrain. I first thought that the images were too unfamiliar, but it later emerged that although the woodgrain was originally perceived as noise, it had in fact been an implicit source of information; where grooves of the woodgrain were present, it was possible to hypothesize that, for instance, the horizontal bar of a 'T' might have disappeared in a groove, which the lack of information on the location of the woodgrain precluded. Familiarity is of course only one of the aspects of the cognitive involvement of experts in their work. As evoked earlier when discussing the polysemy of the word 'feature', skilled vision also is a specific form of cognitive involvement. Investigating the types of cognitive involvement of scholars in their research helps make their methodologies explicit by uncovering processes ranging from conceptual to perceptual processes for which the digital world can help provide triggers and support.[35]

Embarking on investigations into the cognitive underpinnings of experts' research processes does not mean that I have become an expert myself however. I argue that one of the crucial aspects of collaborative work resides in how the narratives about specialist research operate.

4.2 Deep Knowledge and Communicable Knowledge

Domain-specific knowledge creation requires a layered understanding of field-specific concepts; in a collaborative context, experts in a given field need on one hand the deep knowledge that made them experts and on the other hand ways to communicate this deep knowledge in broader brushstrokes so that non-experts might gain enough of an intuitive understanding of the domain to collaborate fruitfully. One approach to achieving this is by exposing the specialist processes.[36] Exposing specialist processes fits with the Digital Humanities transparency agenda,[37] but I contend that this exposing of research processes is intrinsic to the Digital Humanities in a deeper way. Indeed, to engage with, evolve, and create digital tools, it is necessary to understand the underlying methodologies—those same methodologies that are shaped by epistemic cultures and cognitive engagement. My contention is that beyond the transparency agenda, collaborators should not be expected to become experts in a field that is remote from their own. So that more than transparency, what is required is to establish trust between specialists,[38] and this trust can only be built if experts, and/or some skilled intermediaries, know how to communicate intuitively the essence of expert knowledge and methodologies to non-experts. It is through this fine-tuning of field-specific narratives to non-experts that trust can be established and solid foundations set for fruitful and exciting collaborations. The emergence of the transparency agenda in the Digital Humanities has often been brandished as a solution to what is perceived as the computational black box problem, where the inner working of a black box are hidden, generating anxiety towards the interpretability of the output of the black boxes. But black boxes are not the exclusivity of computational tools, experts' cognitive powers are black boxes too. So more than attempting to make black boxes transparent, I contend that unpicking the epistemic and cognitive underpinning of research questions in order to hone interdisciplinary communications between experts will allow us to make methodologies explicit and therefore facilitate the creation of adapted, useful, and trustworthy digital methods.

5 Conclusions

Through describing my experiences as an image processing expert for applications in fields that are as different as computer-assisted surgery and papyrology, I have teased out the aspects that I have found to be critical to the success of interdisciplinary research. One of the salient outcomes of this reflexive take is that methodologies have become, of necessity, a central point of enquiry in Digital Classics, and more generally in the Digital Humanities. The drive to build digital tools therefore has incited a reflexive look on methodologies, and I have reviewed herein the various elements that such an approach can shed a light upon. In substance, engaging in epistemic and cognitive enquiries can only facilitate multidirectional cross-pollination and simultaneously well-balanced knowledge exchanges and field-specific knowledge enrichment. Crucial to interdisciplinary collaborations are the following considerations:

1. an acute attention to communication through the identification of what I have called the T-words (those that ought to Trigger a Terminology Twitch) and the naive questions of and around them in order to uncover the implicit theoretical frameworks they carry with them;
2. an identification of the field-specific epistemic cultures, along with their specific epistemologies and collaborative models, in order to clarify expectations and establish balanced research agendas for all involved;
3. a tuning of narratives where cognitive powers and computational tools are not perceived as black boxes anymore, but rather as trustworthy and adapted tools that serve the common research project as much as the field-specific research agendas.

In this sense, by adopting a decidedly cognitive approach to research, and to understanding a given domain of application, cross-disciplinary exchanges can be facilitated. In particular, cognitive approaches to the study of textual artefacts can inform image processing experts who can then propose not just re-purposed approaches, but re-engineered approaches that might themselves be further re-engineered to benefit the domain of application they were originally inspired by.

Acknowledgements

This work has largely benefited from lengthy conversations with the following people, to whom the author is very grateful: Alan Bowman, Pip Willcox, David

De Roure, Terhi Nurmikko-Fuller, Dominique Stutzmann, Gabriel Bodard and Matteo Romanello, as well as the publisher's reviewers.

Notes

1. Snow 1959.
2. OED *s.v.* "'Feature': <http://www.oed.com/view/Entry/68848> (last accessed November 2015).
3. DigiPal, 'Glossary': <http://www.digipal.eu/help/glossary> (last accessed November 2015).
4. Grasseni 2007; Tarte 2014.
5. Panel 'What is Modeling and What is Not?', chair: Paul Spence, panel members: Van Zundert, JorisJob; Jannidis, Fotis; Drucker, Johanna; Rockwell, Geoffrey; Underwood, Ted; Kestemont, Mike; Andrews, Tara; Sperberg-Mcqueen, Michael; cf. p. 13 <https://dh2014.files.wordpress.com/2014/07/dh2014-conference-program.pdf> (last accessed November 2015).
6. *cf.* for example: Humanist Discussion Group: Vol. 7, No. 0006 (1993); Vol. 16, No. 526 (2003); Vol. 28, No. 74 (2014); on <http://dhhumanist.org/> (last accessed November 2015).
7. OED *s.v.* "model *n.*": <http://www.oed.com/view/Entry/120577> (last accessed November 2015).
8. OED *s.v.* "model *v.*": <http://www.oed.com/view/Entry/120578> (last accessed November 2015).
9. Two options were available, simply visualizing the 3D objects on a 2D screen, or visualizing them using stereoscopic technology that aimed to facilitate actual 3D perception.
10. Letournel & Judet 1993; Tile 1996.
11. Citak et al. 2008.
12. In that project, I was part of a team of image processing experts, hence 'we'.
13. McClelland et al. 2006
14. Tarte 2012.
15. D'Alessio 2009.
16. I use the term 'avatar' here, where others might have used 'facsimile' or 'surrogate'. 'Avatar' simply underlines that this specific remediation of the artefact only captures *some* aspect of its materiality, here its affordance to being rolled.
17. The list goes on, of course: 'multimodal', 'record', 'network', 'fieldwork', 'infrastructure', 'agent', etc.
18. Bischoff et al. 1990.
19. Gonzalez & Woods 2008.
20. Knorr Cetina 1999: 1.
21. Becher & Trowler 2001: 36.
22. Haack 1993, chap. 1.

23 Haack 1993, chap. 1.
24 Hassner et al. 2014.
25 Chap. VII in this volume.
26 Becher & Trowler 2001: 106.
27 Becher & Trowler 2001: 124.
28 Smith et al. 2013.
29 See also Brusuelas (Chap. X in this volume).
30 It will not have escaped to the sagacity of astute readers that this very chapter might be considered a Digital Humanities paper and yet follows the single authorship model of the (more traditional) humanities. This chapter is however written in the first person which is a practice more frequently observed in the sciences (and in the English language). In the context of this volume, this autobiographical voice is a deliberate choice: the use of the personal pronouns 'I' and 'we' serves to reinforce the fact that although the observations presented here are likely to apply in many contexts and have the potential to be widely useful, they carry no claim to universality as they are but mediated by the author.
31 Becher & Trowler 2001: 124.
32 Tarte et al. 2006.
33 Feltovich et al. 2006; Chi 2006.
34 Tarte 2011.
35 Tarte 2014; Terras 2005.
36 As exemplified by the chapters by Vitale (Chap.VIII), Almas & Beaulieu (Chap. IX), Bodard & Stoyanova (Chap. V) in this volume.
37 Ramsay & Rockwell 2012.
38 Hassner et al. 2014.

References

Becher, T. & Trowler, P. R. (2001). *Academic tribes and territories.* (2nd Edn.) Buckingham: The Society for Research into Higher Education and Open University Press.

Bischoff, B., Translated by Ó Cróinín, D. & Ganz, D. (1990). *Latin Palaeography – Antiquity & the Middle Ages.* Cambridge: Cambridge University Press.

Chi, M. T. H. (2006). Two approaches to the study of experts' characteristics. In Ericsson et al. (Eds.). Chapter 2: 21–30.

Citak, M., Gardner, M., Kendoff, D., Tarte, S., Krettek, C., Nolte, L.-P. & Hüfner, T. (2008). Virtual 3D planning of acetabular fracture reduction. *J Orthop Res*, 26(4):547–552.

D'Alessio, G. (2009). On the "Artemidorus" Papyrus. *Zeitschrift für Papyrologie und Epigraphik*, 171:27–43.

Ericsson, K. A., Charness, N., Feltovich, P. J., and Hoffman, R. R. (Eds.) (2006). *The Cambridge Handbook of Expertise and Expert Performance*. Cambridge: Cambridge University Press.

Feltovich, P. J., Prietula, M. J. & Ericsson, K. A. (2006). Studies of expertise from psychological perspectives. In Ericsson et al. (Eds.). Chapter 4: 41–67.

Gonzalez, R. C. & Woods, R. E. (2008). *Digital Image Processing*. (3rd Edn.). Upper Saddle River, NJ: Pearson Education.

Grasseni, C. (Ed.) (2007). *Skilled visions: between apprenticeship and standards*, volume 6 of *EASA - Learning Fields*. New York: Berghahn Books.

Haack, S. (1993). *Evidence and Inquiry: towards reconstruction in epistemology*. Oxford: Blackwell.

Hassner, T., Sablatnig, R., Stutzmann, D. & Tarte, S. (2014). Digital Palaeography: New Machines and Old Texts (Dagstuhl Seminar 14302). *Dagstuhl Reports*, 4(7):112–134.

Knorr Cetina, K. (1999). *Epistemic Cultures. How the Sciences make knowledge*. Cambridge, Massachusetts: Harvard University Press.

Letournel, E. & Judet, R. (1993). *Fractures of the acetabulum*. (2nd Edn.). Heidelberg, Germany: Springer-Verlag.

McClelland, J., Blackall, J., Tarte, S., Chandler, A., Hughes, S., Ahmad, S., Landau, D. & Hawkes, D. (2006). A continuous 4D motion model from multiple respiratory cycles for use in lung radiotherapy. *Med Phys*, 33(9):3348–3358.

Smith, A. M., Lynn, S. & Lintott, C. J. (2013). An introduction to the zooniverse. In *First AAAI Conference on Human Computation and Crowdsourcing*, volume AAAI Technical Report CR-13–01.

Snow, C. P. (1959). *The Two Cultures*. (Canto Edn. 1993). Cambridge: Cambridge University Press.

Ramsay S. & Rockwell G. (2012) Developing Things: Notes towards an Epistemology of Building in the Digital Humanities. In M. K. Gold (Ed.), *Debates in the Digital Humanities*. Minneapolis: University of Minnesota Press.

Tarte, S. (2014). Interpreting textual artefacts: Cognitive insights into expert practices. In Mills, C., Pidd, M., and Ward, E. (Eds.), *Proceedings of the Digital Humanities Congress 2012*, Studies in the Digital Humanities. Sheffield: HRI Online Publications.

Tarte, S., Talib, H., Ballester, M. G. & Langlotz, F. (2006). Evaluating partial surface matching for fracture reduction assessment. In *Biomedical Imaging: From Nano to Macro, 2006. ISBI 2006. 3rd IEEE International Symposium on*, pages 514–7.

Tarte, S. M. (2011). Papyrological investigations: Transferring perception and interpretation into the digital world. *Lit Linguist Computing*, 26(2): 233–47.

Tarte, S. M. (2012). The digital existence of words and pictures: The case of the Artemidorus papyrus. *Historia*, 61(3):325–336 (+bibliog. pp 357–61; fig. pp 363–5).

Terras M. (2005). Reading the readers: Modelling complex humanities processes to build cognitive systems. *Lit Linguist Computing* 20:41–59.

Tile, M. (1996). Acute pelvic fractures: I. causation and classification. *Journal of the American Academy of Orthopaedic Surgeons*, 4(3):143–151.

CHAPTER 7

Cultural Heritage Destruction: Experiments with Parchment and Multispectral Imaging

Alberto Campagnolo*, Alejandro Giacometti[†],
Lindsay MacDonald[†], Simon Mahony[†],
Melissa Terras[†] and Adam Gibson[†]
*University of the Arts, London,
[†]University College London

Abstract

This chapter describes a highly collaborative project in digital humanities, which used tools and expertise from a diverse range of disciplines: medical physics, image science, and conservation. We describe this collaboration through three examples: the use of phantoms taken from medical physics, a historically accurate model of parchment degradation, and a detailed description of the steps taken to run experiments and collect data within a manageable budget. Each example highlights how procedures from a discipline were adapted for the project through collaboration.

Whilst conservation focuses on developing methods to best preserve cultural heritage documents, we describe an unusual collaboration between conservation and image science to document through multispectral imaging the deliberate damage of a manuscript. Multispectral imaging has been utilised to examine cultural heritage documents by providing information about their physical properties. However, current digitisation efforts concentrate on recording documents in their current state. In this project, we aimed at recording the process

How to cite this book chapter:
Campagnolo, A, Giacometti, A, MacDonald, L, Mahony, S, Terras, M and Gibson, A. 2016. Cultural Heritage Destruction: Experiments with Parchment and Multispectral Imaging. In: Bodard, G & Romanello, M (eds.) *Digital Classics Outside the Echo-Chamber: Teaching, Knowledge Exchange & Public Engagement*, Pp. 121–146. London: Ubiquity Press. DOI: http://dx.doi.org/10.5334/bat.h. License: CC-BY 4.0.

of macroscopic document degradation using multispectral imaging, and the digital recovery of the writing using standard image processing methodologies.

This project's success lay in the intersection of knowledge of the processes of parchment deterioration and the specific processes that occur when a document is imaged: this has permitted us to construct a more successful and informed experiment. The knowledge acquired during the project allows us to address the issues related to the recovery of information from damaged parchment documents, and to determine which research questions can be addressed, and through which imaging methodology.

1 Introduction

In this chapter we describe how a highly collaborative project in digital humanities used tools from several disciplines. This collaboration not only made the project more interesting, but was essential to its success. Previous publications and presentations on this research have described in detail the methodology and results.[1] In this chapter, we complement those by focusing on the problems encountered throughout the project and the methodological challenges which could only be overcome though integration of the diverse range of expertise belonging to different, and yet complimentary, disciplines. We describe how this collaboration happened and the specific outcomes in three examples.

These include a description of how we transferred the concept of phantoms from medical physics research into the digital humanities, the methodology we developed to model historically accurate damage to manuscripts in order to reflect macroscopic damage, and a highly collaborative approach we used in order to be able to implement experiments and collect experimental data[2] on a manageable budget. Data acquisition for multispectral imaging projects is relatively straightforward but does, however, require access to specialist—and usually expensive—imaging hardware.[3] Similarly, gaining access to original material on which to experiment can be difficult and even quite costly at times. By bringing in expertise from different fields, we managed to circumvent these problems and each, looking outside their natural echo chamber, managed to hone their methodologies and practices to ensure the success of the common goals within the project.

We started by borrowing the idea of phantom tests from medical physics, and applied it to cultural heritage imaging in order to evaluate methods for recovery of writing from multispectral images of a palimpsest. However, a completely computer-based digital phantom required oversimplification of the problems which occur when parchment degrades. We therefore turned to conservation, seeking practical experience of working with original materials and knowledge of parchment behaviour. This expertise was considered in the context of the use of multispectral imaging on manuscripts. Finally, expertise on colour science was sought in order to optimise the data acquisition within a limited budget.

In this chapter we bring together the experiences of working across a wide range of imaging, computing, and conservation areas, in order to develop best practice guidelines for others working with damaged and deteriorated documents. Working in such an interdisciplinary project, we present here, through three examples, the various factors which led to successful collaboration, including interactive planning, task distribution, consultation, institutional support, and communication.

2 Case Study 1: Phantoms from medical imaging applied to cultural heritage

A first example of how our project had to look outside of the usual echo chamber for its success is the production of imaging phantoms, borrowing a commonly used tool from the medical physics researcher's toolbox. Our approach to investigating multispectral imaging as applied to cultural heritage documents is centred on the design and application of imaging phantoms. These are tools often used in medical physics and for other scientific research. Phantoms are essentially a simplification of a physical research problem where tests and experiments can be carried out quickly and safely. Phantoms are used to test and compare new systems, calibrate prototypes, and iterate improvements quickly.[4] Phantoms in medical physics research are similar to digital surrogates in the humanities; just as these surrogates allow the study of cultural heritage artefacts without further damaging the originals, phantoms allow experiments to be carried out without risking harm to patients.

When designing a phantom test, a researcher attempts to create a controlled environment which replicates a well defined but limited subset of the characteristics of a larger problem. Typically, a phantom in medical physics will include a simplified environment which simulates a patient, or part of a patient such as an organ or similar. The conditions in the experiment are controlled, thus the performance of a system can be tested thoroughly and compared to a known ground truth before testing it on a real patient. This simplified environment provides a fast and robust product development cycle which is independent of concerns about the safety of a patient.

Phantoms can be either a computer simulation of a digital model mimicking a real object on which one can test processing algorithms, or specially designed material objects mimicking specific characteristics of a real object. For example, often in medical imaging phantoms are produced from materials that mimic human tissue but with well-characterised material properties. The phantom can then be imaged with a new experimental technique, providing useful insight into the performance of the new technology. The construction and characterisation of phantoms is an important area of research.[5] For example, Price et al.[6] have developed a material that simulates breast tissue. This material was developed specifically to respond to breast compression and

X-rays in a similar way to breast tissue, so that it can be used by researchers to study the performance of new X-ray imaging techniques. Ionising radiation is dangerous to humans, and phantom materials such as this ensure that the patient is exposed to it only when necessary. Similarly, Levesque, Sled & Pike[7] present an iterative design methodology, aided by a phantom, to optimise systematically, and improve the signal to noise ratio of quantitative magnetisation transfer imaging, a specialised medical imaging technique. Tests can subsequently be performed directly on the patient once the technology and its effects are better understood.

The tradition of phantom development and testing has not yet become established as a research methodology in the humanities. In the world of conservation, and heritage science in particular, however, where new techniques are developed for the assessment, treatment, or recovery of cultural artefacts, the use of controlled degradation and synthetic and virtual models is more common.[8] These tools are used with a similar purpose to that of phantom tests. Examples vary from the determination of the degree of deterioration of parchment samples through comparison with new, artificially-aged, and naturally-aged parchment,[9] to the quantification of the deterioration effects of light damage on parchment through controlled UV irradiation on modern parchment tested before and after irradiation,[10] to the aging characteristics of gelatines and animal glues used in conservation and their reversibility through tests on newly produced adhesive films.[11] These experiments are not directly named as phantoms, but their execution is intended to perform a similar function: testing, comparing, optimising, and validating methodologies. Recently research appears to have begun explicitly utilising phantoms as research tools. Marengo et al.[12] use virtual degradation of multispectral images of documents in order to evaluate an algorithm in controlled conditions. The algorithm they developed monitors the conservation condition of a document, based on information from multispectral images of the document. They manipulate the data in specific ways in order to train the algorithm, which they later apply to unadulterated images.

Finally, recent work in scrolled historical documents has used modelling and problem simplification to develop algorithms to digitally unroll and reconstruct the writing from scanned images of the documents. Scrolls that are too fragile and deteriorated to be physically unrolled present a difficult imaging problem, as most of the text is within the scroll and often is present on both sides of the parchment. Sub-surface imaging techniques have been used to scan these documents, but the writing typically remains illegible. Developing algorithms to digitally unroll these documents is challenging, but the use of laboratory-created scrolls and digital models is proving to be more and more successful.[13]

In this project, we proposed a new method for assessing the effectiveness of image processing algorithms that are currently in use to recover information from degraded documents. The first step was designing and implementing a virtual model phantom to simulate the conditions that are common to palimpsest manuscripts. Figure 1 shows how we constructed a phantom simulation

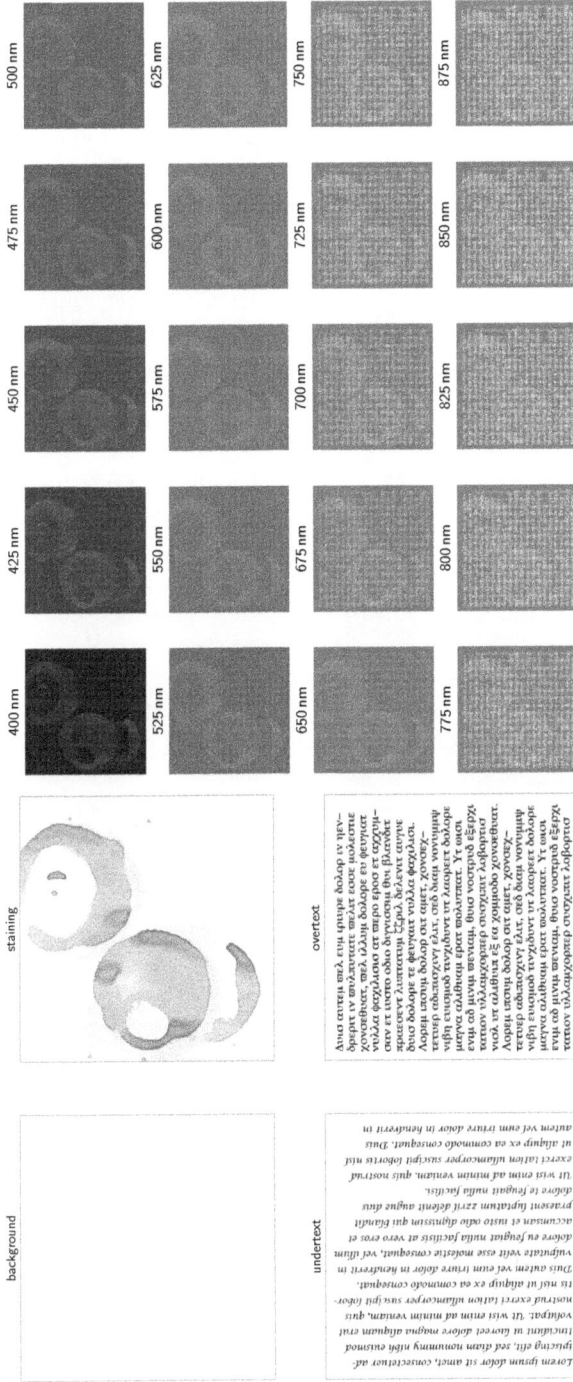

Figure 1: A series of artificial material layers were used in order to construct a virtual model phantom of a palimpsest. By composing the elements in known ways, a method for testing the accuracy of the extraction was devised. Left: materials layers used to compose the phantom. Right: simulation of multispectral images of the phantom based on the material layers (Giacometti 2013).

generated multispectral images with two layers of text, a background layer and a staining layer. A series of image processing algorithms were used to separate the components. *A priori* knowledge of the materials that contribute to the document and their arrangement in the document provides a ground truth which enables the evaluation of how the image processing algorithms perform at recovering the writing from the document. Once a basis for a comparison was available, we were able to propose a method to compare images of recovered information to the ground truth. The phantom was essential in devising an appropriate method to measure that performance. The method proposed later proved capable at handling experimental data. The phantom was based on methodologies from medical physics research. It was only able to be constructed once specific characteristics of palimpsests where understood and in the context of previous experimentation in conservation.

3 Case Study 2: Historically accurate modelling of parchment damage designed for imaging purposes

A second example is the design of a methodology to physically model macroscopic damage to parchment to provide a test platform for multispectral imaging processing algorithms. Following the hands-on approach typically found in conservation research, we identified the different types of damage parchment documents are likely to incur during their lives, from technological mistakes during production, to improper use, unsuitable storage condition, disasters, and natural ageing;[14] we then subjected an original parchment document to a series of treatments aimed at mimicking these deterioration processes. Careful consideration was given to select this set of deteriorating agents which required expertise from conservation and image science.[15]

Accredited archives follow strict guidelines and policies on the deaccessioning of items from their collections. Whilst historical collections are usually preserved, on rare occasions, such as when material is duplicated, non-archival, or of no informational/evidential value, they can be deaccessioned, and disposed of by being transferred to other repositories, returned to owners, sold, or destroyed.[16] Historical items sent to be destroyed may still be of substantial value as physical objects and may be donated to conservation studios or conservation training centres for experimentation and training on historical materials without risking damaging items of incontestable documentary value. We obtained, through this route, an 18th-century parchment document, deemed of no historical value, and deaccessioned from the London Metropolitan Archives' collections in accordance with The National Archives guidance on deaccessioning and disposal.[17] Dated to 11th of August 1753, it is an indenture, or land contract, between a Mr John Sherman and a Mr Christ Gardiner. Apart from some signs of wear and tear, especially around the fold, the parchment document was in overall good condition. The text had been handwritten in metallo-gallic ink on the recto (flesh side), with some information recorded also on the verso.

We chose to focus on parchment documents for our study, given that parchment remains the primary medium of large quantities of culturally important documents in archives, museums, libraries, and private collections. Parchment, prised for its durability and versatility, and used as writing support for centuries, is a material, constituted of structured collagen fibres that is extremely hygroscopic and reacts readily to changes of humidity, resulting in cockling and curling, and is endangered by biological, thermochemical, and mechanical damage.[18] We identified twenty methods of degradation that commonly affect parchment documents, changing their physical characteristics at both microscopic and macroscopic levels.[19] The damage agents were selected so as to affect the properties of the parchment, but also the legibility of text in various ways, for example, shrinking or otherwise deforming the parchment, and obscuring or effacing the writing via physical, chemical, or biological reactions.[20] These degradation methods fall within the main categories of (a) mechanical, (b) thermochemical and humidity, and (c) physical and extraneous substances, all of which act directly upon the writing support, changing its physical characteristics at both microscopic and macroscopic levels. Table 1 summarises the effects of a selection of the damage treatments,[21] and Table 2 puts the treatments into context with the possible causes of damage that can occur to parchment documents during their lives.

In Table 2, the damage categories—*mechanical, thermochemical and humidity, physical and extraneous substances*—highlight what was mainly and primarily affected during the deterioration inflicted on the samples. In conservation, causes of damage are conventionally categorised in discrete groups, even if these are necessarily interrelated, focusing on the main source of damage. For instance, biological damage is caused by mould growing on the material, or insects eating through the material, but for mould to grow, or insects to be lively, the environmental conditions need to be within certain parameters – i.e. high relative humidity and relatively high temperature; at the same environmental conditions the material could already be suffering at the microscopic

Treatment	Description
Mould	In high relative humidity and temperature – micro-organisms and moulds feed on the organic material causing microscopic changes.
Heat	Dry heat above 200°C removes most of the water from the collagen structure. The proteins in the parchment then denature, shrinking and changing the macroscopic shape of the parchment.
Smoking	Smoke alters the colour of the medium, while soot further obscures the writing.

Table 1: A selection of methods used to degrade the parchment.

Degradation Reason		Circumstances	Mechanical	Thermochemical & Humidity	Physical & Extraneous substances
Technological mistakes	During manufacture	lime solution, acidity, finishing	Scraping	Hydrochloric Acid, Calcium Hydroxide	Oil
	During writing	ink acidity		Sulphuric Acid	
	During binding	unsympathetic binding	Mechanical Damage		
Storage	Environmental changes	temperature, humidity		**Heat**, Desiccant, **Mould**	
	Exposure to light	visible light, UV		UV Light, Controls	
	Pollutants, dirt	chemical reactions		**Smoke**, Sulphuric Acid, Controls	
	Natural disasters	fire, smoke, water		**Heat**, **Smoke**, Water	
	Biodegradation	micro-organisms, insects, rodents		**Mould**	
	Mechanical destruction	rubbing, folding	Mechanical Damage		
Use	Erasures, changes to text	corrections, re-usage	Scraping		Iron Gall Ink
	Mishandling, misuse		Mechanical Damage, Scrunching		
	Accidents	spillage		Blood, Red Wine, Black Tea, Iron Gall Ink, Water	Blood, Oil, Red Wine, Black Tea, Aniline Dye, Iron Gall Ink, Indian Ink

Repairs	historical, conservation treatments		WATER, SODIUM HYPOCHLORITE
Rebinding	unsympathetic binding	MECHANICAL DAMAGE	
Palaeographical and conservation experiments	palimpsest text recovery, bleaching		HYDROCHLORIC ACID, OIL
Reformatting, digitisation		MECHANICAL DAMAGE	UV LIGHT
Natural ageing			CONTROLS

Table 2: Summary of different types of degradation (in small capitals), giving the reason for the degradation, the circumstances in which it might occur and the type of degradation. In the table are also highlighted the kinds of degradation that naturally occurred to the manuscript during our experiments; these are identified by the keyword *Controls*. In bold, treatments from Table 1. (Giacometti, et al. 2012a).

level, but these factors are shadowed by the impact of external living organisms on it. Also, when mould grows on paper and parchment, the deterioration process is certainly caused by the chemical reactions following digestion, but deterioration by mould is still usually classified as biological and not chemical damage. In the literature, however, damage classification systems vary from publication to publication: there is no universal standard on damage categorisation and its terminology.[22]

Additionally, we group damage agents that would have similar macroscopic effects on the parchment samples, and that would thus have similar spectral characteristics.[23] In some cases, at the macroscopic level, in our experiments, we have damages that have to be signalled as belonging to more than one category—e.g. any liquid would have similar impact on parchment, but with different overall final result depending on the liquid: all liquids, from neutral water to ink, would have resulted in cockling of the sample and similar physical effects, but inks would have also obscured the writing on the sample, whilst other fluids would have also affected the parchment chemically. The categories help creating subgroups when damaging agents belong to the same group of damage category. We thus group together damages that are usually considered separately in conservation studies, as our groupings highlight similar spectral responses, which is not usually a grouping criterion for conservators. For our purposes, the damage categories can be defined as follows:

> *Mechanical damage*: a physical deterioration originating from a physical force applied to an object, e.g. rubbing, folding, tearing – mostly affecting the legibility of the object but without compromising the chemical structure. This can sometimes provoke changes in the object's structure.
> *Damage by chemical, biological, or environmental factors*: damage caused by substances that react with the original material resulting in a chemical change. Environmental factors such as light, humidity, and temperature can also provoke changes on an atomic or molecular level. The damage is caused by hydrolysis, oxidation or photochemical processes. Biological damage concerns damage to objects caused by living organisms such as moulds, insects, rodents and other living creatures.
> *Damage by extraneous substances*: foreign substances introduced to an object disturbing its legibility.

Once we identified the types of damage that we were going to apply to our document, we cut twenty-three 8 × 8 cm flat square sections from the two pages of the document, each containing written text and avoiding folds (see Figure 2).

The samples were imaged before and after being damaged, thus making it possible to evaluate the efficacy of imaging processing algorithms in recovering the writing from parchment documents suffering from various forms of damage.

Outer Leaf

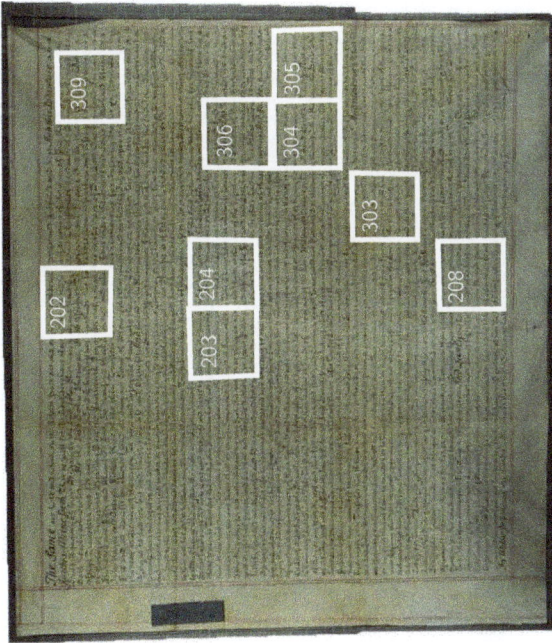

Inner Leaf

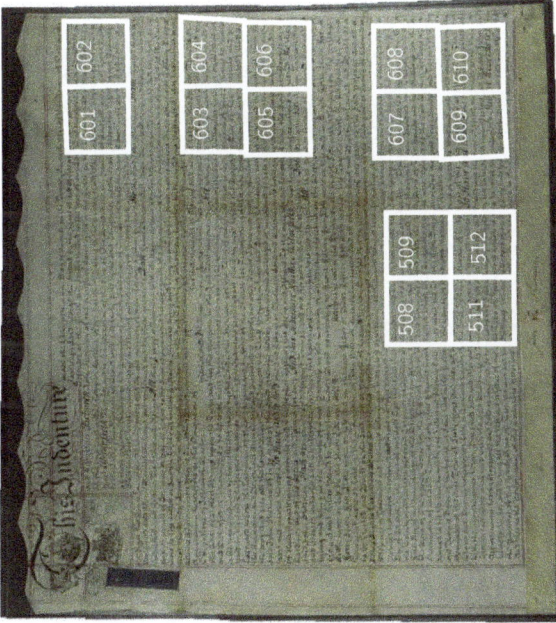

Figure 2: A diagram of the location of the samples cut from both leaves of the iron gall ink on parchment manuscript. Each sample is 8cm square, giving an overall impression of the size of the original parchment (Giacometti 2013).

This experiment was approached from a highly multidisciplinary perspective, applying a methodology taken from medical imaging to a problem in conservation. Expertise in medical imaging and conservation was combined with insights from colour science, chemistry, and image processing in order to develop standardised tests to inform the development of multispectral imaging.

4 Case Study 3: The do-it-yourself spirit of the materials, equipment, and procedures

As the project developed, it became clear that the multispectral images had to be acquired within the project's limited budget. Expertise means having the know how on a subject, and being able to simplify problems and foresee experimental results.[24] In other words, this required an active collaboration with experts from all the domains involved in order to obtain the necessary materials and equipment. As a consequence, this entailed a *do-it-yourself* approach to the production and the acquisition of the experimental data.

4.1 Data production

We were fortunate to be based in a medical physics laboratory, which offered access to basic laboratory equipment and materials, such as a fume cupboard, computer-controlled oven, laboratory glassware, scalpels, nitrile gloves, pipettes, pH indicators, as well as chemicals, human blood, and so on.

As mentioned above, our connections with the conservation world allowed us access to an original, 18th-century parchment document on which to experiment. We cut it into square samples and proceeded to inflict on these the series of damaging procedures illustrated above.

The experience accrued during conservation training and over years of bench work in conservation studios allowed us to optimise the damaging procedures so as to ensure that we limited the effects of each treatment to a single agent or procedure, e.g. we wanted to see the effect of the heat suffered in fire from the smoke. This was an important factor to take into consideration for the production of the physical samples to image: the difference between the images acquired before and after damage had to be well understood for the data analysis to be meaningful, reproducible, and comparable to other exemplars and samples. This required a number of creative solutions that were devised in an ad-hoc manner. Carefully considering the requirements for each one of the procedures, we fashioned simple devices or procedures that allowed us to perform the treatment within our budgetary constraints.

For instance, when parchment is exposed to high temperatures, its collagen structure goes through drastic changes with significant impact on the overall appearance and topography of the sample's surface: heat above 200°C removes most of the water from the collagen structure, it denatures and turns it into a random structure, shrinking and coiling the parchment, which solidifies into a new three-dimensional structure, and becomes extremely brittle, making it impossible to flatten it again.[25] Such a drastic series of changes would have made it extremely difficult to register images taken before and after heating, meaning that we could not be sure that a pixel in one image corresponded unambiguously with the same pixel in another. We therefore had to devise a method to expose the parchment sample to heat, causing its collagen structure to change, without radical changes in the three-dimensional structure of the sample. With this in mind, we placed the parchment sample between two Pyrex® Petri dishes, one inside the other; inside the top dish we placed a series of metal weights (up to about 1 kg), whose purpose was to weigh down the parchment, thus impeding its warping in the third dimension. As a result, as the parchment shrivelled and shrunk in the computer-controlled oven at 225°C, but the trays kept it flat and ready to be imaged (see Figure 3).

Fires in archives and libraries have devastating effects on parchment documents not only for the intense heat to which they are subjected, but also because of smoke stains and soot: particles and dust affect the document's legibility by obscuring text and reducing contrast.[26] Following the principle of isolating different causes of deterioration, we prepared another sample for cold smoking, thus delivering smoke without the effects of heat on parchment. A smoking environment was devised – inspired by instructions from an amateur smoking online community[27]—using a soldering iron, an empty tin, smoking wood chips, aluminium containers, linen thread, and a large plastic box with lid (Figure 4). A hole was drilled on the side of the base of the tin, in order to insert the tip of the soldering iron. The tin was filled with wet wood chips. A linen thread mesh was hand sewn through the aluminium container to create a suspended base for the sample to rest on while being smoked. The components were then placed inside the plastic box to contain the smoke, creating the smoking environment. The soldering iron creates constant heat and slowly burns the wood chips. The sample was left inside the smoking environment for a total of nine hours. The smoke drastically discoloured the parchment, more intensively on the recto, which was facing up, than the verso (see Figure 5). The discolouration pattern on the verso suggested that the smoke penetrated from the recto more prominently through the weaker parts of the parchment (pores, old folds, blemishes).

Documents stored in a damp environment are quickly affected by mould growth. As moulds grow, they feed on dirt particles, and the organic compounds of parchment and inks, leaving coloured stains due to the chemical by-products of the digestion process. Consequently, parchment documents affected by mould are fragile, porous, and often left with permanent discolourations—which can be extremely intrusive—and, in the worst cases, holes. In order to

O610R Heat

O610R Original

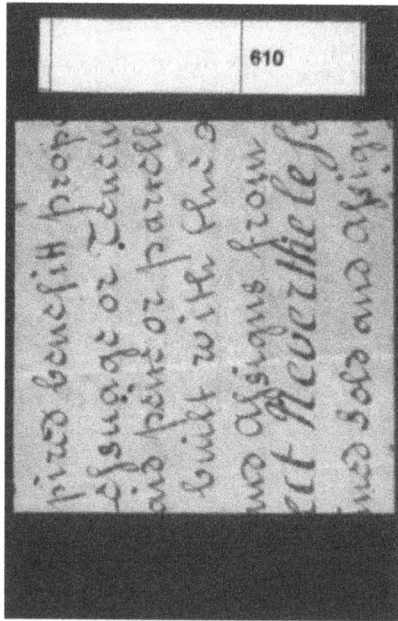

Figure 3: Sample submitted to heat treatment. The sample was placed between glass in order to contain the deformation only in two dimensions (Giacometti 2013).

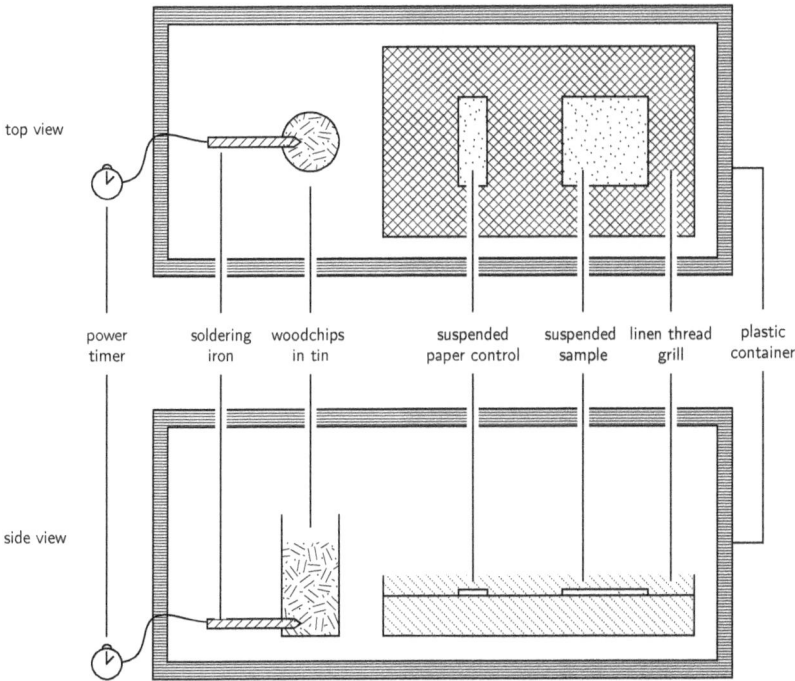

Figure 4: Smoking device constructed in order to treat the selected sample. Its construction was inspired by devices created by amateur smoking enthusiasts sharing their expertise online (see note 27; Giacometti 2013).

accelerate mould growth, a parchment sample was placed inside an airtight plastic container on top of a stack of damp blotters along with a slice of mouldy bread. Moulds that typically grow on bread, such as those of the genera *Aspergillus* and *Penicillium*, as proteolytic fungi, also affect parchment documents.[28] The sample was left inside the container for approximately five weeks in a dark environment at stable room temperature. At the end of the incubation period, the sample presented the characteristic coloured stains, it was rather fragile and porous, and in places it had been completely destroyed (Figure 6).

Limiting the degradation effects by isolating them, whenever possible, allowed for more useful samples for the subsequent imaging process. In a similar way, we had to devise a way to allow successful alignment of the images before and after degradation. In order to create stable reference points for such a registration process, we decided to punch four 1 mm holes using a *Japanese screw punch* into each sample at about a third of the distance from the borders, thus forming a square of holes in the centre of each sample (Figure 7).[29] These holes were later used to visually compare the images of the samples.

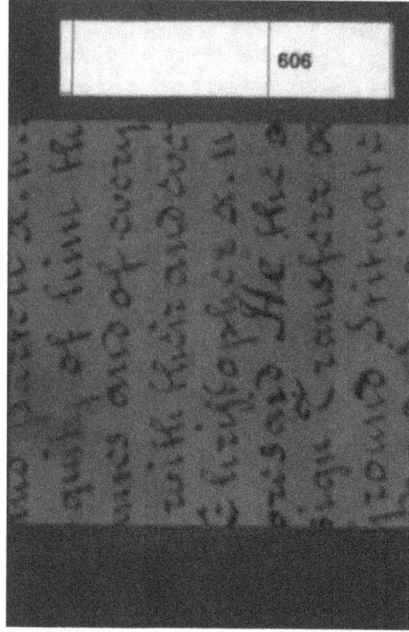

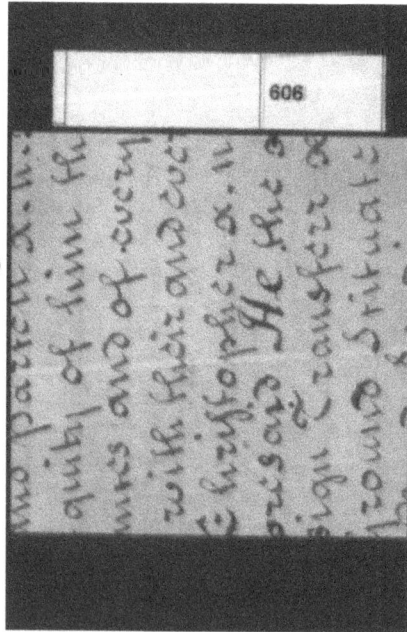

Figure 5: Sample subjected to cold smoke. The after treatment photographs shows the discolouration caused by the exposure to smoke (Giacometti 2013).

O512R Mould

O512R Original

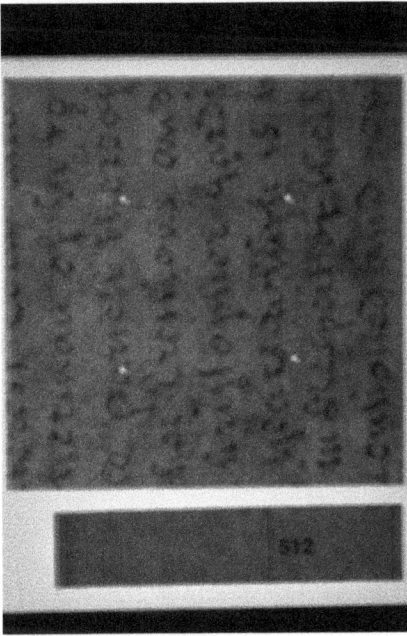

Figure 6: Sample subjected to mould growth. The deterioration of the parchment is significant; and has destroyed any visible signs of the writing (Giacometti 2013).

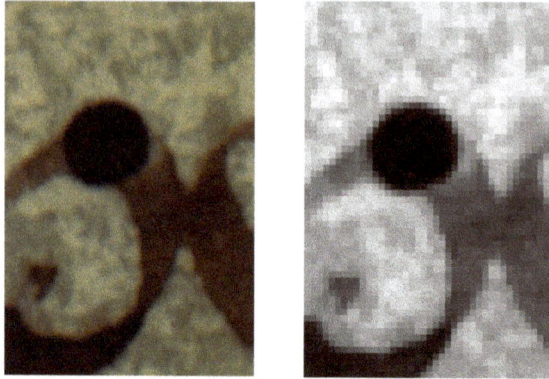

Figure 7: One mm holes were punched into each sample, used as a calibration mark that would survive the conditions that every sample was being subjected to. These images show the difference in resolution of the two cameras used by displaying the punched holes at a similar scale (Giacometti 2013).

A card stencil, the same size of the samples, was used to keep the shape of the square consistent across the samples. These holes were chosen as an effective registration method as they did not affect the integrity of the samples, did not introduce new materials, and they reacted concurrently with the sample when this suffered any changes. This provided a valuable guide when attempting to digitally register the image sets, the holes functioning as detectable features found in both the source and the target image.

These examples show how simple, creative solutions and experimentation aided the development of our approach by borrowing from conservation bench-work experience, simple devices, and advice from an online enthusiast community.

4.2 Data acquisition

This project acted as a pilot which led subsequently to the development of the Multispectral facilities in the UCL Centre for Digital Humanities Multimodal Imaging Suite.[30] However, even this pilot study required access to specialist multispectral imaging hardware.[31] Due to budgetary constraints, we had to assemble a working multispectral imaging suite with minimum expenditure.[32] Having the right set of skills and expertise in the team—between colour science, and data processing and manipulation— made it possible to devise a low-cost, working multispectral imaging system.

The imaging setup was composed of two cameras: a Nikon D200 digital SLR camera with Nikon 105mm f/2.8 lens in combination with 16 Unaxis Optics bandpass filters; and a Kodak Megaplus 1.6i scientific monochrome camera with Nikon 50mm f/2 lens, using 5 Andover Corporation infrared bandpass filters in addition to the previous 16 (Figure 8).

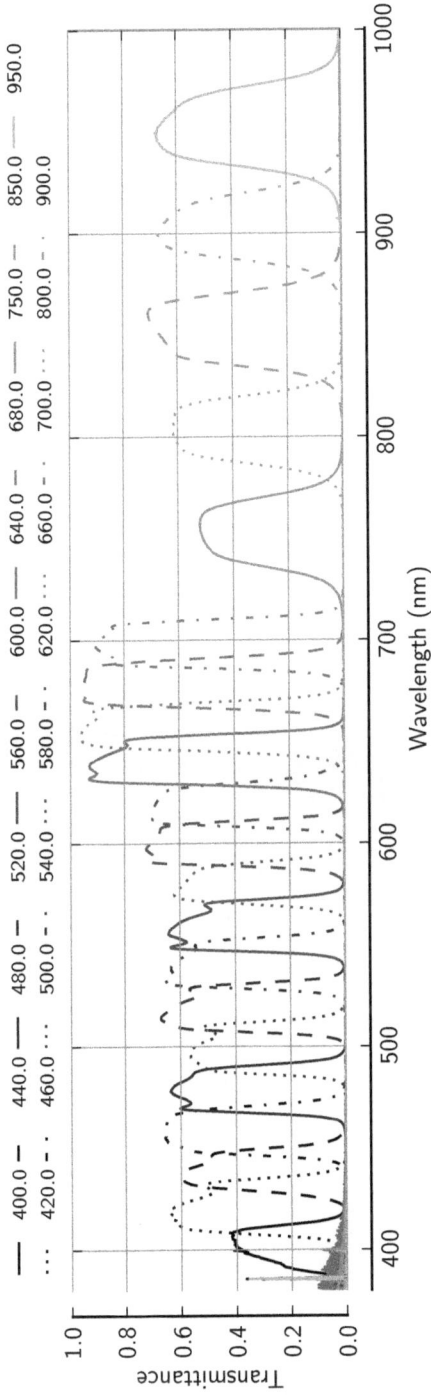

Figure 8: Twenty-one optical bandpass filters centred at regular intervals of measured transmission spectra: 16 Unaxis Optics filters centred at intervals of 20 nm from 400 nm to 700 nm in the visible spectrum and 5 filters with bandwidth of approximately 50 nm in the near-infrared spectrum, from 750 nm to 950 nm (Giacometti 2013).

The 16 Unaxis Optics filters each had a bandwidth of about 20 nm, and were centred at regular intervals of 20 nm from 400 nm to 700 nm. The five infrared filters had a bandwidth of approximately 50 nm, centred at intervals of 50 nm in the near-infrared spectrum, from 750 nm to 950 nm. During initial testing, it was discovered that the four filters above 640 nm in the visible spectrum also transmitted near-infrared light; with these filters, a second infrared blocking filter was used in combination. The five infrared filters were used only with the monochrome camera, as its sensor was sensitive to ranges from approximately 400 nm to 1,000 nm; the Nikon D200 had a built-in infrared blocking filter, and it was thus not capable of capturing images above 700 nm.

The system used two illumination techniques: standard document copystand lighting, and a lightbox backlight. The copystand illuminated the document using four tungsten-halogen lamps set at 45° angles (Figure 9); these lamps provided broadband emission from the ultraviolet into the near infrared. The lightbox backlight was made of two fluorescent lamps behind a flat diffuser, creating a uniform flat source of white light; these lamps illuminated mainly in the visible spectrum, and, for this reason, backlighting was only used with the colour camera. Transmissive lighting allowed illuminating the parchment samples from behind, thus interacting with both the surface, and the structure of the parchment.

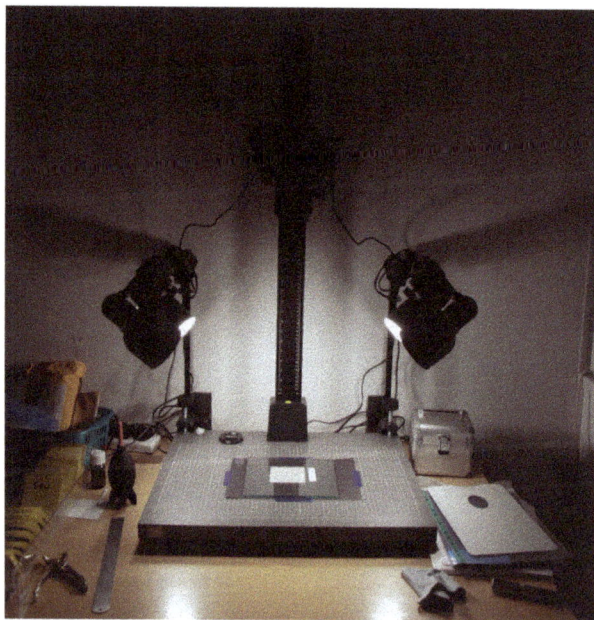

Figure 9: Imaging setup. The camera is locked facing vertically downwards. Four tungsten-halogen lamps illuminate the sample at an angle of 45°. The sample is placed on the copystand over a piece of black card under a sheet of anti-reflective glass (Giacometti 2013).

In total, approximately 3,000 images of samples were acquired during the project in two imaging sessions: before, and after parchment degradation. The data from our experiments forms a set of multispectral images showing both the initial and degraded state of a manuscript. With a *do-it-yourself* attitude towards the equipment, creativity when dealing with problems, and high collaboration with experts in various fields, this project managed to create a large dataset of reference multispectral images of parchment damage within a relatively limited budget. We believe that these can become a valuable resource for both conservation research and libraries and archives undergoing digitisation efforts.[33]

5 Conclusions

Multispectral imaging is increasingly becoming a common tool in cultural heritage, and it is therefore important to understand its applicability to the capture and analysis of our varied written heritage. Our research provides a systematic methodology to evaluate and review the techniques and processing of multispectral images of historical documents, thus allowing a most efficient use of resources.

In our research, we purposefully degraded a real historical manuscript on parchment, which was a necessary step to model successfully the type of damage commonly seen in historical documents. This helped us to understand how different types of damage affect historical documents and their text, both before and after multispectral imaging of the samples. The critical destruction was a fundamental part of the project, since it was essential to the understanding of the effectiveness of multispectral imaging on historical documents.[34]

Often, academic groups experience echo chambers, since their members tend to share information, *modi operandi*, and opinions. This situation is to some extent less critical within the digital humanities—an interdisciplinary field by definition—but looking outside the natural echo chamber for collaborations and knowledge exchanges can prove fruitful and leads to successful projects,[35] as it was the case for the examples outlined in this chapter.

The knowledge exchange for this project was not unidirectional. Gathering information from adjoining fields certainly allowed us to design the phases and components of the project efficiently, however, the results and the analysis are beneficial to fields other than multispectral imaging of deteriorated parchment documents. To conservators and other professionals involved in the preservation of documents, for example, it is helpful to think about how to categorise damage according to what kind of analysis can or needs to be performed on a document to retrieve information (both written information and relative to its state of conservation) as, considering the usually limited resources of these groups of professionals, this would save time and costs.

De facto, by being open about the limited resources we had at our disposal, and the *do-it-yourself* spirit of our materials, equipment, and procedures, we want to highlight how interdisciplinarity and collaboration played a key and fundamental role for the success of our project. We also want to allow replication of our experiments and foster subsequent research and scholarship in the field. We envisage, in fact, that the dataset generated during the project has the potential to become an invaluable asset for libraries and archives, research in conservation, and various image and signal processing sets of problems, and have made all of the data generated from this project freely available online. Our dataset[36] provides physical information of how parchment reacts to various forms of degradation, but also provides consistent process and documentation on acquisition, and will provide a test environment for any future research whilst reducing the need for experimentation on valuable primary historical texts.

Notes

[1] See: Giacometti et al. 2011; Giacometti et al. 2012a; Giacometti et al. 2012b; Campagnolo et al. 2013a; Campagnolo et al. 2013b; MacDonald et al. 2013; Giacometti et al. 2014; with an overview of the whole project available in open access in Giacometti et al. 2015.

[2] The DOI for this dataset is http://dx.doi.org/10.14324/000.ds.1469099.

[3] Terras 2012.

[4] Firbank & Delpy 1993; Krackow, Duncan & Gorten 1973; Levesque, Sled & Pike 2011; Pogue & Patterson 2006; Richard & Webber 1963.

[5] Krackow, Duncan & Gorten 1973; Pekar & Patterson 2010; Richards & Webber 1963.

[6] Price et al. 2010.

[7] Levesque, Sled & Pike 2011.

[8] Fessas, Signorelli, et al. 2006; Dolgin, Bulatov & Schechter 2007; Schellmann 2007; Marengo et al. 2011.

[9] Fessas, Signorelli, et al. 2006.

[10] Dolgin, Bulatov & Schechter 2007.

[11] Schellmann 2007.

[12] Marengo et al. 2011.

[13] Baumann, Porter & Seales 2008; Cao, Ding & Liu 2003; Samko et al. 2014.

[14] Giacometti, et al. in press.

[15] Giacometti, et al. 2015.

[16] The National Archives 2015.

[17] The National Archives 2015.

[18] Reed 1972; Clarkson 1992; Larsen 2007; Giacometti, et al. 2012

[19] Vnouček 2007.

[20] Giacometti, et al. 2015.

[21] A full list of deterioration methods and their explanation can be found in Giacometti et al. 2012, Table 1, pp. 303–304.

[22] Van Camp 2010.

[23] See the *Data acquisition* section below, for a description of the imaging system used for the project.

[24] Ericsson 2006.

[25] Avery et al. 2013; Pal et al. 2013a; Pal et al. 2013b.

[26] Kautek et al.1998.

[27] Fun with Cold Smoking: <http://www.nibblemethis.com/2009/11/fun-with-cold-smoking-macgyver-style.html> (last accessed October 2015).

[28] Berger et al. 1937; Rogerio-Candelera 2014.

[29] Japanese Screw Punch: <http://www.conservation-by-design.com/category.aspx?id=446> (last accessed July 2015).

[30] UCL Centre for Digital Humanities Multimodal Imaging Suite: <https://www.ucl.ac.uk/dh/facilities/digitisation-suite> (last accessed July 2015).

[31] Terras 2012.

[32] Existing equipment was used throughout the project in order to maintain costs down. The cameras, the copystand, some of the filters and some of the lighting were available. In order to reproduce this setup, the bandpass filters would represent the highest cost—around £10,000. A similar Nikon camera and lens combination to the one used could be acquired for approximately £2,000.

[33] The DOI for this dataset is http://dx.doi.org/10.14324/000.ds.1469099.

[34] Giacometti et al. 2015.

[35] Terras 2012; Terras 2010.

[36] DOI: http://dx.doi.org/10.14324/000.ds.1469099.

References

Avery, N., Campagnolo, A., De Stefani, C., Pal, K., Payne, M., Smith, P., Smither, R., Stewart, A.M., Stewart, E., Stewart, P., Terras M., Ward L., Weyrich, T. & Yamada E., 2013. *The Great Parchment Book*. Poster presented at Digital Humanities 2013, University of Nebraska, Lincoln, July 2013, Lincoln.

Baumann, R., Porter, D.C. & Seales, W.B. (2008). The Use of Micro-CT in the Study of Archaeological Artifacts. In: 9th International Conference on NDT of Art. Presented at the 9th International Conference on NDT of Art, Jerusalem, Israel, pp. 1–9.

Berger, J., Johnson, M.J. & Peterson, W.H. (1937). The proteolytic enzymes of some common molds. *The Journal of Biological Chemistry* 117: 429–438.

Campagnolo, A., Giacometti, A., MacDonald, L., Mahony, S., Terras, M., Robson, S., Weyrich, T. & Gibson, A. (2013a). Cultural Heritage Destruction: Measuring Information Recovery from Multispectral Images of Deteriorated parchment. In: British Library, Topic Talk, Collections Care, 11th September 2013. Presented at the British Library, Topic Talk, Collections Care.

Campagnolo, A., Giacometti, A., MacDonald, L., Mahony, S., Terras, M., Robson, S., Weyrich, T. & Gibson, A. (2013b). Documenting and Interpreting Parchment Deterioration by Visual Analysis and Multispectral Imaging, in: Icon PF13, Positive Futures in an Uncertain World, Glasgow, 10–12

April 2013. Presented at the Icon PF13, Positive Futures in an Uncertain World, Glasgow, 10–12 April 2013, Glasgow.

Cao, H., Ding, X. & Liu, C. (2003). A cylindrical surface model to rectify the bound document image. In: Ninth IEEE International Conference on Computer Vision, 2003. Proceedings. Presented at the Ninth IEEE International Conference on Computer Vision, 2003. Proceedings, pp. 228–233. DOI: http://dx.doi.org/10.1109/ICCV.2003.1238346

Clarkson, C. (1992). Rediscovering Parchment: The Nature of the Beast. *The Paper Conservator* 16: 5–26. DOI: http://dx.doi.org/10.1080/03094227.1992.9638571

Conservation By Design Ltd. (2015). Japanese Screw Punch. Retrieved from http://www.conservation-by-design.com/category.aspx?id=446

Dolgin, B., Bulatov, V. & Schechter, I. (2007). Non-destructive assessment of parchment deterioration by optical methods. *Anal. Bioanal. Chem.* 388: 1885–1896. DOI: http://dx.doi.org/10.1007/s00216-007-1410-0

Ericsson, K.A. (2006). An introduction to The Cambridge Handbook of Expertise and Expert Performance. In: K. A. Ericsson, N. Charness, P. J. Feltovich, R. R. Hoffman (Eds.), *The Cambridge Handbook of Expertise and Expert Performance* (pp. 3–20). New York: Cambridge University Press.

Fessas, D., Signorelli, M., Schiraldi, A., Kennedy, C.J., Wess, T.J., Hassel, B. & Nielsen, K. (2006). Thermal analysis on parchments I: DSC and TGA combined approach for heat damage assessment. *Thermochimica Acta* 447: 30–35. DOI: http://dx.doi.org/10.1016/j.tca.2006.04.007

Firbank, M. & Delpy, D.T. (1993). A design for a stable and reproducible phantom for use in near infra-red imaging and spectroscopy. *Phys. Med. Biol.* 38: 847. DOI: http://dx.doi.org/10.1088/0031-9155/38/6/015

Giacometti, A. (2013). Evaluating Multispectral Imaging Processing Methodologies for Analysing Cultural Heritage Documents. (Doctoral dissertation, University College London, London).

Giacometti, A., Campagnolo, A., MacDonald, L., Mahony, S., Robson, S., Weyrich, T., Terras, M. & Gibson, A. (2015). The value of critical destruction: evaluating multispectral image processing methods for the analysis of primary historical texts. *Digital Scholarship in the Humanities*. DOI: http://dx.doi.org/10.1093/llc/fqv036

Giacometti, A., Campagnolo, A., MacDonald, L., Mahony, S., Robson, S., Weyrich, T., Terras, M. & Gibson, A. (in press). Visualising macroscopic deterioration of parchment and writing via multispectral images, in: Care and Conservation of Manuscripts 15, University of Copenhagen 2nd-4th April 2014. Presented at the Care and Conservation of Manuscripts 15, University of Copenhagen 2nd-4th April 2014. University of Copenhagen, Copenhagen, Denmark: Museum Tusculanum Press.

Giacometti, A., Campagnolo, A., MacDonald, L., Mahony, S., Terras, M., Robson, S., Weyrich, T. & Gibson, A. (2012a). Cultural Heritage Destruction: Documenting Parchment Degradation via Multispectral Imaging, in: Electronic Visualisation and the Arts (EVA 2012). Presented at the Electronic

Visualisation and the Arts (EVA 2012), British Computing Society, London, UK, pp. 301–308.

Giacometti, A., Campagnolo, A., MacDonald, L., Terras, M., Mahony, S., Weyrich, T., Robson, S. & Gibson, A. (2012b). Cultural Heritage Destruction: Documenting Parchment Degradation via Multispectral Imaging, in: Digital Classicist & Institute of Classical Studies Seminar. Presented at the Digital Classicist & Institute of Classical Studies Seminar, London, UK.

Giacometti, A., Gibson, A., Hess, M., Hindmarch, J., MacDonald, L., Pal, K., Robson, S., Terras, M. & Weyrich, T. (2014). Heritage Imaging at UCL, in: Annual Conference of Association for Historical and Fine Art Photography (AHFAP). Presented at the Annual Conference of Association for Historical and Fine Art Photography (AHFAP).

Giacometti, A., Terras, M., Gibson, A. & Mahony, S. (2011). Multi-Spectral Image Processing Methods For Analysing Ancient Documents, in: Society for Digital Humanities/Société Pour L'étude Des Médias Interactifs (SDH/SEMI) Annual Conference at the 2011 Congress of the Social Sciences and Humanities. Presented at the Society for Digital Humanities / Société pour l'étude des médias interactifs (SDH/SEMI) annual conference at the 2011 Congress of the Social Sciences and Humanities.

Kautek, W., Pentzien, S., Rudolph, P., Krüger, J. & König, E. (1998). Laser interaction with coated collagen and cellulose fibre composites: fundamentals of laser cleaning of ancient parchment manuscripts and paper. *Applied Surface Science* 127–129, 746–754. DOI: http://dx.doi.org/10.1016/S0169-4332(97)00735-6

Krackow, K.A., Duncan, M.L. & Gorten, R.J. (1973). Use of digital phantoms and a simulation of the scanning process to evaluate techniques of computer focusing of area scans. *International Journal of Nuclear Medicine and Biology* 1: 29–35. DOI: http://dx.doi.org/10.1016/0047-0740(73)90040-5

Larsen, R. (2007). Introduction to damage and damage assessment. In: Larsen, R. (Ed.), *Improved Damage Assessment of Parchment (IDAP): Assessment, Data Collection and Sharing of Knowledge. European Commission, Directorate- General for Environment*, pp. 17–21.

Levesque, I.R., Sled, J.G. & Pike, G.B. (2011). Iterative optimization method for design of quantitative magnetization transfer imaging experiments. *Magnetic Resonance in Medicine* 66: 635–643. DOI: http://dx.doi.org/10.1002/mrm.23071

MacDonald, L.W., Giacometti, A., Campagnolo, A., Robson, S., Weyrich, T., Terras, M. & Gibson, A. (2013). Multispectral Imaging of Degraded Parchment In: S. Tominaga, R. Schettini, A. Trémeau, (Eds.), Computational Color Imaging, 4th International Workshop, CCIW 2013, Chiba, Japan, March 3-5, 2013. Proceedings, Lecture Notes in Computer Science. Springer Berlin Heidelberg, Chiba, Japan, pp. 143–157.

Pal, K., Terras, M. & Weyrich, T. (2013a). 3D Reconstruction For Damaged Documents: Imaging of The Great Parchment Book. In: Proceedings of 2nd International Workshop on Historical Document Imaging and Processing. Washington DC, 24 August, 2013, pp. 14–21.

Pal, K., Terras, M. & Weyrich, T. (2013b). Interactive Exploration and Flattening of Deformed Historical Documents. *Computer Graphics Forum* 32: 327–334. DOI: http://dx.doi.org/10.1111/cgf.12052

Pekar, J. & Patterson, M.S. (2010). Fabrication and characterization of phantoms with tissue-like optical properties from 500 to 700 nm. *Medical Laser Application* 25: 147–153. DOI: http://dx.doi.org/10.1016/j.mla.2010.04.002

Pogue, B.W. & Patterson, M.S. (2006). Review of tissue simulating phantoms for optical spectroscopy, imaging and dosimetry. *Journal of Biomedical Optics* 11: 041102–041102-16. DOI: http://dx.doi.org/10.1117/1.2335429

Price, B.D., Gibson, A.P., Tan, L.T. & Royle, G.J. (2010). An elastically compressible phantom material with mechanical and x-ray attenuation properties equivalent to breast tissue. *Phys. Med. Biol.* 55: 1177–1188. DOI: http://dx.doi.org/10.1088/0031-9155/55/4/018

Reed, R. (1972). *Ancient Skins, Parchments and Leathers.* London: Seminar Press.

Richards, A.G. & Webber, R.L. (1963). Constructing phantom heads for radiation research. Oral Surgery, Oral Medicine, Oral Pathology 16: 683–690. DOI: http://dx.doi.org/10.1016/0030-4220(63)90073-2

Rogerio-Candelera, M.A. (Ed.) (2014). Science, Technology and Cultural Heritage. Balkema, Leiden: CRC Press.

Samko, O., Lai, Y.-K., Marshall, D. & Rosin, P.L. (2014). Virtual unrolling and information recovery from scanned scrolled historical documents. *Pattern Recognition* 47. DOI: http://dx.doi.org/10.1016/j.patcog.2013.06.015

Schellmann, N.C. (2007). Animal glues: a review of their key properties relevant to conservation. *IIC Reviews in Conservation* 8: 55–66.

Terras, M. (2010). The Digital Classicist: Disciplinary Focus and Interdisciplinary Vision. In: G. Bodard, S. Mahony (Eds.), *Digital Research in the Study of the Classical Antiquity.* Farnham: Ashgate, 171–191.

Terras, M. (2012). Being the Other: Interdisciplinary Work in Computational Science and the Humanities. In: P. W. McCarty, P. M. Deegan (Eds.), *Collaborative Research in the Digital Humanities.* Farnham: Ashgate, pp. 213–230.

The National Archives (2015). Deaccessioning and disposal. Guidance for archive services.

UCLDH (2015). Digitisation Suite. Retrieved from https://www.ucl.ac.uk/dh/facilities/digitisation-suite

Van Camp, K. (2010). Damage Atlas for Photographic materials. CeROArt, Conservation, exposition et Restauration d'Objets d'Art. Retrieved from http://ceroart.revues.org/1770

Vnouček, J. (2007). Typology of the Damage of the Parchment in Manuscripts of the Codex Form. In: R. Larsen (Ed.), Improved Damage Assessment of Parchment (IDAP): Assessment, Data Collection and Sharing of Knowledge. European Commission, Directorate- General for Environment, pp. 27–30.

CHAPTER 8

Transparent, Multivocal, Cross-disciplinary: The Use of Linked Open Data and a Community-developed RDF Ontology to Document and Enrich 3D Visualisation for Cultural Heritage

Valeria Vitale

King's College London

Abstract

Scholarly 3D visualisations of cultural heritage are based on a thorough study of excavation records, iconographic documentation, literary sources, artistic canons and precedents. However, the research process is usually not detectable in the final visual outcome, thus bypassing a fundamental principle of scientific method: the reproducibility of the process.

International guidelines define the kinds of information essential to making a 3D visualization an academic resource, but without specifying a technological format or standard for doing so. This chapter proposes the use of Linked Open Data and a dedicated ontology as a synthetic, time- and cost-effective way to document 3D visualisation, connecting the 3D model and its parts, both internally with each other and externally with online information about material remains, as a standard for the community of practitioners involved in the study, preservation and communication of cultural heritage. This semantic network could be implemented, in the number of its elements

How to cite this book chapter:
Vitale, V. 2016. Transparent, Multivocal, Cross-disciplinary: The Use of Linked Open Data and a Community-developed RDF Ontology to Document and Enrich 3D Visualisation for Cultural Heritage. In: Bodard, G & Romanello, M (eds.) *Digital Classics Outside the Echo-Chamber: Teaching, Knowledge Exchange & Public Engagement*, Pp. 147–168. London: Ubiquity Press. DOI: http://dx.doi.org/10.5334/bat.i. License: CC-BY 4.0.

and connections, by different communities sharing the same controlled vocabulary, potentially reaching a richness and complexity of information that no single author, discipline or industry could ever achieve.

This chapter suggests how a community-developed ontology will help creating an inter- and multi-disciplinary network of documented 3D data, moving 3D visualisation from a univocal 'snapshot' of the past to a collaborative virtual laboratory where different voices and different interpretations can be hosted and compared.

1 Opacity and Transparency

'3D visualisation' is a broad term used to define computer generated three-dimensional representations of objects (concrete or abstract). In its application for cultural heritage, it is often divided into '3D modelling,' which involves the use of Computer Aided Design (CAD) software and the creation of 3D content from scratch, and '3D imaging,' which involves the digital recording of information on the shape and colour of existing objects. The division between these two main streams is in no way neat, and there are several intermediate approaches that blend different techniques.

On the one hand, the use of 3D technologies seems to be increasingly common in the study, preservation and communication of cultural heritage and, in particular, of the ancient one. A survey of panel discussions at conferences such as Computer Applications and Quantitative Methods for Archaeology (CAA)[1] or Digital Heritage[2] in the past years, and a look at the online content offered by museums,[3] point out a growing interest towards 3D data. The increasing affordability of 3D technologies and the usability of their interfaces, combined with the recent booming of 3D printing,[4] have made digital platforms to upload, share and download 3D content rather popular among expert and non-expert audiences.[5] On the other hand, 3D visualisation is still not fully integrated in the academic workflow, and it is often considered more an illustration of external research than an investigation tool of its own.[6]

Although it is easy to understand the caution of the academics using 3D tools in their research,[7] the diffidence towards these digital outputs cannot be simply dismissed as resistance to change and technophobia.

One major issue is that, in the vast majority of cases, 3D visualisations are completely 'opaque': it is nearly impossible for the public, or for the academic community, to assess the accuracy of the visual outcome or the soundness of the hypotheses represented. The research around the visualisation, its sources, evidence and references, remain almost entirely hidden, as well as other pieces of information crucial in academic publications such as the date of publication or, sometimes, even the name of the authors.

Generally speaking, opaque digital products are still used in a large number of museums as, traditionally, they tend to present the audience with one single view of the artefact displayed, and seldom share any information on the construction of that particular interpretation, or acknowledge the possible existence of others.[8] In these contexts, 3D visualisations are often used as communication (if not entertainment) tool, meant more to appeal the public for their technological and/or aesthetic value than to actually add anything to the knowledge or investigation of the artefacts represented.[9] Even the Museo Archeologico Virtuale (MAV) in Herculaneum, which is proudly and boldly developed around the idea of having no material artefacts but only information about them and digital reproductions, offers opaque 3D content.[10]

Not knowing enough about the process of building both the 3D visualisation and its interpretation, the public's only choice is to trust the authority of the cultural institution. Although still quite common among museums and cultural heritage sites, this use of multimedia and digital tools has been criticised as it promotes a univocal, authoritative and flat approach to cultural heritage that diminishes its richness, and discourage engagement.[11] Furthermore, when the cultural institutions rely on their prestige to guarantee the quality and accuracy of the 3D visualisation, they reinforce the misconception that the one proposed is the only possible or the only correct 3D image.[12] This issue, which was already evident in the critique of illustrations for museums and historical publications,[13] seems to have been entirely perpetrated in the digital, three-dimensional medium.

Although some cultural institutions find convenient to promote their digital content as 'perfect reconstructions' or 'perfect copies'[14] of artefacts, such a statement is not only untrue but also misleading. First, 3D visualisations are digital representations of objects and, as such, they only display some aspects of their referent. They are, in fact, a *representation of something for purposes of study*.[15] Second, 3D modelling and even 3D imaging are based on a continuous process of decision making and subjective interpretation of the (often incomplete) available information.[16] This would already be true in the visualisation of a still standing artefact, but it is even more apparent when developing hypotheses on the look of no more existing or heavily damaged ones. Last, as an interpretation, every visualisation is subjective in the same way a photograph is. If the idea that photographs always express the point of view of the photographer and not an objective reality[17] is now commonly accepted, the same assumption is curiously ignored (even by practitioners[18]) in the case of 3D visualisations, and especially 3D imaging.

If an opaque and univocal digital visual product seems to be (arguably) considered acceptable in a commercial environment, it definitely cannot pass the threshold of academic publications, and cannot join the scholarly debate, regardless the rigour of the research and the value of the hypotheses behind it. With most part of the informative value hidden, 3D visualisations are as useless in academia as would be a paper missing the authors' names, methodological discourse, bibliography and footnotes. Insufficient documentation makes the process not repeatable and, thus, not complying with the scientific standards.

2 The London Charter: its Applications and Limits

The scarcity of exhaustive documentation for academic 3D visualisations can be attributed to several different causes. According to Goodrick and Earl (2004), the initial enthusiasm for the technology has driven the application of 3D tools to academic research more than a methodological reflection on it. Also, disseminating the documentation opens more than few technical issues that span from the publication of the 3D content per se (only recently made dramatically simpler) to strategies to correlate text and images to 3D environments. Last, being the commissioners of 3D visualisations of cultural heritage usually only interested in the final visual product, researchers often have to argue (and not always successfully) for the documentation to be included in the project's budget.

All these issues involving authorship, peer review, digital publishing technologies, preservation strategies and their implications in the development of 3D visualisation as a scholarly tool were already a concern of the first pioneers in the field.[19] The interest in a proper scientific methodology for scholarly 3D visualisation led to the publication of the London Charter[20] (2006): a set of guidelines for the use of 3D technologies for cultural heritage. The Charter makes some excellent points, among which:

> *Sufficient information should be documented and disseminated to allow computer-based visualisation methods and outcomes to be understood and evaluated in relation to the contexts and purposes for which they are deployed.* (The London Charter. Principle 4: Documentation)[21]

However, ten years after the publication of those guidelines, the number of documented 3D visualisations is surprisingly very low, even within academic projects.

There are, of course, examples of approaches to documentation of scholarly 3D visualisation. One is the work on the Villa of Livia at Prima Porta.[22] The 3D component, in the form of an explorable environment with narrative elements, was distributed on a CD-ROM alongside a traditional printed publication covering the archaeological research on the material evidence, plus some chapters about the specific challenges of the 3D representation. Although this approach may sound safe as it follows more traditional scholarly conventions, it does not unfold the correlation between the look of the 3D model and the archaeological research, but presents the two outcomes separately, often asking the viewer to believe that the model is nothing else than the natural outcome of the discussed archaeological finds. Again, the viewer has to trust the competence of the virtual archaeologists, and cannot really challenge specific aspects of the 3D model, or know on what other sources, not published in the book, the researchers have relied.[23]

Another strategy to document 3D visualisation that seemed affordable and easy to use in the past years was the use of blogs, like, for example, in the case of the 3D visualisation of the Abbey Theatre in Dublin at the time of its inauguration in 1904.[24] However, the information provided remains quite generic, and when looking for the resource related to a specific part of the model, the user has to read the entire documentation in order to find any particular piece of information, if available. Other projects, such as Digital Pompeii,[25] use some of the digital 3D models to browse and access, on click, the images, hosted in an internal archive, that are related to the specific element selected, showing past or contemporary pictures of the actual remains. Although this seems to be an informative and interactive way to access archaeological resources while offering, at the same time, some documentation about the 3D environment, the system can only deliver information when the source is part of that single digital repository.

A more rigorous approach is the one followed by University of California Los Angeles (UCLA) researchers and showed, for example, in projects like the Digital Roman Forum[26] or Digital Karnak.[27] In both cases, some of the main components of the buildings modelled are discussed on the project's online platform and connected with visual or verbal sources and with bibliographical references. Although very promising, the methodology does not seem to be followed systematically for all the buildings' components, and the provenance of information remains often not declared.

Although incomplete and partly flawed, all these attempts can be seen as steps forward towards a more scientific use of 3D visualisation. Besides their differences, they share some common issues in the process of documentation. None of the mentioned cases, for example, records what happens when the researcher has no direct information about a given element. Likewise, no-one mentions alternative and conflicting sources and how the author has dealt with them. None of them mentions alternative hypotheses or interpretations.

What this very brief review wants to highlight is, mainly, the range of variety and degrees of accessibility in the existing approaches, and how their different formats, structures and criteria make the documentation hardly comparable and searchable. The lack of a standard and a consolidated workflow contributes to make documentation a confusing and time-consuming process. Last, 3D visualisations, especially extensive and complex ones, are usually the work of more than one person.[28] The number of authors, often with different skills and interests, makes it even more difficult to follow a single, well-defined standard.

This overview of the difficulties in documenting 3D visualisations for cultural heritage stresses that, after agreeing on the need of documentation, it is also necessary to define a documentation standard that makes the process time and cost effective, and allows comparisons. Here, we want to suggest that the use of Linked Open Data (LOD) technology[29] and the creation of a dedicated resource description framework (RDF) ontology can be an effective approach to documentation, and also open new possibilities that were not foreseen in the London Charter, including a more multivocal approach to the representation of cultural heritage, and a process of knowledge exchange with non-academic partners such as cultural tourism, museum management, urban planning and education.

3 Why Linked Data?

LOD is an existing technology that has already been tested, and has proven its usefulness in successful digital projects on the ancient world such as the Pleiades[30] gazetteer of ancient places, Pelagios[31] or the Perseus Digital Library.[32] It is a low cost technology producing lightweight outputs that create less concern than average about their preservation. It is easy to learn and use even for people that are not particularly familiar with digital technology.

LOD establishes connections between data through statements (roughly) in the form of subject-predicate-object. These statements are expressed using controlled vocabularies.[33] Thus, the nature of LOD makes it quite suitable to be applied as a standard to describe a 3D visualisation and its production, implicitly acting as a constraint, and making, eventually, documentation comparable and not idiosyncratic.

The use of LOD allows us to attach specific information to each element of the 3D visualisation and to annotate it. Moreover, being open and non-hierarchically structured, a documentation expressed in LOD will allow multiple authors to annotate and add information about the same entity, encouraging the idea that a 3D visualisation is the representation of only one of the many possible hypotheses and interpretations. Last, LOD is both human and machine readable. It means that it can be read as comprehensible synthetic documentation for a 3D output, but also that, once online, the information can be harvested by APIs, and connections automatically identified and showed to the users.

Linked data is becoming a fairly popular technology and its applications are widely investigated in many different disciplines. There is in fact a growing number of ontologies[34] meant to describe specific domains or processes. Museums are one of the fields that show a strong interest in linked data[35] and are the cradle of one of the most widely known and applied ontology, the CIDOC CRM.[36] Looking at museum ontologies seemed the first natural step in sketching a language to document cultural heritage. However, an attempt to use the existing ontologies, even in combination, to document a 3D visualisation, pointed out some crucial gaps, and suggested the necessity to draft a purpose-specific new ontology. In the first place, the museum ontologies tend to focus on the material artefacts and not on their digital representation. In general, none of the existing ontologies offers a vocabulary that describes the specific process of producing a 3D model or image of an existing or destroyed artefact on the grounds of academic research.[37]

Writing a new ontology, even a basic one, is not to be considered a task for a single researcher for both practical and methodological reasons. Form the practical point of view, the amount of work does not seem likely to be undertaken by a single person in the time of an average academic project. Even more important though is the methodological objection: 3D visualisation is a very wide and diverse field that includes under its umbrella a large number of approaches and techniques, from Computer Aided Design (CAD) models, to laser scanning, to the use of footage produced by drones. Writing an ontology that describes a production process requires a deep understanding of the process itself and of the real issues met in the attempt of recording it consistently and synthetically. Moreover, writing an ontology is a knowledge representation process, i.e. it models a view of the world. An ontology modelled on the assumptions, expertise and needs of a single researcher would be of limited use for the rest of the community. For all these reasons, the suggested purpose-specific ontology, named SCOTCH (Semantic Collaborative Ontology for Three-dimensional visualisation of Cultural Heritage), is meant to be intrinsically collaborative, and requires that different communities of practitioners engage with its refinement and implementation, according to their own specific point of view. However, as a proof of concept, the author has started drafting a first subset of the ontology that, according to her direct knowledge and use of 3D visualisation, focuses on documenting the process of 3D modelling ancient buildings.

4 The SCOTCH Ontology

Expressing documentation in LOD requires that the 3D file is divided into smaller units first, each of them receiving a specific Unique Resource Identifier (URI). It is, obviously, possible to connect all the information to the single main file (and to one single URI), but that would diminish the effectiveness and specificity of the documentation, and make less easy the debate around a given element of the visualisation. Dividing a 3D representation of an object (in this specific case of a building), though, is not a straightforward task. A model developed with a CAD software generally allows to identify and isolate different elements up to the level of the single vertex.[38] It is not possible to define a level of granularity that suits all the cases, as different researches focus on different aspects (and scale) of cultural heritage, from urban landscape to microscopic analysis of the single artefact. LOD allows the addition of both further specifications and further generalisation without affecting the pre-existing data, facilitating, for example, the practice of building on top of previous research zooming in or out its original scope.

When visualising ancient heritage, and in particular architecture, it may appear a natural decision to rely on the many and very detailed available taxonomies.[39] However, using semantically charged labels would make the 3D visualisation fall again into that univocality that we were trying to avoid, or at least minimise. Calling a building 'temple' or a space 'kitchen' is already a (subjective) interpretation and could be challenged by other scholars, especially when describing ancient buildings and settlements where so much information is missing.[40] The SCOTCH ontology aims at dividing and naming the space in the most neutral way possible. Labels about the name or the function of a given element will then be linked to it, each connection expressing the statement of a specific author and, possibly, a bibliographical reference. Obviously, more than one label could be attached to the same element.

After naming the parts of the 3D visualisation in a consistent way[41] and assigning each a URI, the primary purpose of SCOTCH is to make visible the connection between each element and the related sources and documents. In this respect, the present research does not intend to create redundancy with existing ontologies that already successfully model both explicit and implicit citations, such as the Citation Typing Ontology (CiTO),[42] but to fill the gaps related to the specific domain of 3D visualisation, and to create a conceptual framework that maps and harmonises the useful parts of various available ontologies, especially when they are already well received by part of the academic community.

Looking at other digital projects, including LOD based ones, the most common way to express relationships with the sources, especially when they tend to be fuzzy, is through a degree of certainty.[43] Nonetheless, SCOTCH prefers to avoid the use of the word, and in general the concept of, 'certainty'. First, rating the certainty of a source may suggest a quantitative approach to documentation that is not in the SCOTCH agenda. 'Certainty' is an ambiguous concept and can be perceived differently by different researchers. There are no guidelines or shared conventions on what it takes for a source to be labelled as 'certain'. It is not clear if, for example, primary sources should be considered more or less certain than secondary ones, or what would happen if there are inconsistencies between them. Is the source rated with the highest level of certainty always the most accurate? In addition, in the specific case of archaeology, information is often a work in progress, and new evidence can always arise and contradict or complement the previous one. These characteristics make a quantitative assessment of the sources of limited use and problematic application. But, above all, simply communicating the degree of certainty about a visual hypothesis does not actually contribute to making it more transparent. The use of values of certainty may also suggest that there is a degree of preferability among types of sources. SCOTCH advocates that not only all sources can be debatable in their own respect, but also, and mainly, that it is beyond the scope (or the interest) of this ontology to assess the 'quality' of the sources. SCOTCH simply aims at showing the methodological relationship between an element in the 3D visualisation and the information that motivated the visual output.

Instead of degrees of certainty, SCOTCH prefers to refer to types of sources, indicating, for example, if a given element is based on direct observation of still standing artefacts or on secondary historical sources; if it is deduced from material clues or imagined according to external references; if it is based on the expert knowledge or even intuition of the researcher and so on. As there are many possible purposes for the visualisations (including purely recreational ones), there are no types of sources that are discredited *a priori,* as long as their use is clearly documented. Those elements that appear in the 3D visualisation only to add contextualization value,[44] when not mere 'colour,' are very likely to lack any actual historical evidence, but they can be nonetheless useful in particular research outputs. All types of sources can be part of a documentation when it becomes clear that the 3D visualisation does not aim at representing the material artefact, but the knowledge of the author about the artefact. In this view, showing a lack of historical sources can be as informative as communicating which are the sources that have actually been analysed and investigated. As mentioned, the main aim of SCOTCH is, basically, to point out at the source of information (in the form of link to online digital resource, bibliographical information or annotation). However, also stating the type of the source (choosing from a controlled vocabulary of available choices) appears as a useful option that will allow us, for example, to render the 3D visualisation highlighting or hiding the elements that are based on a particular type of sources.[45]

Each of the subsets of SCOTCH will cover and model, through the ontology, specific issues related to the technology of choice or the field of application, from the research process to the simplifications, normalisations and post-editorial choices. However, for the purpose of this paper, it is no use to discuss them in depth[46] and it seems more appropriate to remain on a methodological level, stressing that, basically, the application of LOD and the development of a dedicated semantic ontology will allow us to attach information of different kinds to specific parts of the 3D output, and to introduce 3D into the growing pool of data about cultural heritage that is already published online in LOD format.[47] This approach allows different authors and different datasets to dialogue in spite of their differences, as long as they refer to the same element (identified via a URI) and the same vocabulary (the ontology that is community developed).

5 What would be the Benefits?

The first major benefit in the use of LOD to document 3D visualisation will be, obviously, the enhanced transparency of the 3D output. It will also open the door to aspects of the academic research from which 3D visualisations are currently excluded such as repeatability of the process (because other researchers will access detailed information about sources analysed and methodology followed), peer review (because the quality of the hypotheses represented and the provenance of the sources will be assessed) and citation (because information about authorship will be attached to the single 3D element). Furthermore, it will force researchers to reflect critically on their sources, on their choices and on their methodology.

5.1 Within Academia

The use of LOD, and a dedicated ontology, will affect scholarly 3D visualisation both from the inside (in the way it is carried out and disseminated) and the outside (in the way it is received). The opportunity to attach information (as annotation, bibliographical references, alternative sources and hypotheses) will not only open a discussion between different researchers in the same discipline—like two archaeologists comparing their research on the same artefact—but it will turn the 3D visualisation into a multidisciplinary portal where scholars from various discipline can link information and add annotations that are relevant to their own research. As a consequence, on the one hand the 3D visualisation will be an open-ended aggregator of multidisciplinary information on the same object, on the other, the 3D visualisation will see its informative value dramatically increased thanks to the different perspectives and variety of sources connected. Even when not interested in the 3D visualisation per se, members of the scholarly community may want to use it as a digital, searchable portal of information on a given artefact. The 3D visualisation of a Roman temple, for example, could gather information, expressed in linked data, from archaeologists interested in the material remains as well as from art historians interested in the wall paintings. The subject depicted could be linked to taxonomies of art techniques and/or proposopography of mythological characters, and so on. The examples could be countless and varied, potentially involving any discipline from anthropology to engineering.

5.2 Outside Academia: Knowledge Exchange

The availability of a documentation for 3D visualisation, its openness and multivocality potentially lead to a wider use of the visual outputs outside academia, consolidating mutually beneficial relationships with members of the private sector. To mention a few examples of possible exchange:

Museums and Archives

As discussed, 3D visualisations displayed in museums do not seem to be successful in engaging the audience because the information delivered, despite the technological novelty, is often still mono-dimensional and authoritative.[48]

Making the documentation available to the public (along with the opportunity to filter the information according to competence and interest) can change this attitude, and contribute in enhancing the audience experience in museums. First, allowing the public to see the 'behind the scene' process of research around the artefact and its visualisation will include them in the process of meaning-building, as advocated in the constructivist approach.[49] Second, showing the existence of conflictual and incomplete information and the existence of open ended questions is likely to solicit curiosity in the visitors and stimulate a more critical thinking.[50,] The opportunity to evaluate how much of a 3D visualisation for cultural heritage is actually based on speculation will stress the fact that many hypotheses are possible, even starting from the exact same evidence and sources. In the most optimistic view, an open and interactive documentation can encourage the public to add their own annotations to the 3D visualisation. Then, it is each institution's decision how to manage the access to their data and to what extent allow users to add information. Different models can be adopted from open-to-all access to more or less strict moderation, involving editorial boards or the most suitable vetting process.

Likewise, all the other examples of knowledge exchange, the benefits will be bidirectional. On the one hand, disseminating more engaging 3D products for cultural heritage will make them more popular among cultural institutions, reinvigorating the use of 3D visualisation in academic research and reinforcing the idea that documentation is actually a crucial and necessary component of the final output, even in commercial contexts. On the other hand, the annotations from the public carry a considerable informative value of their own when considered as both subject and object. They enrich the 3D visualisation in the number and variety of connections expressed, can identify new sources, point out inconsistencies and propose new alternatives. Also, members of the public can be the last witness of lost information about cultural heritage in the form or family archives and personal memories. But, besides this, the annotations from the public are a corpus of data in its own right that could be subsequently analysed in other researches investigating, for example, reception of cultural heritage. Although this scenario appears like a step forward towards the representation of more voices in the study and communication of cultural heritage, it remains clear that it is by no means a solutions to the issue of underrepresented minorities, and, at the moment, the technology is still likely to be used almost exclusively by a specific segment of population.[51]

Another line of collaboration between academic 3D visualisation and museums goes through 3D printing. The printed replica, of course, only reproduces some aspects of the original artefact. Nonetheless, the manipulation of facsimile seems to be a promising strategy in enhancing the understanding of the artefact and to make it partially accessible to the visually impaired. Some museums are already sharing with the general public 3D scans of their artefacts that can be easily 3D printed.[52] Making available not only the 3D files but also their documentation, museums can offer a much bigger value than just a file to download at home. Also, if properly documented with information about authorship, copyright and a description of the sources, external 3D files can be used by smaller museums (that cannot afford their own digitisation program) in order to engage the public.

The potential exchange with museums does not only involve directly the general public. 3D visualisations documented in LOD will help museums' and archives' catalogues to interlink meaningfully their resources (sometimes already in linked data format) according to different criteria, from commonality of provenance to subject depicted. Making these relationships visible will create a straightforward digital unification, even just at an informative level. Also, highlighting connections between different collections and archives may suggest new discoveries that would have not been possible when looking at only one repository. The web of connections around the 3D visualisation will also work as a possible starting point for museum exhibitions (in the traditional physical form or in an entire virtual space). Lastly, it will help pointing out gaps and inaccuracies in the museums and archives' own documentation, generating, when possible, more correct and reliable information.[53]

Teaching and Education

The application of LOD to 3D scholarly visualisations will make them part of the new family of digital tools and strategies used in educational environments to teach students about the ancient world while using their inputs to populate databases and annotate texts and images. For example, when a building or artefact is mentioned in an ancient text, or reproduced in an archive document, students involved in theses digital programs will be invited to include 3D visualisations in their annotations, making the amount of information connected to the 3D files vaster and deeper than the one any single group of researchers could ever achieve.

From a pedagogical point of view, the exercise of connecting historical documents (from digitised ancient text to excavation reports, journal entries and historical depictions) will promote among the students the idea that all representations of cultural heritage are subjective and culturally biased. Moreover, the act of establishing connections between the same source and more than one 3D visualisation will show how everything we know about the past (and the way we represent it) is always incomplete and hypothetical.

Artefacts and Building Restoration

Documented 3D visualisations can be a valuable tool for curators and restorers to monitor changes and degradation of artefacts and buildings, displaying accurately to what part of the object the measurements, reports and analysis refer. Even when the scientific information will not be fully available to the public for copyright issues, it could be linked as bibliographical reference, facilitating dialogue and contacts between different laboratories and professionals. A comparison between measurements of the same object, taken at different times or with different equipment, can also help identifying biases and problems that are due to technologies more than methodology. The various connections to other artefacts showed through the documentation and annotations can lead restorers to the identifications of useful precedents or similarities and, as a consequence, to the development of new restoration hypotheses.

Geography and Urban Planning

Laser scanning the archaeological digs to record different stages of the excavation process is presented by virtual archaeologists as a more effective means to document the excavation, compared to traditional bidimensional representations.[54] According to Dell'Unto (2014), 3D images offer a better and more detailed record of the archaeological site as it was before and during the intrinsically destructive process of excavation. Especially when combined with haptic technologies or oculus rift, a 3D imaging of the site, theoretically, allows to re-examine the excavation later on, even when the actual place and the archaeological evidence do not exist anymore.

An annotated 3D digital record of the landscape and the terrain stratigraphy can prove extremely interesting for geological and hydrological surveys. It will maximise the usefulness of the archaeological investigation, producing data that are, potentially, accessible by various industries. The opportunity to link together, to the same 3D visualisation, both academic and commercial reports will produce a very rich and unprecedented pool of information. Commercial companies may analyse the 3D scanning of archaeological excavations (and the related and connected reports) in order to avoid or reduce preliminary investigations in the same area, and archaeologist could have their study of the terrain enriched by the annotations of other professionals that will use different approaches and, probably, different technologies. In a few years, the availability of these kind of 3D records might become a crucial source of information in understanding the changes in the area, and how human or natural activities have influenced the environment. Likewise, annotated 3D scanning of underground areas of a city (such as those recently performed in Rome[55] or London[56]) could be shared with the local municipality and contribute to a more efficient planning of urban works like, for example, the improvement of the underground transportation system.

What the examples above want to point out is that the availability of 3D data as such is not likely to have a significant impact as long as the information remains opaque and univocal. But, as soon as it is documented, and, even better, it is documented in an open, multivocal and multidisciplinary way, then its usefulness increase dramatically and can be potentially of interest of many different public and commercial fields, not necessarily immediately related to the cultural heritage sector.

5.3 Engaging the Academic Community

Although the focus of this paper is on the impact of scholarly research outside academia, it seems appropriate to conclude this overview started with public engagement and multidisciplinarity, with few words on the engagement of scholars within academia. A virtual transparent 3D environment that links and discuss information from different fields and perspectives, can be a promising premise to a cross-disciplinary dialogue. The collaborative nature of the semantic ontology is not only a necessity driven by the variety and complexity of the matter, it is also a means to engage the academic community on the shaping of the knowledge representation process and to make the documentation standard as widely known and familiar as possible. Every project involving 3D visualisation, in this view, is never finished, but always open to new sources, to new debates, to new variants and hypotheses.

6　Potential Issues

The documentation of 3D visualisations for cultural heritage in LOD format is still at an experimental stage, and there is not enough evidence available yet to predict its success or foresee its limits. Furthermore, this application is based on some assumptions that have not been proven.

6.1　Who is the author?

The first one is that 3D visualisations of cultural heritage are developed by the same person(s) that are in charge of the historical or archaeological research. Such professional figures do exist in academia and belong to a well-established trend in the Digital Humanities (and especially Digital Classics). There are several cases in which, for example, 3D visualisations of ancient places and artefacts are used to teach, at the same time, 3D techniques and Classics.[57] However, there is an opposite trend that sees the 'humanists' undertaking the academic research, and then 3D 'technicians' making the humanists' research visible producing the 3D output.[58] In this case, it is easy to imagine how the process of documentation, and the whole attribution of authorship and intellectual ownership, becomes more complicated.

6.2 Are contributors willing to share information?

The second assumption is that all potential contributors, inside and outside academia, are willing to share the outcome of their work. It is a fact that the amount of data available on line (sometimes already in linked data format) is constantly growing, but, of course, many things still have restricted access. The issue could be theoretically overcome considering that links can be established with documents and pieces of information that are not actually online, but that can be identified through their metadata or URIs. Following the example of platforms like Recogito,[59] the LOD documentation only aims at connecting information, without duplicating, or publishing the documents. Nonetheless, copyright issues and a certain reluctance among private companies is not unlikely to manifest.

6.3 Are researchers willing to be assessed?

Another concern seems to be that many researchers using 3D technologies have been quite comfortably hiding behind the screen of opacity and actually do not want each and every one of their intellectual choices to be scrutinised by the entire community; including all those implicit simplifications and regularisations that are part of the visualisation process, and that are almost automatic to 3D practitioners. It is not unlikely that virtual archaeologists (and other researchers using 3D technologies) are, even at an unconscious level, reluctant to the idea of stating on how many occasions they work without referring to any specific source but relying on their experience and intuition, feeling that such an admission will undermine their entire research. It is important to change the expectations in the expert and non-expert audiences about 3D visualisations and stop promising 'perfect replicas' of things from the past. More realistically, and more interestingly, scholarly 3D visualisation should be presented as the expression of a researcher's point of view on an ancient artefact, with all their biases and gaps, but open to discussion, confrontation and implementation.

6.4 Is the community interested in expanding the ontology?

The last major assumption is that the community of users is willing to be engaged in the development and refinement of the various subsets of the SCOTCH ontology. It will require the organisation of testing and discussion groups, and the sharing of the first results of the application of the ontology to the different sub-fields of 3D visualisation. Also, the process of decision making to judge if a new term should be introduced in the ontology, or if changes have to be applied needs to be completely set up. Even if based on the voluntary contribution of the users, a community built ontology will require a considerable investment in terms of time and resources.

6.5 *What is the most appropriate technology?*

At this stage, SCOTCH is mainly a conceptual framework that aims at harmonising elements from pre-existing ontologies and new ones created ad hoc to describe the specific process of producing a scholarly accurate 3D visualisation, identifying methodological similarities in the workflows of different 3D techniques. More than a ready-to-use application, it is an attempt of modelling, among other issues, the complex and multifaceted relationship between cultural heritage, the present and past research about it, and its digital, three-dimensional representations.

Effective ways to connect the linked data to the single 3D elements, and to display, meaningfully and clearly informative relationships and/or the outcome of a query, have to be further investigated and tested. The use of a cross-platform application programming interface (API) such as OpenGL[60] seems, so far, the most likely direction to go, but the question remains open. Moreover, a suitable user interface, able to present together the 3D visualisation and the LOD based information related to each element, still has to be designed. Useful lessons can be learned looking at the interfaces of other, successful LOD projects, but the intrinsic stress on visual information is likely to require specific features to be designed and discussed. A potential involvement of public and private IT companies at the stage of 3D software development, in order to include a user friendly documentation tool may prove a promising collaboration.

7 Conclusions

This research was mainly driven by the necessity to constrain and standardise the documentation of 3D visualisations, making it time and cost effective, and thus more likely to be retained in a project's budget. However, we believe that the application of LOD technology and a dedicated ontology to 3D visualisations also presents a number of other potential benefits. In general, it will allow documented 3D visualisations to join and enrich the growing network of linked digital resources on cultural heritage, making 3D visualisations human and machine searchable, connecting them with contemporary and historical sources. It will also encourage comparison of different visualisations and interpretations of cultural heritage, as the same resource will be connected to all the related visualisations that share the same vocabulary. Likewise, it will facilitate citations, re-use and peer-review of 3D visualisations, as every 3D element (and its author) will be always identifiable and linkable through the URI.

We see the value of SCOTCH especially as a means to change the ways 3D visualisations of cultural heritage are perceived and experienced by both expert and non-expert audiences; to move from a univocal display of traditional research to a collaborative virtual environment that can be shared and implemented by different authors.[61] We envision SCOTCH, and the research around it, as a step towards a shift in perspective: from the static representation of a material artefact to the dynamic and open-ended representation of the knowledge around that artefact.

With the caution due to the involvement of many and different actors in the process of creating a 3D visualisations, and the various degree of openness that are convenient to each partner, this approach seems to facilitate a large number of fertile and mutually beneficially interactions between different disciplines within academia, between public and private sectors and between authors and consumers of 3D visualisations.

Several theoretical and practical issues remain open to discussion and improvement, from the management and coordination of the collaborative effort to the need of a shared and well established naming conventions for the component parts of 3D visualisations. We see stimulating and channelling such a discussion and its outcomes, as one of the first and most profitable outcome of this research.

Notes

[1] For example, a quick survey of the panels presented at the 2015 CAA in Siena, Italy, shows that, of the 44 discussed, 27 had at least one paper that was explicitly about the creation or management of 3D data. Full program at <http://caaconference.org/wp-content/uploads/sites/14/2014/07/Detailed-program_CAA-20155.pdf>.

[2] See also Digital Heritage conference, 2015: <http://www.digitalheritage2015.org/>.

[3] Cf., for example, the 3D content offered by The British Museum on the sketchfab platform at <https://sketchfab.com/britishmuseum>, or the X 3D Explorer application developed by the Smithsonian at <http://3d.si.edu/> and related models.

[4] According to the Wohlers report (AAVV 2014), 3D printing has experienced a growth of 34.9% between 2013 and 2014, and of 346% between 2008 and 2011.

[5] The platform to upload and share 3D content that are, currently, most frequently used for reproductions of cultural heritage artefacts are Sketchfab, Autodesk 123D catch, 3DHOP

[6] Hermon 2008.

[7] Frisher et al. 2002; Denard 2012.

[8] Parry 2007.

[9] Favro 2006.

[10] One of the 3D products displayed at the MAV in Herculaneum, a fly-through of the 3D model of the House of the Tragic Poet in Pompeii, was also part of the British Museum exhibition *Life and Death in Pompeii and Herculaneum* (2013).

[11] Cameron & Robinson 2007.

[12] Forte & Pietroni 2009.

[13] James 1997.

[14] Cf., for example, the 3D models of Pompeian houses advertised as 'perfect reconstructions' on the MAV website.

[15] McCarty 2004.

[16] Baker 2012.

[17] Walsh 2002.

[18] For example, statements such as: 'The possibility of obtaining a virtual, exact replica of reality in a limited amount of time makes the laser scanning method ideal for studies of 3D digital restoration' in Stanco et al, 2012: 212.

[19] Ryan 2001.

[20] London Charter: <http://www.londoncharter.org>.

[21] London Charter, Principle 4: Documentation: <http://www.londoncharter.org/principles/documentation.html>.

[22] Forte 2007.

[23] The publication also highlights the consequences, overlooked at the time, of the lack of long term preservation strategies: the model on CD rom it is now hardly accessible on the most commonly used computers.

[24] Abbey Theatre, available: <http://blog.oldabbeytheatre.net/>.

[25] The project is developed by the University of Arkansas, available: <http://pompeii.uark.edu/>.

[26] Digital Roman Forum: <http://dlib.etc.ucla.edu/projects/Forum>.

[27] Digital Karnak: <http://dlib.etc.ucla.edu/projects/Karnak/>.

[28] For example, they can be the students' output of teaching modules in 3D visualisation, digital cultural heritage or digital classics. Or they could be produced by commercial companies with different employees in charge of the different phases of the development.

[29] As defined by Europeana on their Linked Open Data page 'Linked Open Data is a way of publishing structured data that allows metadata to be connected and enriched, so that different representations of the same content can be found, and links made between related resources'. Available: <http://labs.europeana.eu/api/linked-open-data/introduction/>.

[30] Pleiades: <http://pleiades.stoa.org/>.

[31] Pelagios: <http://pelagios-project.blogspot.co.uk/p/about-pelagios.html>.

[32] Perseus Project: <http://www.perseus.tufts.edu/hopper/>.

[33] Best practice would be to have the terms of the controlled vocabularies defined and available online. Cf., for example, the DBpedia ontology at

<http://dbpedia.org/ontology/> or the FRBR Term Summary at <http://vocab.org/frbr/core.html>.

34 There are domain ontologies to express concepts in Linguistics, Politics, Archaeology, Show Business, Videogames and many other fields. Major institutions such as the BBC and the British Museum have developed their own in-house ontologies.

35 Although not necessarily open.

36 See also: <http://www.cidoc-crm.org/>.

37 CRMdig offers a useful basis to express metadata of a 3D file, but also some kind of annotations. Cf. <http://www.ics.forth.gr/isl/CRMext/CRMdig/docs/CRMdig3.0.pdf>.

38 Each vertex has unique x, y, z coordinates in the virtual environment.

39 Cf., for example, the Thesaurus of Art and Architecture developed and made available by the Getty Research Institute at <http://www.getty.edu/research/tools/vocabularies/aat/>.

40 The building in Pompeii located at VII.9.7, 8, 19, 42 has been identified during the years as a Pantheon, a temple of Serapis, a fish market, a macellum, a college of the Augustales (only to mention some of the attributions).

41 There is not, at the moment, a widely adopted naming convention to define space in built environments. The researcher has drafted a new one in order to apply SCOTCH. The discussion of the naming convention, although a crucial issue in the development of a LOD documentation, is beyond the scope of this article.

42 See also <http://vocab.ox.ac.uk/cito>.

43 Cf. for example the assessment of certainty in a 3D visualisation project such as The Digital Roman Forum: (see n. 26) or a LOD project such as the Pleiades gazetteer: <http://pleiades.stoa.org/>.

44 Such as plants and other ornaments, passers-by, dirt or other traces of human activity.

45 For example, the user could decide to render only the elements that are derived from still standing archaeological evidence, or only those that are inspired by Vitruvian rules. The user could combine more than one selection or, on the contrary, select everything but a specific type of sources, for example the elements that are entirely speculative.

46 The documentation of a 3D visualisation of a piece of archaeological heritage (the Iseum in Pompeii) using RDF triples and the dedicated ontology SCOTCH is discussed in the author's doctoral thesis, due in 2016.

47 Cf. platforms such as Europeana <http://www.europeana.eu/portal/>, OpenGLAM <http://openglam.org/> or Ariadne <http://www.ariadne-infrastructure.eu/About>.

48 Dallas 2007.

49 Merriman 2004.

50 Graffieti et al. 2010. See also the issue discussed in various venues such as: Issues in Education <https://www.informs.org/ORMS-Today/Public-

Articles/April-Volume-38-Number-2/ISSUES-IN-EDUCATION>, Education World <http://www.educationworld.com/a_curr/responsiveclassroom/responsiveclassroom014.shtml> or Canada Education <http://www.cea-ace.ca/education-canada/article/engaging-students-through-effective-questions>.

[51] See also Rainie 2013.

[52] Cf., for example, the 3D printable files made available by institutions such as African Fossils <http://africanfossils.org/search>, the Museo di Arte Orientale di Torino through the Google Art platform <https://www.google.com/culturalinstitute/u/0/collection/museo-d-arte-orientale?v.view=grid&hl=it> or El Museu d'Arqueologia de Catalunya via Sketchfab <https://macb3d.sketchfab.me>.

[53] After error and inaccuracies have been identified, it could be valuable to study them as a corpus in its own right.

[54] Forte 2010.

[55] ScanLAB's project *Rome Invisible City*. See also: <http://scanlabprojects.co.uk/projects/bbcrome>.

[56] ScanLAB's London project *Mail Rail*. See also: <http://www.wired.com/2015/04/laser-scans-london-new-way-see-world/>.

[57] Cf., for example, the 'Tesseract' program at University of Arkansas, teaching Classical Mythology combined with development of 3D gaming environment <http://tesseract.uark.edu/classes/4>, or the Digital Silchester module offered at the University of Reading <http://www.reading.ac.uk/modules/document.aspx?modP=CL3SIL&modYR=1213>.

[58] Bakker et al. 2003.

[59] Pelagios, 'About Recogito', available; <http://pelagios.org/recogito/about>.

[60] See also <https://www.opengl.org/documentation/>.

[61] Johanson 2009.

References

AAVV (2014). *Wohlers Report 2014. Additive Manufacturing and 3D Printing State of the Industry. Annual Worldwide Progress Report*. Wohlers Associates.

Baker, D. (2012). *Defining Paradata in Heritage Visualization*. In A. Bentkowska-Kafel, H. Denard, & D. Baker (Eds.). *Paradata and Transparency in Virtual Heritage*. Farnham: Ashgate.

Bakker, G. F., Meulenberg, F. & de Rode, J. (2003). Truth and credibility as a double ambition: reconstruction of the built past, experiences and dilemmas. *The Journal of Visualization and Computer Animation*, 14(3): 159–167.

Cameron, F & Robinson, H. (2007). Digital Knowledgscapes: Cultural, Theoretical, Practical and Usage Issues Facing Museum Collection Databases in a Digital Epoch. In F. Cameron, & S. Kenderdine (Eds.)m *Theorizing Digital Cultural Heritage. A critical discourse.* Cambridge, MA: MIT Press.

Dallas, C. (2007). *Archaeological knowledge, virtual exhibitions and the social construction of meaning.* Established by: Mauro Cristofani and Riccardo Francovich.

Dell'Unto, N. (2014). The use of 3D models for intra-site investigation in archaeology. *3D Recording and Modeling in Archaeology and Cultural Heritage. Theory and best practices.*

Denard, H. (2012). A New Introduction to the London Charter. In A. Bentkowska-Kafel, H. Denard, & D. Baker (Eds.), *Paradata and Transparency in Virtual Heritage*, Ashgate.

Favro, D. (2006). In the eyes of the beholder: Virtual Reality Recreations and academia. *Journal of Roman Archaeology Supplementary Series Number* 61(2006): 321–334.

Forte, M. (Ed.). (2007). *La villa di Livia: un percorso di ricerca di archeologia virtuale* (Vol. 41). L'Erma di Bretschneider.

Forte, M. & Kurillo, G. (2010). Cyberarchaeology: Experimenting with teleimmersive archaeology. In *Virtual Systems and Multimedia (VSMM), 2010 16th International Conference on* (pp. 155–162). IEEE.

Forte, M. & Pietroni, E. (2009). 3D Collaborative Environments in Archaeology: Experiencing the Reconstruction of the Past. *International Journal of Architectural Computing*, 7(1): 57–75.

Frischer B., Niccolucci F., Ryan N. & Barcelò J. (2002). From CVR to CVRO. The Past, Present, and Future of Cultural Virtual Reality. In F. Niccolucci (Ed.) *Proceedings of VAST 2000.* British Archaeological Reports 834 (Archeo-Presss, Oxford) 7–18.

G. Goodrick & G. Earl (2004). A manufactured past: virtual reality in archaeology. *Internet Archaeology* 15.

Graffieti, M., Scagnetti, G., Ricci, D., Masud, L. & Porpora, M. (2010). TELL THEM ANYTHING BUT THE TRUTH: THEY WILL FIND THEIR OWN. Paper presented as a contributed talk at Arts | Humanities | Complex Networks – a Leonardo satellite symposium at NetSci2010. May 20, 2010 Boston MA.

Harte, T. & Bors, A. G. (2002). Watermarking 3D models. In *Image Processing. 2002. Proceedings. 2002 International Conference on* (Vol. 3, pp. 661–664). IEEE.

Hermon, S. (2008) Reasoning in 3D: a Critical appraisal of the role of 3D modelling and virtual reconstructions in archaeology. In B. Frischer & A. Dakouri-Hild (Eds.), *Beyond Illustration: 2D and 3D Digital Technologies as Tools for Discovery in Archaeology*, BAR International Series 1805 (Oxford).

Johanson, C. (2009). Visualizing History: Modeling in the Eternal City. *Visual Resources: An International Journal of Documentation*, 25(4): 403–418.

McCarty, W. (2004). Modeling: a study in words and meanings. *A companion to digital humanities, 26.*

Merriman, N. (2004). Involving the Public in Museum Archaeology. In N. Merriman (Ed.), *Public Archaeology.* London/New York: Routledge.

Parry, R. (2007). *Recoding the Museum: Digital Heritage and the Technologies of Change.* London: Routledge

Rainie, L. (2013). The State of Digital Divides. *Pew Research Internet Project. November.*

Ryan, N. (2001). Documenting and validating virtual archaeology. *Archeologia e Calcolatori,* (XII), 245–273.

Walsh, K. (2002). *The representation of the past: museums and heritage in the post-modern world.* London: Routledge.

Wang, Y. P. & Hu, S. M. (2009). A new watermarking method for 3D models based on integral invariants. *Visualization and Computer Graphics, IEEE Transactions on, 15*(2): 285–294.

SECTION 3

Public Engagement

CHAPTER 9

The Perseids Platform: Scholarship for all!

Bridget Almas* and Marie-Claire Beaulieu†

*Perseus Digital Library,
†Tufts University

Abstract

It is rarely possible for students, members of the public, and other non-traditional scholars to access ancient documents such as texts, inscriptions, and manuscripts. The Perseids collaborative editing platform offers a gateway to scholarship which is open to all, regardless of native language, background, and level of expertise. Within this fully integrated online environment, participants can view, edit, translate, and annotate ancient documents (texts, manuscripts, inscriptions), while contributing to an ever-growing repository of open access humanities data sets. The variety of tasks available, which ranges from textual criticism to annotation of personal names and geographical entities, ensures the inclusion of all participants, and offers them a chance to learn and perform increasingly difficult tasks as they gain expertise. At the core of the platform is the integration of two pre-existing frameworks, the Son of Suda Online (SoSOL) and the CITE services. The former enables collaborative editing by providing workflow tools on top of a Git-based revision control system, supporting a built-in, versioned review process whereby each contribution is examined by a board and receives feedback before being approved for publication. The latter provides standards and APIs designed to link the resources, provide a citation scheme for texts and images, and support dynamic presentation of digital editions. Together, along with a variety of other integrated tools, standards, and services, these systems enable the Perseids platform to support communities of participants, who can collaborate based on participation in a class, shared interest in a literary work, or interest in a category of documents.

How to cite this book chapter:
Almas, B and Beaulieu, M-C. 2016. The Perseids Platform: Scholarship for all!.
In: Bodard, G & Romanello, M (eds.) *Digital Classics Outside the Echo-Chamber: Teaching, Knowledge Exchange & Public Engagement,* Pp. 171–186. London: Ubiquity Press. DOI: http://dx.doi.org/10.5334/bat.j. License: CC-BY 4.0.

1 Introduction

Current practice in Digital Humanities focuses heavily on crowdsourcing as a model for producing knowledge, vetting contributions, and in general, dealing with large datasets.[1] In Classics, the rapid growth of digital repositories and the increasing number of largely unedited and untranslated documents available online for processing—thousands of Greek and Latin inscriptions, 900 medieval manuscripts from e-codices and 250 from the Walters Art Museum, to name only those few—practically force us to abandon traditional single-scholar approaches to adapt to the realities of the digital age.[2] The needs are simple, yet challenging: we must process more documents, but we must do so in a manner that is sustainable, upholds the established standards of quality in the discipline, and will result in the production of fully interoperable, transferable data.

The advantages to the method are obvious: a well-organized crowdsourcing effort can accomplish far more work than any lone scholar and the work ultimately produced benefits from the variety of perspectives included in its user base. Furthermore, crowdsourcing helps break down the social and geographical barriers that have long kept ancient documents and scholarship in a limited number of hands. However, the pitfalls of crowdsourcing are numerous, such as ensuring the reliability and consistency of the data being produced and ensuring the longevity of projects by renewing and growing the user base.[3] Finally, as crowdsourcing is more and more frequently practiced in classroom settings, questions arise with respect to pedagogy.[4] Does crowdsourcing change traditional teaching methods in Classics, and if so, how? In this new disciplinary landscape, what is the relationship between teaching and scholarship?

The Perseids platform,[5] nested within the Perseus Digital Library,[6] offers an online collaborative editing and annotation environment in which to test different approaches to crowdsourcing and pedagogy. Users can form communities based on participation in a class, in a research project, or individual interest in a particular type of document or question. The flexibility of the platform and the variety of tools offered ensure that users at every level of expertise and from a variety of fields can undertake editing and annotation work. Such broad participation leads us to rethink the role that scholarship plays in pedagogy, and in general the role that Classical scholarship can play in engaging Perseids users with the past.

2 The Audience of Classics Scholarship

Classics scholarship, in the form of interpretative essays, critical editions, and other forms of highly specialized publications, has long been strictly targeted to established scholars such as university professors and other professionals in the field. The objective of such publications is generally understood to bring knowledge further by engaging specialists in a conversation among themselves.

This is certainly useful: in all fields, it is important for new discoveries and new ideas to be examined carefully by those who know the most about the field and therefore can cast a critical eye at the work being done and express informed opinions.

Yet Classics, by its very nature as a field that encompasses disciplines as diverse as history, philosophy, archaeology, art history, rhetoric, grammar, linguistics, and many others, engages a large body of stakeholders who are not specialists. In fact, this is precisely the reason why the discipline of Classics has been conceived as part of the core educational curriculum in the West until recently. For this reason also, the teaching of Latin (and to a lesser degree, Greek) has recently regained some of its popularity in high schools, as parents and educators search for means to introduce children to the Humanities and the study of languages.[7] The question then becomes, how to accommodate these different aspects of the field without compromising either quality or accessibility, and in general, how to promote the study of Classics?

The Perseus Digital Library, within which the Perseids platform is nested, has long served such a diverse audience. Perseus' broad mission is 'to make the full record of humanity – linguistic sources, physical artifacts, historical spaces – as intellectually accessible as possible to every human being, regardless of linguistic or cultural background'.[8] Naturally, such a mission can never be fully realized, yet the infrastructure that we design now will materially enable or constrict how the next generation will be able to read languages from the past, scrutinize ancient artifacts, and explore historical spaces. With these goals and caveats in mind, the Perseids collaborative editing platform was designed to enable a broad audience to contribute to Perseus, and in general to participate in the creation of knowledge in the Humanities.[9]

The Perseids platform makes a range of tasks available to its users, from micro-tasks to multi-step editorial projects.[10] Students can undertake entire editorial tasks individually or in groups, as was done in Marie-Claire Beaulieu's Medieval Latin class in 2013 with the Tisch Miscellany Collection, a group of manuscript leaves and folios from early printed books preserved in the Tisch Library at Tufts University.[11] This project served as a test bed for tasks that were later to be made available in an integrated workflow on the Perseids platform. Now, students have started using the Perseids platform for such tasks. Editing and translation work has started on a 14th-century compendium of English Forest Law preserved in the Tisch Library (see Fig. 1),[12] and we intend to finish the edition and translation of the Tisch Miscellany Collection. Within these broad tasks, students can be assigned micro-tasks such as morpho-syntactic analysis through treebanks and named entity annotation through a variety of means including Perseids interfaces, through data imported from Google Spreadsheets or via integration with tools from the Alpheios and Pelagios projects.[13] By opening up the possibility for a wide range of external and third party tools to be used for annotation, we test different approaches to scholarship and pedagogy but recognize that an integrated fluid user experience is essential to

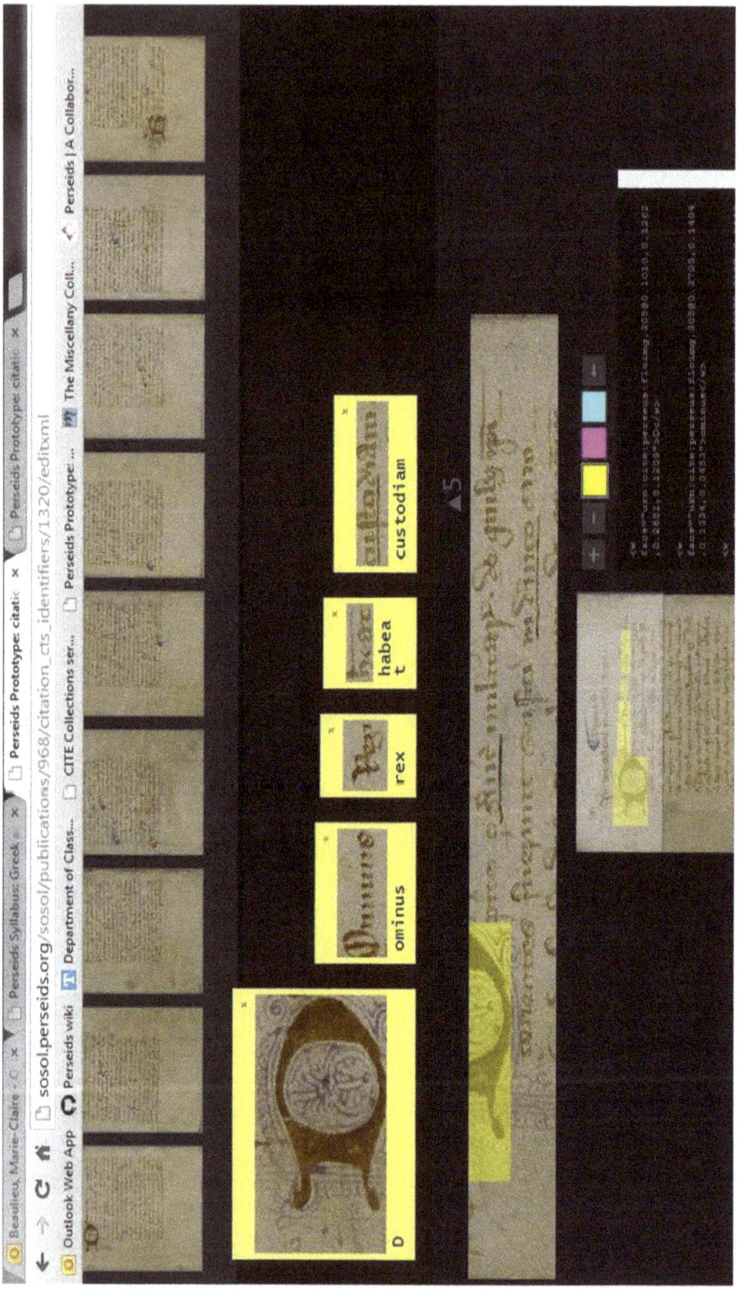

Figure 1: Ongoing editing work on the Carta de Foresta, 14th century compendium of English Forest Law, Tisch Library, Tufts University.

successful uptake and use of the platform. For this reason, we have also now integrated the Arethusa client-side annotation framework, which enables rapid development of new interfaces for different types of annotations and documents, within a single consistent user interface paradigm (see Fig. 2).[14]

The methodology behind the development of the Perseids platform is consistent with the project's goals for openness and accessibility. Underlying all architectural decisions is the premise that all texts and data produced on the platform must be fully accessible to the creator of the data at any time, and also available to other users of the platform.

There are different aspects to accessibility. First, in terms of user access, all that is required to create an account on the platform is an account with a Social Identity Provider that supports the OpenId protocol.[15] The most common type of account for this is a Google email address, but Yahoo and AOL addresses are also accepted and additional OpenId provider services can be added. We have also included support for authentication via a user's educational institution, through support for the SAML/Shibboleth protocol.[16] The user can choose to link this account with her social identity, so that if the user changes institutions, she can retain a consistent single identity on the platform associated with her publications. Support for the OpenID and SAML/Shibboleth protocols also puts the amount of private information made available to the Perseids platform and its end users in the primary user's own control. Perseids never has access to authentication credentials (such as passwords) and the only information a user is required to provide is a nickname for their user id. Although a user may choose to provide their email address, full name, and affiliation, this is purely optional.

Next, in terms of legality, all the data produced on Perseids is published under the Creative Commons CC-BY-SA license.[17] In addition, at no time is the data locked into a closed database under proprietary formats. Instead, we use the git version control system to store and manage all texts and data,[18] and while the current deployment of the platform uses a git repository which is local to the infrastructure components that read and write data, there are various means by which this data can be retrieved by the end users.

All publications at any stage of editing are downloadable via links in the Perseids user interface, serialized according to standard and widely accepted data formats (the standards used will be discussed further below). In addition, version history and comments for any given file are available to any user of the platform through the user interface. No access controls are imposed on either download or history and commenting functionality, although in order to accommodate needs for use in the classroom, we have given the user the responsibility to share links into their publications, rather than advertising them broadly through the user interface. By the end of the first implementation phase of the project, we will also establish a public-facing clone of the master branch of the local git repository on the GitHub platform. This branch contains all committed publications, i.e. those which are no longer under review.

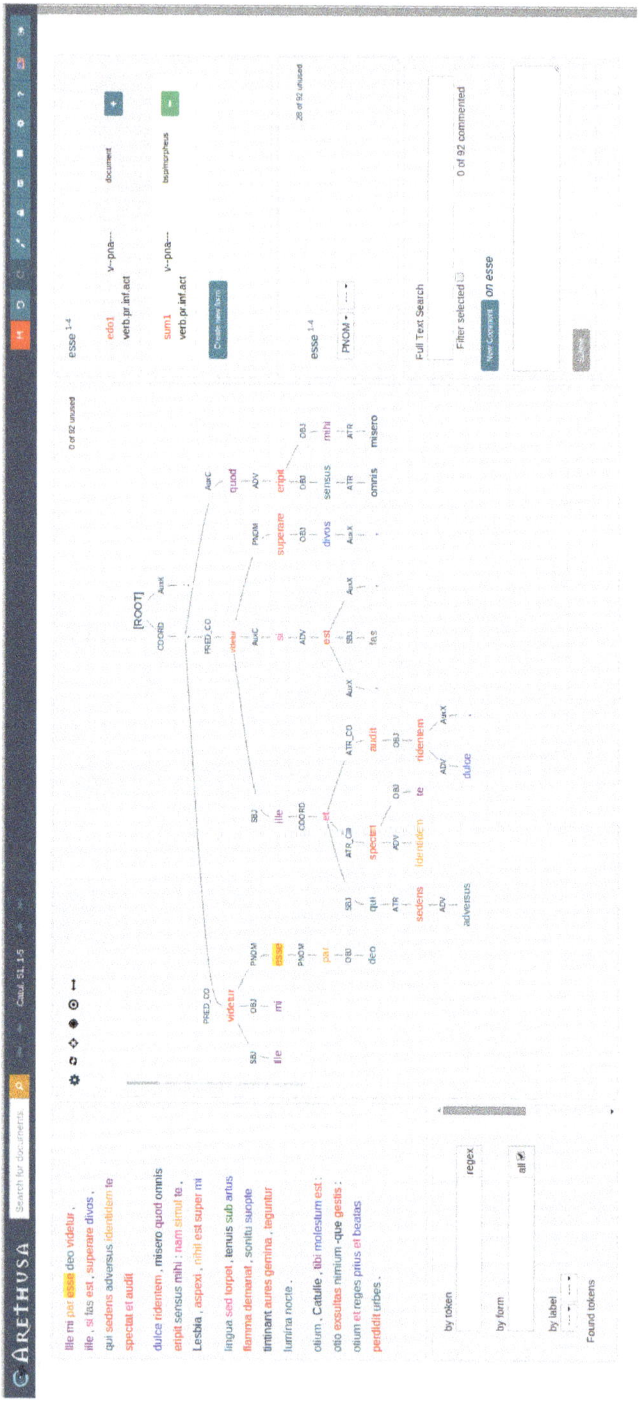

Figure 2: Arethusa Annotation Framework showing a morpho-syntactic annotation of Catullus 51.

Finally, the tools themselves used to create, curate, and annotate texts and data are all open source components, available in public version control repositories such as github, sourceforge, and bitbucket. Public contributions to these code bases are encouraged, and – subject to review by Perseids project staff – will be accepted and deployed on the platform. Should a user or set of users wish to add functionality to one or more of these tools that is not deemed to be in line with the project priorities or goals, these users are free at any time to fork the code bases and deploy their own version of the tools, taking their data with them. The tools themselves are connected via documented APIs and standard RESTful web protocols.

A different avenue we are pursuing for accessibility is via integration with other projects in the domain. The Europeana network of Ancient Greek and Latin Epigraphy (EAGLE) project[19] has setup a multilingual Wiki for the enrichment and enhancement of epigraphic images and texts, to provide a basis for future translations of inscriptions into other European languages. However, the wiki approach with open editing practices is a new model for traditional scholarship in the field, and Perseids is integrated with the EAGLE wiki to provide an alternate review workflow which allows translations to go through an editorial board. Perseids is in this case serving as a bridge between fully open wiki editing models and the more closed review circles, by providing an open platform to enable peer and board review for wiki-based publication.

3 Pedagogy and Scholarship

When Perseids is used in class to edit, translate, and analyze ancient documents, traditional pedagogical models give way to a new model in which the teacher becomes a collaborator, guiding students through the process of research. In such a pedagogical setting, traditional top-down teaching methods where the teacher is in control of projects and outcomes and individual students all produce work on the same texts are set aside. Rather, work is produced in small teams or as a broad group with distinct tasks. Such a pedagogical method has proved motivating for students, who expressed enthusiasm at the idea of producing original work. Furthermore, this collaborative method can easily be combined with more traditional lectures or drills in order to vary classroom activities and stimulate different types of learners, from the more passive to the more pro-active students.[20]

Furthermore, collaborative teaching methods provide a new model for evaluating student work. While traditional assignments are produced on a one-time basis and usually go through only one grading cycle, collaborative assignments can be evaluated multiple times, formally or informally. This component of the Perseids platform is an extension of the Son of SUDA Online (SoSOL) application, which was developed by the Papyri.info project (where it is called the Papyrological Editor).[21] This tool supports a workflow that leverages the

Git version control system and in which a publication can consist of multiple linked documents, each identified by a stable Uniform Resource Identifier (URI).[22] There are no fixed editions; everything is potentially in flux but each change is carefully recorded and vetted via an approval process which passes the documents in a publication through one or more targeted review boards made up of editors and community members. In a classroom setting, the board can be the teacher and teaching assistants, while in other projects the board can be composed of invited experts, or simply all the members of a project team. Such a review method is commonly used in research and forms the basis of the peer-review system on which modern scholarship relies. In a classroom setting, multiple reviews allow students to learn from their mistakes and correct them, cut down on stress, and allow for a longer-term formative experience that shifts the emphasis from grades to learning. The students and the teacher make sure the task is done optimally rather than simply evaluating how it meets a certain standard at first try. Furthermore, the process serves to train students as researchers as they get to experience the many stages of review through which any work of scholarship must go before publication.

Our aim is to support a wide range of publication types for the texts and data produced on the Perseids platform, from micro or nano publications[23] to full-fledged digital editions which adhere to scholarly standards such as those outlined by publications like RIDE.[24] Some examples of micro publications already supported include the commentary annotations produced by Marie-Claire Beaulieu's mythology students and published on the Perseus Digital Library,[25] additions and corrections to linked data sets like the Perseus Lexical Inventory,[26] and named entity and date annotations produced via the use of tools like TimeMapper and preserved via ingest into the Perseids repository from Google spreadsheets.[27] We also support complete digital editions comprised of multiple documents including transcriptions and translations of source text in TEI XML, complete morpho-syntactic annotations on the text in the form of treebanks, translation alignments, accompanying commentary, bibliography, and other related information. The Fragmentary Texts and Bodin prototypes are demonstrations of possible web based presentations of such editions, always backed by the raw XML, and annotations that are the substance of the data behind the edition.[28] Through tools like Arethusa, mentioned previously, we are also exploring approaches to living publications, where members of the community can distribute links to their work in progress and invite feedback. The goal is to support as small or large a contribution to the scholarly discourse as an individual is willing and able to make, always preserving the history of the work, recording provenance information according to standards for research data like the PROV ontology so that work is credited and attributable.[29] Perseids team members have also been participating in international research data efforts like those of the Research Data Alliance to ensure we are informed of and follow the best practices in the scientific and scholarly communities for preservation and publication of the data that makes up our publications.[30]

Collaborative teaching methods also give permanence to student work. While traditional classroom assignments will usually get thrown out after the semester is over and are rarely expanded into further work, the work done through Perseids is published to the web in the form of editions, translations, and annotations, where it serves to support further scholarship and learning activities. In this way, the students learn by producing concrete results, much in the way students in the sciences learn by participating in experimentation in laboratories or students in trade schools learn by working on actual products. In this way, Perseids not only democratizes access to publication, but also gives value to small contributions as well as to large ones.[31] For this reason, Perseids will soon implement an e-portfolio module,[32] which will pull together all of a user's contributions to scholarship through the platform and make them available as a body of work. The module can be used as a tool for global classroom evaluation, for capstone projects, or as material for graduate school and job applications.

4 What is Scholarship?

Opening up participation in scholarship in this way brings us to ask the question, what exactly is scholarship, and do these methods change it? According to the American Heritage Dictionary, scholarship is 'the methods, discipline, and attainments of a scholar or scholars'. According to this definition, scholarship is about the ways in which knowledge is produced as well as the result of this production, namely, contributions to the advancement of knowledge. Thus, over the centuries, scientific research methods have evolved in order to ensure maximum accuracy of the results. These methods apply to all science, regardless of the field, whether it is in the Humanities or Natural Sciences. At their core, they involve relatively simple principles that correlate the collection of accurate data and its interpretation. In Classics, these principles are seen at work in language training, which is essential in order to understand and use the information provided by ancient documents to the fullest, and in the principles that guide the conduct of textual criticism, archaeological digs, etc. All these methods are designed to collect data in a way that is as accurate as possible so as to form the basis for sound interpretation.

Perseids helps Classicists to uphold these scholarly standards and to make them accessible to a broader population than ever before. Many of the tools offered on Perseids facilitate language acquisition, such as morpho-syntactic analysis through treebanking, which provides a visual and kinetic method to analyze language, as words and clauses are moved around the screen to show sentence structure. This is an effective method not only to gain understanding of language, but also, to display one's understanding of a sentence or group of sentences and justify interpretations. In this way, morpho-syntactic analysis offers learning tools that are also intrinsically scholarly.[33] Similarly, alignment tools developed by the Alpheios project offers readers who have no knowledge of the original language insight into the text itself, and also allow justifying translation choices.[34] As for textual criticism, the editing tools available in Perseids are designed to make the collation of textual data as transparent as possible. The Imgspect tool, the design of which was inspired by the Image Citation Tool of the Homer Multitext Project, allows us to link transcriptions directly to an image of the document (this is particularly helpful in the case of inscriptions and manuscripts) in order to justify readings and show the evidence directly to the audience.[35] Furthermore, transcriptions of inscriptions and manuscripts are encoded following the EpiDoc standards, which are ultimately based on the Leiden conventions, long accepted in the field as the scientific standard for presenting epigraphical and manuscript texts.[36] Finally, the built-in review process available in Perseids and the collaborative focus of the platform helps to uphold the standards of peer review, which are crucial in establishing credibility in any field.

The Canonical Text Services Unique Resource Name (CTS-URN) specification, developed by Chris Blackwell and Neel Smith, working with the Center for Hellenic Studies, is a core standard of the Perseids platform and enables us to connect the work we do today with the long standing tradition of scholarly citation in the classics.[37] The CTS-URN specification allows us to translate canonical citations such as Thuc 2.44 and Liv. 1.34 (which have long described chapter 44 of book 2 of Thucydides and chapter 34 of book one of Livy) into a technology independent and machine actionable form.[38]

These URNs, when combined with the http://data.perseus.org namespace, allow us to provide persistent, stable, resolvable identifiers for any canonical text, passage, or even word as the target for our annotations in a manner that adheres to best practices for linked data.[39] We make this data interoperable and sharable by other projects in the field by serializing all annotations. This includes the simple identification of named entities, to commentaries on texts, to the more complex morpho-syntactic analysis, according to the Open Annotation (OA) data model, including provenance information for the creators, contributors, and reviewers of these annotations.[40] The inclusion of provenance information allows consumers of the data to make their own quality assessments about the data. And in addition to the persistent URIs for the primary source texts which are the target of the annotation, we can reference and contribute to other established data sets in the domain, such as the Pleiades Gazetteer and the annotations on ancient places aggregated by the Pelagios Project.[41]

In addition to these methodological principles, the American Heritage Dictionary offers a second definition for scholarship, explaining it as the knowledge resulting from study and research in a particular field. Thus, according to this definition, Perseids users become scholars by the very fact that they engage in such activities. We note that the dictionary does not characterize scholarship or scholars as possessing definitive knowledge on a topic. Rather, both definitions imply a process that results from the practice of scholarly activities through which knowledge is produced, with new data and new interpretations constantly replacing old ones. Knowledge advances on a continuum, with contributions big and small paving the way to discovery. In Perseids, this aspect of scholarship is represented in the equal value given to all contributions, whether they are large editing tasks or the correction of typographical errors.[42] For this reason, all contributions will appear in a user's e-portfolio, showing all the aspects scholarship can take.

5 Conclusions

Perseids permits the practice of scholarship in the traditional sense of the word. Yet, Perseids also transforms scholarship by offering broad access to and engagement of individuals at all levels of expertise, not only to the practice of scholarship, but also to its valued outcome, publication. We encourage and enable users to take responsibility for the scholarly data they produce on the platform, offering the opportunity for it to be published, after review, by the Perseus Digital Library as part of a larger collective body of work while also leaving them free to take it with them and re-imagine its publication by itself or as part of other projects, such as that of the EAGLE network. As a result of this process, the undergraduate students who currently make up the large majority of our user base learn that they are part of a global community of interconnected scholars sharing the responsibility for making more ancient texts than ever before available for analysis and study by all, while still upholding the long-established standards of quality of the discipline. Some of these students begin to see themselves as research partners with their professors, rather than just as students completing an assignment, and discover that they are empowered to publish and disseminate their knowledge in a wide variety of forms and venues. As undergraduates in multidisciplinary courses of study, many of our users will go on to fields well outside of traditional academic structures and we hope that we have planted a seed they will carry with them, leading to their future engagement in opportunities for scholarship, whatever they may be.

Acknowledgements

This work was made possible by a grant from the Andrew W. Mellon Foundation, 'Developing Perseids: Enhancements to a Collaborative Editing Platform for Source Documents in Classics', 2013–2015. This work was supported by a Digital Humanities Start-Up Grant from the National Endowment for the Humanities [grant HD-51548-12]. Any views, findings, conclusions, or recommendations expressed in this article do not necessarily represent those of the National Endowment for the Humanities. This work was also supported by a

Tufts Innovates Grant from the Office of the Vice Provost at Tufts University. This project is made possible by a grant from the U.S. Institute of Museum and Library Services [grant LG0611032611].

Notes

1 Crowdsourcing has become so common within the digital humanities, a recently published anthology was dedicated to the topic with various chapters authored by significant projects; see Ridge 2014.

2 Indeed the growing importance of crowdsourcing to humanities research and cultural heritage infrastructure has been explored by both Dunn & Hedges 2013 and Owens 2013.

3 Both Oomen & Aroyo 2011 and Rockwell 2012 offer good overviews of both the potential and the challenges of humanities crowdsourcing.

4 For one recent project exploring crowdsourcing and digital humanities pedagogy, see Gilchrist et al. 2014.

5 Perseids: <http://sites.tufts.edu/perseids/>.

6 Perseus Digital Library: <http://www.perseus.tufts.edu/hopper/>.

7 E.g. Los Angeles Times, December 2, 1998: <http://articles.latimes.com/1998/dec/02/local/me-49820>; New York Times, October 6, 2008: <http://www.nytimes.com/2008/10/07/nyregion/07latin.html?pagewanted=all&_r=2&>. In 2013, 3,545 high school students took the Latin Advanced Placement exam, a dramatic increase from 1,927 in 2003. See: <http://apreport.collegeboard.org/>; Gephardt 2011.

8 Perseus, 'Research': <http://www.perseus.tufts.edu/hopper/research>.

9 For further discussion of the Perseids platform and its initial development, see Beaulieu & Almas 2012 and Almas & Beaulieu 2013.

10 This feature of supporting a range of user tasks in a collaborative annotation environment addresses recent criticisms of standard approaches to crowdsourcing in cultural heritage, see Walsh et al. 2014.

11 The Miscellany at Tisch Library: <http://www.library.tufts.edu/tisch/ematlocalstorage/miscellany_collection/home.html>.

12 Images of the manuscript and other holdings in the Tisch Library Special Collections available at: https://www.flickr.com/photos/tischlibraryspecialcollections/sets/72157627007916920/.

13 Alpheios: <http://alpheios.net/>; Pelagios: <http://pelagios-project.blogspot.com/p/about-pelagios.html>. For more on the recent work of the Pelagios project, see Isaksen et al. 2014.

14 Perseus, 'Announcing the Arethusa Annotation Framework': <http://sites.tufts.edu/perseusupdates/2014/09/19/announcing-the-arethusa-annotation-framework/>.

15 OpenID: <http://openid.net/>.

16 Shibboleth: <http://shibboleth.net/>; Oasis Security Services (SAML), available: <https://www.oasis-open.org/committees/security/>. The SAML/ Shibboleth protocols are also being supported by large research infrastructures such as DARIAH and CLARIN.

17 Creative Commons Attribution license: <http://creativecommons.org/licenses/by-sa/4.0/>.

18 Git: <http://git-scm.com/>.

19 EAGLE Portal: <http://www.eagle-network.eu/>. For more on the development of the EAGLE project and its future plans see Orlandi et al. 2014.

20 The pedagogical models illustrated in the use of Perseids in the classroom including meaningful research collaborations between student and professor, project-based student teamwork and student publication of their contributions at earlier stages have been highlighted elsewhere as key potential contributions of digital humanities pedagogy to broader humanities teaching, see Bonds 2014, and Hirsch 2012.

21 SoSOL in Github: <https://github.com/sosol/sosol>; for more on the development and current status of work on SoSOL see Baumann 2013; Papyri. info: <http://papyri.info/>; Papyrological Editor: <http://papyri.info/editor/>.

22 Git: <http://git-scm.com/>; for a good definition of URIs, see Wikipedia, 'Uniform resource identifier': <http://en.wikipedia.org/wiki/Uniform_resource_identifier>.

23 Nanopub Guidelines: <http://nanopub.org/guidelines/working_draft/>. For more on on the definition of micro or nano-publications, see Groth et al. 2010 and Clark et al. 2014. And for an initial consideration of some of their potential for publication within the humanities, see Drucker 2013, and Hall 2013.

24 RIDE Guidelines: <http://ride.i-d-e.de/reviewers/guidelines/>.

25 Student Commentaries Published in Perseus: <http://sites.tufts.edu/perseusupdates/2014/05/29/student-commentaries-published-in-perseus/>.

26 Announcing the Perseus Lexical Inventory – an Open Linked Data Set: <http://sites.tufts.edu/perseusupdates/2014/03/21/announcing-the-perseus-lexical-inventory-an-open-linked-data-set/>.

27 TimeMapper: <http://timemapper.okfnlabs.org/>.

28 Fragmentary Texts demo: <http://perseids.org/sites/berti_demo/>; for more on this work see Almas & Berti 2013. Bodin prototype: <http://perseids.org/sites/bodin/>.

29 PROV Ontology: <http://www.w3.org/TR/prov-overview/>.

30 Research Data Alliance: <https://rd-alliance.org/>; see Krohn 2014.

31 For a similar discussion of the importance of recognizing and publishing both student contributions and smaller forms of scholarly publication, see Blackwell & Martin 2009; Presner 2012.

[32] For a recent overview of e-portfolios and their use and importance in higher education see Jenson & Treuer 2014.

[33] For the uses of treebanks in teaching and scholarship see Bamman et al. 2009; Mambrini (Chap. V in this volume).

[34] Alpheios Installation: <http://alpheios.net/content/installation>. An example of an aligned translation of Od. 1. is available at <http://alpheios.net/alpheios-texts/Perseus.text.1999.01.0135/book1_card1.html>.

[35] Imgspect: <https://github.com/PerseusDL/imgspect>; Image Citation Tool: <http://kleos.chs.harvard.edu/?p=521>.

[36] EpiDoc Collaborative: <http://epidoc.sourceforge.net/>; for a discussion of the Epidoc standard and its basis on Leiden, see Cayless et al. 2009.

[37] CTS-URN: <http://www.homermultitext.org/hmt-docs/specifications/ctsurn/>; for more on the development and history of the CTS URN specification see Smith 2009 and for an example of it in use see Blackwell & Blackwell 2011.

[38] For further examples of how this works in practice see Almas et al. 2014, and Crane et al. 2014.

[39] Best Practices for Publishing Linked Data: <http://www.w3.org/TR/ld-bp/>.

[40] Open Annotation: <http://www.openannotation.org/>.

[41] Pleiades: <http://pleiades.stoa.org/>.

[42] The need to open up the task of editing and to redefine levels of contribution and publication has previously been articulated by Crane 2010.

References

Almas, B. & Beaulieu, M.-C. (2013). Developing a new integrated editing platform for source documents in classics. *Literary and Linguistic Computing* 28(4): 493–503.

Almas, B. & Berti, M. (2013). Perseids collaborative platform for annotating text re-uses of fragmentary authors. In *Proceedings of the 1st International Workshop on Collaborative Annotations in Shared Environment: Metadata, Vocabularies and Techniques in the Digital Humanities*, DH-CASE '13, New York, NY, USA. ACM.

Almas, B., Babeu, A. & Krohn, A. (2014). Linked data in the Perseus Digital Library. In *ISAW Papers 7: Current Practice in Linked Open Data for the Ancient World*, New York University : Institute for the Study of the Ancient World. Retrieved from http://dlib.nyu.edu/awdl/isaw/isaw-papers/7/almas-babeu-krohn/

Bamman, D., F. Mambrini & G. Crane. (2009). An ownership model of annotation: The ancient greek dependency treebank. *TLT 2009-Eighth International Workshop on Treebanks and Linguistic Theories*. Retrieved from http://hdl.handle.net/10427/70399

Baumann, R. (2013). The Son of Suda On-Line. In S. E.S Dunn & S. Mahony (Eds.), *The Digital Classicist 2013*. University of London., Institute of Classical Studies. Retrieved from http://hdl.handle.net/10161/8414

Beaulieu, M.-C. & Almas, B. (2012). Digital Humanities in the classroom: Introducing a new editing platform for source documents in classics. In *Digital Humanities 2012*. Retrieved from http://www.dh2012.uni-hamburg.de/conference/programme/abstracts/digital-humanities-in-the-classroom-introducing-a-new-editing-platform-for-source-documents-in-classics/

Blackwell, C. & Martin, T. R. (2009). Technology, collaboration, and undergraduate research. *Digital Humanities Quarterly*, 3(1). Retrieved from http://www.digitalhumanities.org/dhq/vol/3/1/000024/000024.html

Blackwell, C. & Blackwell, A. H. (2011). Image 'quotation' using the C.I.T.E. architecture. *Ariadne* (67). Retrieved from http://www.ariadne.ac.uk/issue67/blackwell-hackneyBlackwell/

Bonds, E. L. (2014). Listening in on the conversations: An overview of digital humanities pedagogy. *CEA Critic* 76(2): 147–157.

Cayless, H., Roueché, C., Elliott, T. & Bodard, G. (2009). Epigraphy in 2017. *Digital Humanities Quarterly* 3(1). Retrieved from http://www.digitalhumanities.org/dhq/vol/3/1/000030/000030.html

Clark, T., Ciccarese, P. & Goble, C.A. (2014). Micropublications: a semantic model for claims, evidence, arguments and annotations in biomedical communications. *J. Biomedical Semantics* 5: 28. Retrieved from http://arxiv.org/abs/1305.3506

Crane, G. (2010). Give us editors! Re-inventing the edition and re-thinking the humanities. In *Online Humanities Scholarship: The Shape of Things to Come*, University of Virginia: Mellon Foundation, 2010–03. Retrieved from http://cnx.org/content/m34316/latest/

Crane, G., Almas, B., Babeu, A., Cerrato, L., Krohn, A., Baumgart, F., Berti, M., Franzini, G. & Stoyanova, S. (2014). Cataloging for a billion word library of Greek and Latin. In *Proceedings of the First International Conference on Digital Access to Textual Cultural Heritage*, DATeCH '14, New York, NY, USA. ACM: 83–88. Retrieved from http://dx.doi.org/10.1145/2595188.2595190

Dunn, S. & Hedges, M. (2013). Crowd-sourcing as a component of humanities research infrastructures. *International Journal of Humanities and Arts Computing* 7(1–2): 147–169.

Drucker, J. (2013). Scholarly publishing: Micro units and the macro scale. *Amodern 1*. Retrieved from http://amodern.net/article/scholarly-publishing-micro-units-and-the-macro-scale/

Gephardt, L. (2011). Classics in American schools. *Expositions* 5(2): 9–13.

Gilchrist, M., Wolfe, J., McElroy, K. & Keegan, T. (2014). Crowdsourcing in the curriculum: Engaging undergraduates through collaborative manuscript transcription. In *Digital Humanities 2014*. Retrieved from http://dharchive.org/paper/DH2014/Poster-763.xml

Groth, P., Gibson, A. & Velterop, J. (2010). The anatomy of a nanopublication. *Information Services and Use* 30(1): 50–56.

Hall, G. (2013). The unbound book: Academic publishing in the age of the infinite archive. *Journal of Visual Culture* 12(3): 490–507.

Hirsch, B. D. (2012). </Parentheses>: Digital humanities and the place of pedagogy. In *Digital Humanities Pedagogy: Practices, Principles and Politics.* Open Book Publishers: Cambridge, pp. 1–30.

Isaksen, L., Simon, R., Barker, E. T. E. & de Soto Canamares, P. (2014). Pelagios and the emerging graph of ancient world data. In *Proceedings of the 2014 ACM Conference on Web Science* (WebSci '14), pp. 197–201.

Jenson, J. D. & Treuer, P. (2014). Defining the E-Portfolio: What it is and why it matters. *Change: The Magazine of Higher Learning* 46(2): 50–5.

Krohn, Anna (2014). So You Want to Track Provenance: Concepts and Considerations. RDA/US Scholars Program Internship Abstract and Poster. Retrieved from https://rd-alliance.org/group/research-data-provenance/wiki/rdaus-scholars-program-internship-abstract-and-poster.html

Oomen, J. & Aroyo, L. (2011). Crowdsourcing in the cultural heritage domain: opportunities and challenges. In *Proceedings of the 5th International Conference on Communities and Technologies.* New York, NY, USA: AC, pp. 138–149.

Orlandi, S., Giberti, L. M. & Santucci, R. (2014). EAGLE: Europeana network of ancient greek and latin epigraphy. making the ancient inscriptions accessible. *Lexicon Philosophicum: International Journal for the History of Texts and Ideas* 2. Retrieved from http://lexicon.cnr.it/index.php/LP/article/view/408

Owens, T. (2013). "Digital cultural heritage and the crowd." *Curator* 56 (January 2013): 121–130.

Presner, T. (2012). How to Evaluate Digital Scholarship. *Journal of Digital Humanities* 1(4).

Ridge, M. (2014) (Ed.), *Crowdsourcing our cultural heritage.* Farnham: Ashgate.

Rockwell, G. (2012). Crowdsourcing the humanities: social research and collaboration. In *Collaborative Research in the Digital Humanities*, Farnham: Ashgate, pp. 135–154.

Smith, D. N. (2009). Citation in classical studies. *Digital Humanities Quarterly*, 3(1). Retrieved from http://www.digitalhumanities.org/dhq/vol/003/1/000028.html

Walsh, B., Maiers, C., Nally, G., Boggs, J. & Team, P. P. (2014). Crowdsourcing individual interpretations: Between microtasking and macrotasking. *Literary and Linguistic Computing* 29(3): 379–386.

CHAPTER 10

Engaging Greek: Ancient Lives

James Brusuelas
University of Oxford

Abstract

Since July 2011, Ancient Lives has recorded well over 1.5 million transcriptions of ancient Greek papyri (over 9 million characters), the work of over 105,000 unique online collaborators. The result was not simply the creation of big data, but the inception of an entirely different way of conceiving and interfacing ancient digital texts. Put simply, Ancient Lives has created something that has never existed before: a database of unedited Greek. We have strings of Greek characters without word division or any modern editorial convention. The purpose of this chapter is to discuss, first, the Ancient Lives' methodology of public engagement, the inclusive process by which the public participates in the fundamental tasks of papyrology (this includes both untrained and the unique users targeted by Almas and Beaulieu). Next, the success of any crowdsourcing project depends not only on data input but also how that data is subsequently processed and utilized. An overview of current development then follows, which particularly addresses Ancient Lives' interest and continual use of machine intelligence and genetic sequence alignment algorithms (examples of successfully repurposed field-specific algorithms, an often challenging process as discussed by Tarte), to process multiple transcriptions of a single fragment (version control), query, data mine, and edit these crowdsourced transcriptions within an innovative digital environment. More importantly, in providing public access to data that was for a century viewed only by a handful of scholars, Ancient Lives continues to engage in changing models of traditional scholarship.

How to cite this book chapter:
Brusuelas, J. 2016. Engaging Greek: Ancient Lives. In: Bodard, G & Romanello, M (eds.) *Digital Classics Outside the Echo-Chamber: Teaching, Knowledge Exchange & Public Engagement*, Pp. 187–204. London: Ubiquity Press. DOI: http://dx.doi. org/10.5334/bat.k. License: CC-BY 4.0.

1 Introduction

It's madness. Within the field of Classics and its subset Papyrology, that phrase, in one form or another, was often the response to even the slightest mention of Ancient Lives (hereafter AL) in 2010, when I arrived at Oxford to begin work on the project.[1] A collaboration between Oxford Classics and Astrophysics,[2] AL was to join the many other crowdsourcing projects hosted by the Zooniverse.[3] As one might guess, upon hearing the word crowdsourcing, such a reaction usually came from senior academics. But perhaps the most colorful comment I can recall was the description of AL as the 'bastardization of the papyri,' uttered by a young postgraduate student at an academic gathering in Leiden in 2012, months after the project had launched—I happened to be sitting on the other side of the table and, with arguably too much delight, responded, 'Oh yes, my project.' What a thought, an experiment indeed. Let anyone, trained or untrained, transcribe a papyrus fragment of ancient Greek online. Let the world assist in transcribing the seemingly countless papyrus fragments from the ancient city of Oxyrhynchus, housed in the Sackler Library of the Ashmolean Museum.

Since their discovery this body of well-known fragments has reintroduced to the world texts that have not been seen since antiquity, such as the Gospel of Thomas and the poetry of Sappho,[4] and although Oxford has held them for over a century, the opportunity for discovery still lingers seductively; due to the sheer volume of fragments, more texts and authors are still waiting to be found. From its very inception, then, AL touched a distinct nerve: access. Looking back, it was not so much about crowdsourcing but access to viewing unpublished material. What happens if someone with no formal training accurately transcribes a fragment? Worse still, what happens when a self-taught individual, using the same tools available to scholars, contextualizes or even identifies a fragment? The cardinal rule, after all, of working with ancient manuscripts is that their text looks nothing like the modern printed editions through which students and the vast majority of scholars engage their content. A Greek papyrus fragment is a perfect example. It is just a string of characters without word division and little to no punctuation, not to mention issues such as scribal errors, variant readings, new words, and cursive handwriting reminiscent of a doctor's prescription. It is not a simple reading experience. Accordingly, a distinct scholarly identity has been constructed around them; one that, as noted above, cuts across generations. For the laymen to walk in off the street and successfully perform certain academic and papyrological tasks, even if only at a rudimentary level… That idea was not just brushed off, but seemed threatening to some. It seemed that any success achieved by AL would be at the expense of Papyrology and even Classics, or at least demystification of the academic process to a certain degree.

Be that as it may, I found myself in a peculiar position. I was tasked with creating a dialogue between academics, our beloved primary source material, and ... everyone else. Better (or worse) still, I had to create this dialogue even if certain segments of my field simply were not interested. Now, it is not that AL was devoid of supporters in the beginning. There were, and still are, many colleagues interested in engaging the general public about Classics, classicists, and the Greek and Latin languages in a living dialogue rather than from any position or notion of 'gatekeeper;' these languages are not oracles nor are we the Delphic priestesses and priests uniquely capable of interpreting them. And so many colleagues and friends have long suggested I write something about my involvement with AL and my ongoing role as its leading voice. For the invitation to contribute to this book, I am thus very grateful for the opportunity (or, better put, the motivation of a deadline) to write a simple essay about my involvement in the development of Ancient Lives and what the project has thus far achieved.

As I write, AL is in the process of being rebuilt for re-launch. This is both to improve its functionality, its overall frontend and backend design (a Rails app about to become a Backbone.js app), and to upgrade the application to conform with current Zooniverse standards. AL is changing, morphing into something else.[5] What follows now is nothing more than a simple reflection on how AL initially produced millions of transcriptions of useable data, engaged in machine learning for processing this data, and dabbled in Bioinformatics for the purposes of automated text identification.

2 Patterns and Users

With the lure of discovering new texts of Greek literature or even a new gospel, we always expected classicists of all skill levels to play with the interface. And they did. Nevertheless, although AL embraces the volunteer community as a whole, including trained classicists, development of the interface was always focused on the individual with no knowledge of ancient Greek. So, how does one produce an environment that facilitates participation and contribution from those outside of academia? Pattern recognition.

The fundamental premise upon which AL operates is pattern recognition. It is a task at which the human brain excels. And so one does not need to know the dynamics of ancient Greek grammar and syntax to recognize the triangular shape of alpha and delta (A, Δ) or especially a familiar shape like nu (N). A simple image and a keyboard of Greek characters are all one needs (Figure 1).

Be that as it may, like any evidence of human generated script, character shape is not consistent and the degree of cursive can be slight to severe. Moreover, the alphabet present in the papyri is devoid of any cognitive notion of modern upper or lower case; there really is only an 'upper' case, even though it appears to mimic those distinctions, such as the case of alpha being triangular (A) or round (α). From a development standpoint, that caused a bit of a

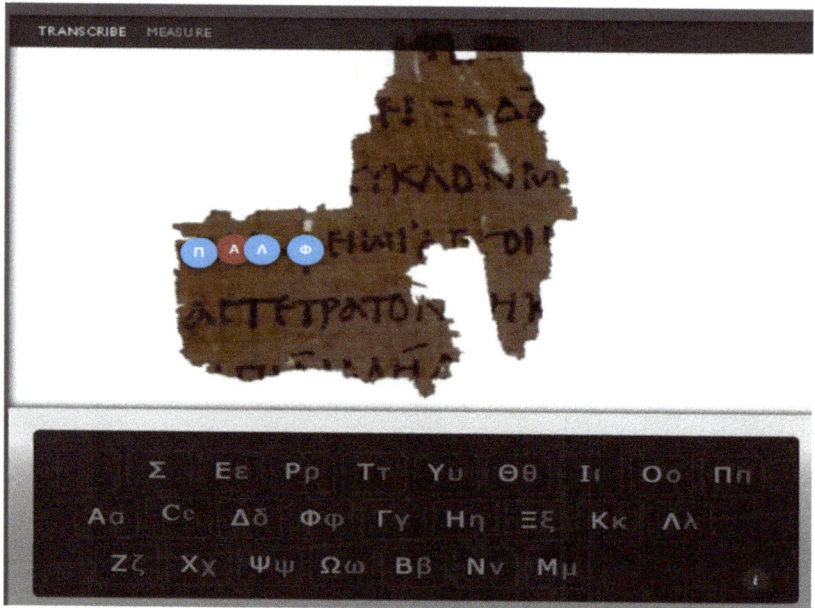

Figure 1: Current AL keyboard.

dilemma. There is no 'paleographical' keyboard devoted to the character shapes found in ancient papyri. For a virtual keyboard we only have Unicode character shapes, of which many directly correlate to the later Byzantine Greek minuscule preserved in parchment codices. Moreover, to produce useful data, it is indeed those Unicode characters that are the required input. In a papyrological context, while a trained user could immediately recognize that they are looking for lunate sigma (c) and not medial and final sigma (σ, ς), or that delta (Δ) does not look like the minuscule form (δ) in papyri, the question over what visual data to provide the crowd lingered. Furthermore, from the crowdsourcing standpoint, users not only needed to focus on finding patterns and matching character shapes, but also the intuitive freedom to provide data without being bogged down in a host of variables that would cause hesitation. In other words, that first moment of interface is not a moment for actual training or official indoctrination in Greek manuscripts. Motivation to engage in the task of classification must arise from the simple notion of pattern matching, not necessarily knowledge of ancient Greek or Greek paleography. The user must recognize that the digital tools before them facilitate their contribution. If there were even the slightest hint that formal training was needed, participation by the general public would have most likely been stifled to a large degree. Accordingly, the solution at the time was to provide users with a standard Greek Unicode keyboard, including both shapes that appear in papyri and even those that do not. In addition, to assist with the difficulty that arises as letter shapes become cursive, images of cursive forms were made available by hovering over a given character.

In psychological parlance, AL would most likely straddle both the 'template matching' and 'feature analysis' theories of human pattern recognition. Some literary hands are nearly font-like, and users are explicitly pairing character shapes in an image with a character 'template' in the keyboard. But as documentary hands become more and more cursive, the general feature of epsilon (Figure 2), for example, must be recalled when classifying cursive character shapes.

In late July of 2011, when AL went live, the Zooniverse had a community of roughly 400,000 users – it is now over 1 million. To a large extent, and considering the positive reception during beta testing, we knew the Zooniverse community would provide data, at least enough data to evaluate the experiment. But would the general public engage in transcribing ancient Greek papyrus fragments? The question still remained. Fortunately, the answer was not only a resounding 'yes,' but AL, due to the media attention we received, even brought in new users into the Zooniverse. The general public was and is indeed interested in what papyrologists do. Moreover, the characters shapes themselves, both clear and cursive, and the random bits of ancient art visible on some papyrus fragments inspired the imagination of the volunteer community.[6] And as the world outside academia became more informed about this vast number of papyrus fragments from Oxyrhynchus, the idea of contributing to the discovery of a lost work was a profound source of motivation. By the end of the first year of the project, AL recorded 1.5 million transcriptions, roughly 7 million Greek character classifications – currently over 9 million have been recorded. What became immediately apparent, and not unexpected in the Zooniverse, was the appearance of so-called 'power' or 'super' users, individuals who contribute hundreds of transcriptions as opposed to the majority of users that were only producing a few.[7] And so there was this segment of the crowd that wanted to talk with papyrologists and classicists about what they love, discuss ancient literature and history, and simply help. This nodal point of interaction and outreach is unique. This is Classics in culture, happening in real time and not defined by the parameters of a classroom or even a university campus.

Despite such interesting variables, however, no in-depth study of AL users, both in the context of the Zooniverse community as a whole and in relation to other crowdsourcing projects, has been conducted. To get a feel for the AL community one must visit Talk. Every Zooniverse project is equipped with a Talk section, a place where the members of a specific community of a given project talk to one another, as well as project members. This is a place to isolate interesting images, flag them, ask questions, and essentially acquire further knowledge about a project's data. For the AL community we should note their engagement in self-learning. As an expert, one of the unique aspects of working with users in Talk is not being the never-ending voice of 'no' or 'wrong.' They may be there to help you, but they did not sign up for your class. This is an

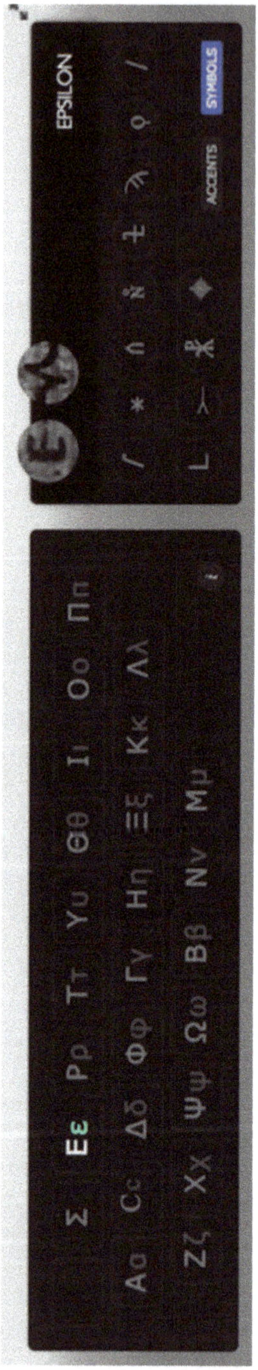

Figure 2: Cursive shapes.

exploration in real time, in their private time. The biggest mistake would be to drive volunteers away by constantly hammering home what they do not know. The user who actively engages in Talk is someone that wants more information, wants to improve the accuracy of their classifications. As an expert, your voice is simply one of information, not evaluation. After providing basic guidance it is often better to step back and let the users help each other. After AL launched and users began to get acquainted with the various kinds of handwriting present, it was not long before individuals began posting online links for Greek paleography, especially those showing examples of the more difficult cursive forms of certain Greek characters. Soon users were helping each other classify the more difficult forms of cursive epsilon, for example. And discussion pertaining to the AL keyboard and characters shapes not present in the papyri become commonplace, especially the topic of lunate sigma vs. the medial and final sigma forms of the later Greek minuscule.

How did AL generate so many crowdsourced transcriptions? We simply gave the crowd images, a virtual Greek keyboard, and an intuitive task.[8] With so many users in the Zooniverse, AL then generated what can be described as Big Data, a term not necessarily devoid of ambiguity. But in our case, since AL creates multiple transcriptions of a given fragment, processing the data posed a great challenge.

3 Enter the Machine: Consensus, Line Sequencing, and Greek BLAST

Having over a million transcriptions tucked away in a MySQL database allowed for easy interaction with AL data, if one knew how to write a MySQL query. The number of papyrologists and classicists that can, however, never seems to be very large. Consequently it became rapidly clear that AL required serious computational support if its data was going to be made useful to those without any knowledge of coding.[9]

One of the principal tenets of papyrology is that more than one pair of eyes is always better. Whether a student or an experienced scholar, establishing a transcription and eventually a final edition is not produced in isolation. We often see different shapes, and in reconstructing a fragmented ancient text the most accurate product is never the result of just one pair of eyes. The size of ALs papyrological database may have been unprecedented, but the required methodology for processing was no different. For each fragment we needed a consensus transcription. How to extract a consensus from the database then emerged as a machine learning challenge. We needed an algorithm that could be trained to batch process millions of transcriptions. Accordingly, it also offered the opportunity to bring the transcription data face to face with the experts.

To tackle this problem AL collaborated with the Minnesota Supercomputing Institute (MSI) and the departments of Classics and Near Eastern Studies and Physics and Astronomy at the University of Minnesota. Dr. Haoyu Yu from MSI was tasked with writing a consensus algorithm. In doing so, one must remember that AL is very different from a transcription project like Transcribe Bentham, whose input is plain text and supplemental XML tags.[10] Again, if you want the world to help transcribe ancient Greek, one cannot assume their varied devices are equipped with the necessary Greek keyboard. Instead of recording plain text, a virtual mapping is employed. For each click on a papyrus image, the database not only stores the Unicode character selected, but also the relative click location as x,y coordinates. For the aggregation of user clicks, the initial approach was written in Matlab, employing kernel density estimation—that is, mathematically inferring the likelihood that a variable will take on a given value—to isolate consensus clicks and letters. Besides giving different transcriptions, users will also not click the same exact location on an image, resulting in both multiple characters and multiple sets of x,y coordinates for one character position. Looking at the multiple transcription data of one fragment, the algorithm essentially takes the x,y coordinates for each click position and distributes them into a number of bins according to the search radius, a number determined by multiplying a user-specified kernel width by 2 (the default value is 8 if no kernel width is specified). Within each bin the algorithm finds a consensus letter by identifying the highest kernel density peaks. The x,y coordinates of those peaks are then clustered to create consensus characters and their locations (pixel locations), whereby a virtual image of the fragment can be visualized (Figure 3).

Training the algorithm to successfully render consensus also meant evaluating the resulting user consensus. This was accomplished by performing kernel density estimation against a select group of fragments transcribed by volunteers and then compared with the transcription of expert papyrologists. On this select group of fragments, which included examples of clear literary hands, semi-cursive, and cursive documents (marriage certificates, land leases, personal accounts, private letters, etc), we created a correspondence between the expert's characters and locations and that of the consensus. For clear literary book hands, as seen in Table 1, comparison yielded the following.

Number of expert locations	Number of consensus locations	Number of overlapping locations	Percent coverage of expert locations by consensus locations	Number of matches in the overlapping locations	Percent match in the overlapping locations
100	150	95	95.00	85	89.47

Table 1: Consensus evaluation.

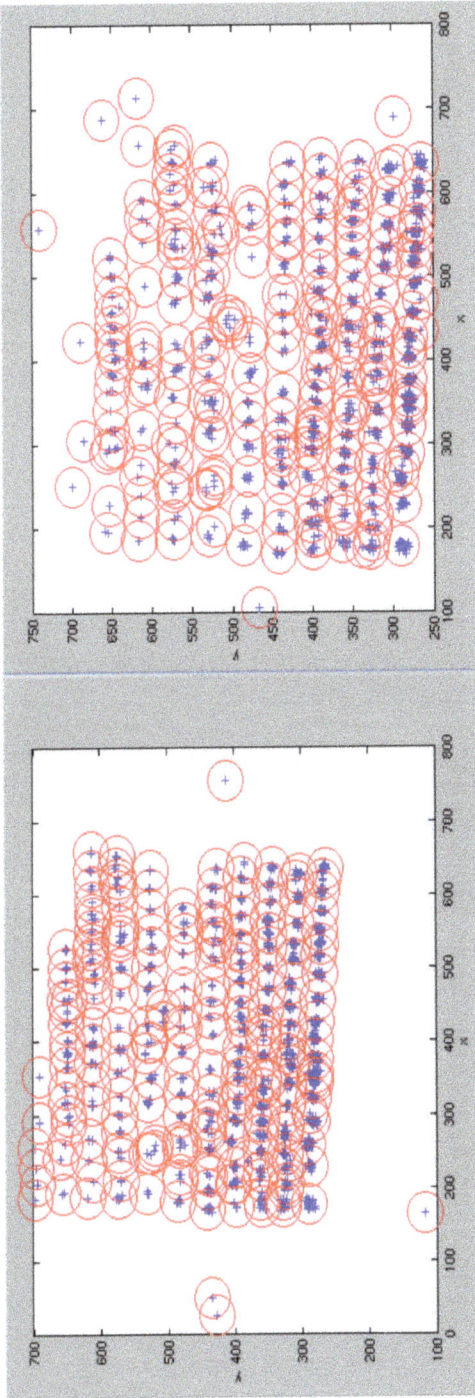

Figure 3: Kernel Density Clustering. This image shows how clustering the highest kernel density peaks (user clicks storing character and x,y coordinate data) in Matlab also reveals an abstract image of the papyrus itself.

AL volunteers, as a community, could thus provide excellent data. Users were capable of providing transcriptions that were nearly identical to those given by experts. That said, gathering good data from a clear literary hand was never really in question. It was the idiosyncratic hand styles and cursive writing that posed the largest potential problem. Conducting further isolated investigations we began to see what was expected. Looking at 31 examples of semi-cursive scripts, the percentage of agreement dropped to 65%, while 14 examples of very difficult cursive hands yielded a percentage agreement of only 51%.

Although consensus characters could be successfully gathered, kernel density estimation in Matlab proved to be a computationally cumbersome task. It took multiple days, hundreds of hours, to process the data. More recently we addressed this issue at Oxford. Alex Williams, research programmer on the Proteus project,and Dr. John Wallin of Middle Tennessee State University developed the stepwise approach using the high level programming language Python.[11] This new method utilizes the recently established concept that members of the Zooniverse community who complete more classifications, the so-called 'super' user, demonstrate a higher ability to correctly classify data than those who complete fewer classifications. This new algorithm thus identifies the user that has made the most number of clicks first and isolates their character positions as potential nodes of consensus. The remaining clicks are then either merged according to pre-existing locations or, depending on their frequency, established as another possible node of consensus. Once finished, a centroid of each agglomeration of clicks is isolated, yielding a consensus letter. Unlike Matlab, the Python script processes the data in minutes. In a Big Data context, this was quite an achievement. However, we did not intend stepwise to supersede kernel density estimation entirely, as both have their merits. Speed is obviously the benefit that comes with stepwise. But the Matlab approach, though slow in processing time, records and allows visualization of all the user data for a given fragment. In comparing user transcriptions of cursive documents with expert transcriptions, we noticed instances where the correct character was essentially hidden under the incorrect consensus character. More evaluation needs to be conducted in order to fully grasp how the AL pipeline might processes the more difficult cursive manuscripts.

The purpose of AL was to explore new methods that could potentially increase the pace at which scholars study and organize this massive body of fragmentary ancient texts, and the fundamental way to do that is through transcriptions, which are important for identifying and contextualizing fragments. This is how we determine what is Homer, Demonsthenes, Simonides, Pindar, etc. Although both the stepwise and kernel density methods could extract a consensus transcription, the output consisted only of characters and x,y coordinates, not an actual text file of Unicode characters in lines corresponding to the papyrus image. To create lines, Dr. Wallin created another Python script to identify the presence of lines based on gaps of vertical space between neighboring y-coordinates. As shown below in Figure 4, the code smartly deduces lines.

The creation of usable strings of Greek Unicode was perhaps the most important achievement for AL; it also completed the initial AL pipeline (Figure 5). From the moment of launch, we proved that the crowd was interested in transcribing, but the onus was always on us to turn their volunteer efforts into useful data. And with these strings there was always one target in the distance: algorithmic identification of fragments.

When I first arrived at Oxford, I was given a few boxes of black and white images and asked to identify whatever fragments I could. After a few weeks of compiling a long list of identifications, it became clear not only how time consuming the process was – and this was just a tiny fraction of the total number of fragments – but authors we expect to find due to the canon in ancient education, like Homer and Plato, were indeed in great abundance. There was so much Homer! For every high priority discovery, such as a new text or the first papyrus evidence for a known author, one had to slowly make their way through multiple copies of works like the *Iliad*. But with the creation of Unicode transcriptions, AL had the opportunity to leverage them against a database of known Greek texts for rapid algorithmic matching. This would not only result in discovering important texts, specifically works only known through select quotation by other ancient sources, but also allow us to quickly isolate and batch known material, and thus turn our attention to the literary texts that could not be matched.

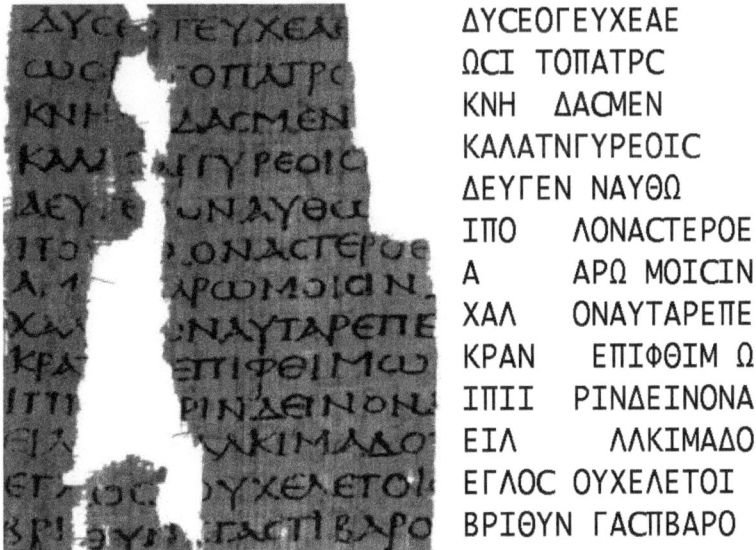

```
ΔΥСΕΟΓΕΥΧΕΑΕ
ΩϹΙ ΤΟΠΑΤΡϹ
ΚΝΗ  ΔΑϹΜΕΝ
ΚΑΛΑΤΝΓΥΡΕΟΙϹ
ΔΕΥΓΕΝ ΝΑΥΘΩ
ΙΠΟ    ΛΟΝΑϹΤΕΡΟΕ
Α      ΑΡΩ ΜΟΙϹΙΝ
ΧΑΛ    ΟΝΑΥΤΑΡΕΠΕ
ΚΡΑΝ   ΕΠΙΦΘΙΜ Ω
ΙΠΙΙ   ΡΙΝΔΕΙΝΟΝΑ
ΕΙΛ    ΛΛΚΙΜΑΔΟ
ΕΓΛΟϹ ΟΥΧΕΛΕΤΟΙ
ΒΡΙΘΥΝ ΓΑϹΠΒΑΡΟ
```

Figure 4: Line sequencing.

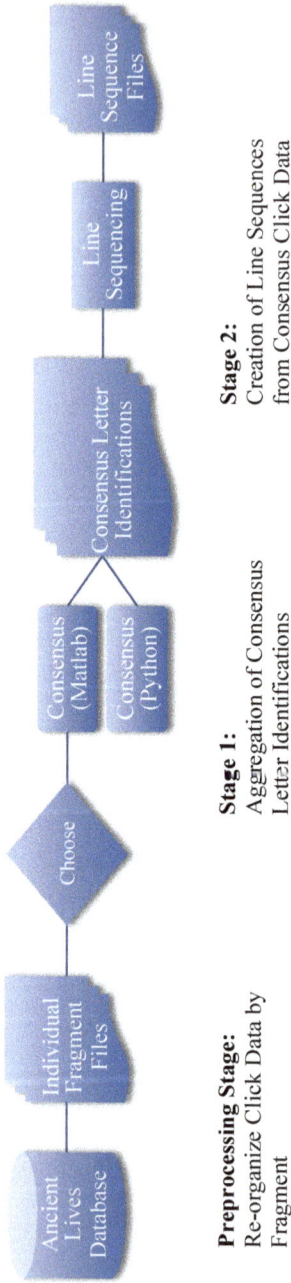

Preprocessing Stage:
Re-organize Click Data by
Fragment

Stage 1:
Aggregation of Consensus
Letter Identifications

Stage 2:
Creation of Line Sequences
from Consensus Click Data

Figure 5: AL pipeline.

Instead of creating another algorithm for this task, we instead decided to repurpose one from Bioinformatics. The Basic Local Alignment Search Tool (BLAST) is the standard tool for matching amino acid sequences in proteins or nucleotide sequences in DNA.[12] Genes are digitally represented by a sequence of continuous letters, in which each letter represents a specific nucleotide or amino acid. Figure 6 below shows the typical BLAST output.

The serendipitous realization that occurred was that BLAST was essentially thinking in terms of an alphabet, especially in the case of proteins in which twenty amino acids are found. Better still, when comparing genetic sequences an exact match is not necessarily the goal. Thus BLAST was already equipped to account for gaps between aligned sequences. The Greek alphabet not only consisted of 25 characters, but a papyrus text is nothing but a string of Greek characters often separated by gaps, the literal holes in a papyrus, let alone the appearance of variant material such as changes in spelling and scribal errors. All we had to do was simply substitute the characters of the Greek alphabet for those representing amino acids, supply a database of known strings for comparison, and alter how the algorithm scores the identified relationships. In a short period of time BLAST was beginning to think in Greek, as shown in Figure 7.

And so we have Greek-BLAST, which, instead of using the BLOSUM (BLOcks Substitution Matrix)[13] substitution matrix for scoring alignments between protein sequences, now has the Greek Letter Oriented Substitution Matrix (GLOSUM). Put simply, scoring is critical for evaluating instances of match and mismatch resulting from alignment. Greek-BLAST, in particular,

Score = 98.6 bits [244],   Expect = 1e-23, Method: Compositional matrix adjust.
Identities = 42/66 (64%), Positives = 57/66 (86%), Gaps = 0/66 (0%)
Frame = -2

```
Query 199 VAPSITNTPLAQRLLSSSDKEEASAKRHPLHRVGKAKDIGSMAAFLLSDQSGWMTGAILG   20
          +APS+TNTPLA++LLS+ +K++     +RHPL RVG+AKDI +M   FLLS++S WMTGQ+LG
Sbjct 162 IAPSLTNTPLAEKLLSNDEKKKKMDERHPLKRVGEAKDIANMVVFLLSEKSSWMTGQVLG 221

Query 19  VDGGLS   2
          +DGGLS
Sbjct 222 MDGGLS   227
```

Figure 6: BLAST.

Score = 68.4 bits (154), Expect = 8e- 13

Ancient Lives fragment: 131383

```
FRAGMENT ΠΑ?ΑΔΟ?Ι?ΑΓΑΘΗΚΑΙΠΑΝΔΩΡΗΜΑΤΕΛΕΙΟΝΑΝΩΘΕΝΕ?ΤΙΝΚΑΤΑΒΑ
TEXT     ΠΑΣΑΔΟΣΙΣΑΓΑΘΗΚΑΙΠΑΝΔΩΡΗΜΑΤΕΛΕΙΟΝΑΝΩΘΕΝΕΣΤΙ-ΚΑΤΑΒΑ
SIMILAR  ΠΑ ΑΔΟ Ι  ΑΓΑΘΗΚΑΙΠΑΝΔΩΡΗΜΑΤΕΛΕΙΟΝΑΝΩΘΕΝΕ ΤΙ ΚΑΤΑΒΑ

FRAGMENT ΙΝΟΝΑΠΟΤΟΥΠΑΤΡΟ?ΤΩΝΦΩΤΩΝ
TEXT     ΙΝΟΝΑΠΟΤΟΥΠΑΤΡΟΣΤΩΝΦΩΤΩΝ
SIMILAR  ΙΝΟΝΑΠΟΤΟΥΠΑΤΡΟ ΤΩΝΦΩΤΩΝ
```

Figure 7: Greek-BLAST.

evaluates letter-pair matches uniquely, taking into account the frequency of the letter in the known database and confusion likelihood from AL volunteers. Recalling again the reality that literary papyrus fragments are not always a verbatim match with the tradition of medieval manuscripts, which was the principal source of transmission from antiquity, a positive match will not always be an exact one. Consequently, Greek-BLAST needs to bring to our attention output that shows both exact matches and those of potentially interesting similarity. In early 2016 Greek-BLAST will begin interrogating the AL database of papyri from Oxyrhynchus.

4 The Papyrologist in the Shell

As I said in the beginning, Ancient Lives is transforming, becoming something else. In its next iteration new projects based on other collections and even new languages will be incorporated. So this essay is somewhat timely. In the end, what have I learned from AL and crowdsourcing? More importantly, what has AL done? How does AL fit within the community of Digital Classics? What is its significance?

Crowdsourcing, in the context of moving beyond one's niche academic community, works. But this should not come as a surprise. The Zooniverse model has been in operation since 2007. Using that model, AL was also launched successfully without even conducting prior workshops, case studies, or surveys. That may sound cavalier. But AL was and still is more about directly engaging the world outside academia; not employing academic methods was crucial in this respect. Moreover, if untrained users can, as they have shown, produce good transcriptions, that certainly does not come at the expense of Papyrology. AL simply gathers transcriptions in order to re-think how the vast collection of papyrus fragments from Oxyrhynchus might be studied. It is certainly not about the mass publishing of papyri; oversight of the study and publication of these fragments is maintained by the Egypt Exploration Society and the Oxyrhynchus Papyri Project. In aggregating these transcriptions AL has produced something that has never existed before: a database of largely unedited and unpublished ancient texts. Looking at the raw data, there are just strings of information, including that data ultimately removed in the editing process. It is also devoid of XML or any markup convention or standard. Regardless of the kind of manuscript processed through AL in the future, this is what it does. Consequently, this is predominately why AL has been slow to collaborate with other Digital Humanities or Digital Classics projects. Its data is something else. The methods needed for data analysis thus did not exist and required new thinking. We had to invent as we went along, designing the consensus, line sequencing, and Greek-Blast methods.

With this unique database our initial focus has been on fragments of Greek literature. This is primarily due to the research interests of project staff and the quality of data generated from literary fragments. Although Greek-BLAST has yet to be fully deployed, its ability to advance and expedite the identification process has great promise. Bringing to light new texts, whether that means more Sophocles, Aristotle, or even unknown uncanonical gospels, is one way AL can impact the production of new knowledge. But users have also engaged the more cursive documents, the texts of everyday life. How ALs database can impact the study of ancient documentary evidence is very much a topic of future research. And as more data is gathered over time, there are possibly more ways to analyze and visualize this vast dataset that spans roughly from the first century BCE/CE to the Muslim conquest of Egypt in the 8th-century, such as studying and modeling scribal errors and habits, the development and spread of Koine, and the rate and characteristics of bilingualism. I did not even mention the fact that we take measurements of margins, and that AL is potentially housing data that can statistically either prove or modify the way we think about the aesthetics of ancient bookrolls.[14] Machine learning and automated algorithmic mining is the way forward. And it is perhaps time to start thinking not so much about so-called Omega, in the textual criticism sense of trying to reconstruct what an ancient author actually wrote, but the reality of ancient reading and cognition. In the end, one can continue to invent methods for exploiting AL data.

In creating this database I have also been asked numerous questions about digital editing and digital editions – rightfully so if so many transcriptions have been generated. Naturally, this was the next step Dirk Obbink and I took. The year 2016 will not only see the re-launch of AL but also the launch of Proteus, a new ecosystem for digital philology and the creation of born digital critical editions and the textual criticism that underwrites them. Our initial focus is on Greek literary (primarily those constituting direct evidence for an author and/or text) and subliterary papyri (i.e. commentaries, lexica, glossaries, anthologies, etc.). Proteus is a virtual space for parallel critical editing, a process whereby multiple scholars and students can produce digital editions, suggest conjectures, and submit critical notes and translations. As the data from these fragments evolves over time through the re-editing process, Proteus provides a way to interface and examine this change through its search platform; it is designed to not just house multiple editions of a given text, but to spawn multiple editions while simultaneously applying version control. The architecture consists of two components: the Proteus Search Interface and the Digital Editor for Classical Philology (DELPHI). The project is implemented using Python, HTML5, CSS, JavaScript, PostgreSQL database management system, and Apache Solr for search. Its new Digital Editor for Classical Philology (DELPHI) allows for the creation of all the attributes that make an edition critical and citable: critical apparatus, testimonia, paleographical apparatus, diplomatic transcriptions, even the ability to edit marginalia. Along with updating the TEI/EpiDoc/XML standards for Greek literary and subliterary fragments by creating the necessary tags required for creating digital critical editions, DELPHI also employs a markdown concept similar to the Leiden+ system in the SoSOL editor used by Papyri.info and the Perseids project. DELPHI, however, provides automated translation of markdown into full XML and HTML5 in live time; XSLT stylesheets are not used. Moreover, for accents and diacritics, the editor employs a built-in on-screen menu inspired by the Apple OS X Character Accent menu. Proteus' ecosystem is also not Oxyrhynchus-centric. Born digital critical editions of fragments from any collection can be produced. But in order to integrate AL data into the scholarly process of editing, DELPHI will have a user workflow for those working on unpublished fragments from Oxyrhynchus. For those fragments the consensus transcription produced by AL will be provided to their editors. This is an important step for unpublished material. The capture of the digital edition at the inception of the *editio princeps* will remove the need for another party to encode the text at a later stage for use in other projects and digital research.

To conclude, I should say that I am very fond of coding and promote coding literacy whenever possible. As a Classicist, Papyrologist, or any other humanities scholar, coding may not be your job, but whether you are managing or just participating in a Digital Humanities or Digital Classics project, coding literacy ensures that you actually understand the nature of your data. This also facilitates communication with the developers and computer scientists involved. As of now, if your data is going to be useful to your colleagues, new digital tools will most likely be required. When your development team asks what you want to do with your data, the correct answer needs to reflect an actual knowledge of the data. There is a saying in the entertainment industry that it takes just as much time, effort, and money to make a bad movie as it does a great one. Development, especially academic development, is not immune. We can build as many digital tools and algorithms as we like, but if these tools and their output are not being used and cited by the field of Classics at large, then there is a disconnect that needs to be addressed. In that context AL still has more work to do.

Notes

[1] Ancient Lives: <http://ancientlives.org/>.
[2] The project is led by Dirk Obbink (Classics) and Chris Lintott (Astrophysics).
[3] Zooniverse: <http://zooniverse.org/>.
[4] For an introduction to the city of Oxyrhynchus and the importance of the Oxyrhynchus papyri collection, see Bowman et al. 2007 and Parsons 2007.
[5] Ancient Lives will no longer focus on transcribing Greek papyrus fragments from Oxyrhynchus. But other collections and even Coptic manuscripts will be included. Along with this transformation Ancient Lives is now a full partnership between the University of Oxford and the University of Minnesota.

[6] User comments and discussions within AL Talk document a wide range of reactions to the content and images found in Oxyrhynchus papyri. Their opinions and expressions, however, are their own. Since Talk is not open to the public, but a forum for registered users, I encourage exploration of the Ancient Lives site to get a feel for its community.

[7] See Prather et al. 2013.

[8] For a recent study on crowdsourcing in the humanities, see Dunn & Hedges 2013: 147–169.

[9] For further reading on the algorithms involved, see our computational papers: Williams et al. 2014a: 100–105 and Williams et al. 2014b: 5–10. For support in creating these algorithms, I would like to thank the following funding bodies: The John Fell Fund, Minnesota Futures, The Arts and Humanities Research Council, and the National Endowment for the Humanities. Images provided by Alex Williams.

[10] Moyle et al. 2011: 347–356.

[11] Proteus, available: <http://www.proteusproject.uk>; see also <http://www.papyrology.ox.ac.uk/ProteusProject/>. Python: <https://www.python.org>.

[12] Altschul et al. 1990: 403–410.

[13] Henikoff & Henikoff 1992: 10919.

[14] To date Johnson 2004 remains the only comprehensive study of the aesthetics of the ancient papyrus bookroll; the dataset notably comprises of only 413 papyri fragments.

References

Altschul, S. F. et al. (1990). Basic local alignment search tool. *Journal of molecular biology*, 215(3): 403–410.

Bowman, A. K., Coles, R. A., Gonis, N., Obbink, D. & Parsons, P. J. (2007). Oxyrhynchus: a City and its Texts. *Egypt Exploration Society*, 93.

Dunn S. & Hedges. M. (2013). Crowd-sourcing as a Component of Humanities Research Infrastructures. *International Journal of Humanities and Arts Computing*, 7(1–2): 147–169.

Henikoff S. & Henikoff, J. G. (1992). Amino acid substitution matrices from protein blocks. *Proceedings of the National Academy of Sciences*, 89(22): 10915–10919.

Johnson, W. A. (2004). *Bookrolls and Scribes in Oxyrhynchus*. Toronto, University of Toronto Press.

Moyle, M., Trona, J. & Wallace, V. (2011). Manuscript transcription by crowdsourcing: Transcribe Bentham. *Liber. Quarterly*, 20(3/4): 347–356.

Parsons, P. J. (2007). *City of the Sharp-Nosed Fish: Greek Lives in Roman Egypt*. London, Weidenfeld & Nicolson.

Prather, E. E., Cormier, S., Wallace, C. S., Lintott, Raddick, M. J. & Smith, A. (2013). Measuring the Conceptual Understandings of Citizen Scientists

Participating in Zooniverse Projects: A First Approach. *Astronomy Education Review*, 12(1).

Williams, A. C., Wallin, J. F., Yu, H., Perale, M., Carroll, H. D., Lamblin, A-F., Fortson, L., Obbink, D., Lintott, C. J. & Brusuelas J. H. (2014a). A Computational Pipeline for Crowdsourced Transcriptions of Ancient Greek Papyrus Fragments. *Big Data, IEEE International Conference on*, 100–105.

Williams, A. C., Carroll, H. D., Wallin, J. F., Brusuelas, J., Fortson, L., Lamblin, A-F. & Yu, H. (2014b). Identification of Ancient Greek Papyrus Fragments using Genetic Sequence Alignment Algorithms. *e-Science, 2014 IEEE 10th International Conference on*, 2: 5–10.

CHAPTER 11

Ancient Inscriptions between Citizens and Scholars: The Double Soul of the EAGLE Project

Silvia Orlandi

Sapienza University of Rome

Abstract

The mission of the European project EAGLE (Europeana network of Ancient Greek and Latin Epigraphy) is 'to make ancient inscriptions accessible'. This means not only to create a useful research tool for classical scholars so that they can find online high quality information about epigraphic texts and artefacts, but also to allow a broad public—consisting of students, teachers, tourists, curious and interested citizens—to understand and appreciate inscribed monuments, even if they are written in ancient languages and alphabets. Digital technologies can help not only to preserve, at least in a virtual archive, our archaeological heritage that is often in danger, but also to improve knowledge of, and therefore respect for said heritage. The EAGLE project has given particular importance to this 'civic' aspect, developing two applications (a mobile app, that uses an image based recognition system, and a storytelling application), which show that even ancient inscriptions are not so out of reach as they seem, and can also be fun.

1 Preliminary Thoughts

In her interview with the *Huffington Post* on 31 January 2014, Perry Hewitt, Harvard University's Chief Digital Officer, has illustrated the 10 Best Practices

How to cite this book chapter:
Orlandi, S. 2016. Ancient Inscriptions between Citizens and Scholars: The Double Soul of the EAGLE Project. In: Bodard, G & Romanello, M (eds.) *Digital Classics Outside the Echo-Chamber: Teaching, Knowledge Exchange & Public Engagement*, Pp. 205–221. London: Ubiquity Press. DOI: http://dx.doi.org/10.5334/bat.l. License: CC-BY 4.0.

for dealing with digital transformation.[1] As the scientific coordinator of a project which focusses on digital technologies, I carefully read this list. One point in particular caught my attention: 'Don't do digital for the sake of digital: figure out how digital impedes or advances your key objectives and goals'.

The enormous growth of projects, papers, blogs and other initiatives being published on the Web has put at everyone's disposal a huge (and ever-growing) amount of data, documents and images. Sometimes these data are of high quality; sometimes they are not completely reliable and sometimes simply flawed or out of date. This means that having access to a larger amount of information, in a manner that is much faster than before, does not necessarily translate into an improvement of our knowledge, given the need to check and critically appraise what we find online and to collect and compare materials often scattered in different and disconnected online archives. To make digital projects actually useful and effective for meaningful cultural development, better and ever-improving technology undoubtedly helps, but it is not enough: much depends on how content is conceived and prepared in order to be made available, as well as on several crucial choices made with regard to the target audience and to the scenarios of access and of use of said content. In short, one must carefully consider the overall vision (or lack thereof) that lies behind every digital project.

A solid concept indeed lies at the very root of the EC-funded project Europeana Network of Ancient Greek and Latin Epigraphy (EAGLE),[2] that forms the background of what is discussed in this essay. The latter was born in 2003 as a federation of four epigraphic databases that had agreed to make their geographically separated collections accessible through a common online interface (i.e. a single portal).[3] Most importantly, the four partners shared the same idea of what an inscription is and what information we need in order to deal with it: epigraphic documents should not be regarded as mere texts, but as inscribed objects and monuments within specific topographic and geographic contexts. Each inscription should be presented and studied as a whole, examining material and archaeological characteristics along with textual and philological aspects. EAGLE was founded on the bedrock of this approach.

To reach a goal of this kind, scanning a book and quickly filling in just a couple of metadata fields is not enough: both the epigraphic text and the remaining information must be ingested carefully and critically. This means checking the text, whenever possible, against the original stone engraving, or at least against a good photo or drawing of it, and giving the user the chance to accomplish the same. This is not easy, and not quick, but a good and reliable documentary corpus is the necessary starting point of every research work. Therefore, it is worth investing time and energy in order to produce it. The only way to ensure both quality of content and quantity of items is by bringing together different people, projects, institutions, which for their knowledge and experience are in the best position to provide high quality content, and letting them work together towards a common goal. In other words, in order to become a really useful resource, a digital project must be structured and organised according to the wills and needs of experts in the field.

2 On the Usefulness of Digital Resources—an Example

To give an idea of how such a collaboration can result in more informed and richer digital editions, I have deliberately chosen the smallest possible example.

Among the hundreds of inscriptions found at the beginning of the twentieth century in Rome, there is a fragment of a marble slab, which was dug up from a vast necropolis site between via Salaria and via Pinciana. The fragment is thus featured in the sixth volume of Corpus Inscriptionum Latinarum (Figure 1):

Reproducing this apparently meaningless sequence of letters faithfully but uncritically would add a new item to our digital archive, but it would be of no help to an in-depth study of the context to which this fragment used to belong or to a development of its historical importance. Additional data that complement the text with other layers of information (such as an image of the monument and other details about its spatial and social context) help lift the veil of ambiguity. Thanks to the work of American colleagues who are working on a digital edition of all the Classic Greek and Latin inscriptions hosted by US collections, we now learn that this fragment is preserved in the J.B. Speed Art Museum of Louisville, Kentucky, and its photograph, which is also available on line, tells us that it is the left part of a *columbarium* (niche for funerary urn) inscription.[4]

In turn, putting these two resources in relation with one another allowed us to infer three things: firstly that small *columbaria* were part of the ancient landscape of the funerary area between via Salaria and via Pinciana; secondly that the inscription can be dated to the beginning of the 1st century AD, when such artefacts were mostly used; and thirdly, that the dead person mentioned in the text is probably a member of the lower classes of Roman society, for which this kind of funerary monuments were conceived. Thanks to the additional information collected through different sources, we can also go beyond the simple reading of the surviving letters and propose an integration and an

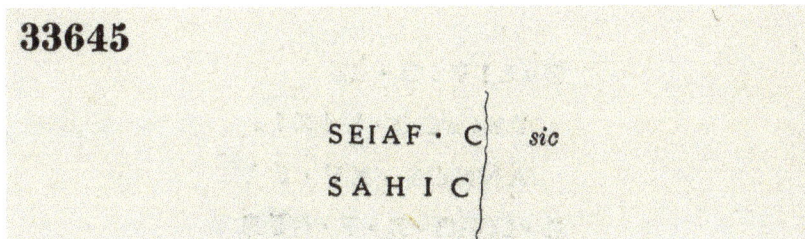

Figure 1: *CIL*, VI 33645.

interpretation of the text, which is actually the epitaph of a woman, whose family name in genitive, Seiae, was written in the wrong form 'Seiaf' because of a mistake of the stonecutter. Seiae was probably followed by the cognomen of the dead person, which was lost, together with the right part of the stone, and by the formula 'ossa hic sita sunt' ('Her bones lay here'), which is typical of this kind of text and which can be completely restored. Therefore the digital form of our inscription in the Epigraphic Database Roma goes beyond the simple reproduction of the corresponding CIL edition, allowing a more interpretative and meaningful transcription of the text: *Seia*ᵉ*e*ᵓ *C[--- os]/sa hic [sita sunt]*. [5]

This is but a small example of the kind of achievements that collaboration between researchers, coupled with a critical approach to ancient sources, can give. If we apply this method systematically to every possible epigraphic document, the result is a large digital archive to which many scholars contribute by providing high quality content, in order to build together a real state-of-the-art research asset.

Moreover, the application of data mining methods may help to reveal interesting relationships among, for instance, linguistic style, positioning and dating of inscriptions, thus creating new links between different pieces of data, and trying to give 'quantitative measurements' of intuition. [6]

3 EAGLE and Europeana: Online Digital Resources for Everyone

The idea of a collaborative project to share both data and knowledge about inscriptions led to the original EAGLE federation in 2003, as well as to the 'new' EAGLE project, which kicked off in 2012. In fact, 2012 is the year when EAGLE 'grew up'—so to speak— to become a consortium of 19 partners from 12 different European countries. [7] The new consortium constitutes what the European Commission calls a Best Practice Network, aimed at making accessible most of the ancient Greek and Latin inscriptions through a single Web portal, as well as through Europeana, the European digital library. [8]

Within the EAGLE consortium, besides the four 'historical' members (EDB, EDH, EDR and HEpOl), there are new important content providers, including some of the most important European projects in digital epigraphy—such as The Last Statues of Antiquity project by Oxford University, Ubi erat lupa (based in Salzburg and collecting material from different Eastern European countries), the new version of the existing PETRAE project, which has put on line the inscriptions of Roman Aquitania and not forgetting the key role played by the Arachne project, which is currently digitising the huge photographic archive and part of the library of the German Archaeological Institute.

All this content comes from different repositories with different architectures, interfaces and data structures. Hence, it must be first of all harmonised and aggregated according to a common metadata model in order to be made accessible through a single search tool. In this field, the technical partners of the EAGLE consortium have a fundamental importance, starting from the Catholic University of Leuven, whose task is to 'disambiguate' content coming from different archives but related to the same object. No less important is the role played by the IT staff working at CNR-ISTI in Pisa, as well as of Promoter, Gogate and QED Productions, three companies with a great deal of experience in EC-funded projects. Thanks to the concerted efforts of all these entities, EAGLE is becoming not only a large database of aggregated content, but also— and this is perhaps one of its most interesting and promising aspects—a virtual platform over which other people and institutions sharing the same spirit of the EAGLE community can join the consortium and put at everyone's disposal the epigraphic content on which they are working. This in turn generates interesting synergies between different geographically separated institutions and people.

In other words, we are gradually moving from the idea of collecting large amounts of digital data that can be searched easily and quickly, to the idea of working in a digital environment; a world where collaboration and interoperability are the keywords for a real cultural (not only scientific) progress. To put it another way, the successful digital aggregation project is as much an inspiring operation of social and institutional engineering as it is a technical IT challenge.

This became clear when, for example, EAGLE signed a Memorandum of Understanding with the Pelagios consortium[9] in order to share geographic information to improve the digital atlas of the ancient world, and also through the Cooperation Agreement with the project led by Alison Cooley and focused on the Latin inscriptions of the Ashmolean Museum,[10] or when the EAGLE content was enriched by the thousands of English translations of Greek inscriptions provided by the Attic Inscriptions Online.[11] In fact, the use of new technologies integrated in a virtual environment allows possibilities that are not limited to the academic world. A 'virtual environment' is by definition an open space, not an ivory tower that can be reached only by few scholars, but a room with open doors that can be entered by academics as well as by interested and curious people, not just 'customers' but users.[12]

A good example of what can be done collecting and making accessible primary sources of historical interest is given by the big Europeana 1914–1918 initiative—untold stories and official histories of WW1: a wide range and number of digital materials (letters, postcards, photographs, videos, audio files...) coming from both public and private archives, intended to be used to discover more about our past, learn history in a more interactive way, research new aspects of well-known events and above all share this knowledge with the whole community. To collect materials telling interesting stories about people, families and little communities (war nurses, chaplains, Old Etonians...) that escaped the attention of the great historians, different initiatives were taken and different engagement strategies were applied. Museums and libraries have organized 'Collection days', when letters, photos and other documents were physically collected in order to be digitized and put at disposal of the project.

Registered users can also contribute any time through the page 'Add your story!' of the Europeana 1914–1918 website.[13] Thousands of documents have been added, enriched and displayed in this way.

User engagement is, in fact, one of the key issues of every digital initiative that aims to bring a real improvement and a long term change in our culture and society. As many papers, lectures and interviews have recently underlined, no legal or political action to protect our cultural heritage is better than the involvement of the citizens, and respect can only rise from the consciousness of the importance of the past.

4 Digital is also Useful for Preservation

Ancient inscriptions are part of this cultural heritage and a fundamental source for our knowledge of classical civilizations. But at the same time, as all the relics of the ancient world, inscriptions—or what is left of them—are fragile and perishable: the majority of the millions of inscribed objects and monuments that were produced in the Classical world did not survive to this day. Indeed, most of the inscriptions that were still known to exist only a few centuries ago are now lost. To preserve this important heritage is therefore the first requirement and civic duty of a digital project like EAGLE, since past and present experiences teach us that:

i) inscriptions can be destroyed.

As we can read in the *Corpus Inscriptionum Latinarum*, the epitaph of a Roman soldier which had been found re-employed as a slab of the floor of the San Pietro in Vincoli church in Rome, got lost when troops occupied the church during the conflict against the papal army in the time of the Repubblica Romana in 1849 (anno 1849 coenobio a militibus occupato periit, vel certe ab eo inde tempore latet) (Figure 2). Hence, this fragment is known only thanks to a manuscript (CIL, VI 2597).[14]

Soldiers can be dangerous for cultural heritage not only in war actions, but also during their free time, as is witnessed by the history of an ancient inscription with bronze letters found in the floor of the Odeon in Pompeii at the end of the 18th-century (CIL, X 845).[15] In the following years, some of the letters were stolen by soldiers visiting the archaeological site, and only some of them were given back to the custodians—as can be read in the comment of CIL, X 845 (Figure 3), before being almost completely lost today.[16]

More recently, on July 29th 1993, the San Giorgio al Velabro church in Rome was the target of a terrorist attack (Figure 4).

The inscriptions displayed in the portico were damaged and made inaccessible, as we can read in one of the entries of the supplementary volume of CIL,

2597 fragmentum tabulae marmoreae. *Nel ri-fare il pavimento di S. Pietro in Vincoli sotto il card. Galli* MONS. In bibliotheca coenobii S. Petri ad vincula anno 1842; anno 1849 coenobio a militibus occupato periit, vel certe ab eo inde tempore latet ROSSI.

. . . .

ARTIVS SIGNIFER COH V

PRAET · ALVMNE BENE MI:

*re*NTI · FECIT

Descripsit de Rossi. Exhibent schedae Mon-sacrati in bibliotheca S. Petri ad vincula ad-servatae.

Figure 2: *CIL*, VI 2597.

VI edited in 2000 by Géza Alföldy: post pyroboli diruptionem ab hominibus terrorem excitantibus effectam (Figure 5).[18]

ii) Inscriptions can be stolen.

A fragment of one of the inscriptions of the Colosseum mentioning the senators who had the right of sitting in the first rows of the amphitheatre was the protagonist of a famous theft some years ago and mentioned by different newspapers.[19] Beyond this, a large number of inscribed objects have become impossible to find, whilst sometimes some of them suddenly reappear on the antiquarian market.[20]

845 [= 2242] litteris aere incrustatis.   Pompeiis in pavimento theatri minoris ACTA 14 Nov. 1793 [ed. 1, 2, 54].

M · OCVLATVS · M · F · VERVS · II · VIR · PRO · LVDIS

Descripsi et recognovi.   Marini Arv. p. 661; Vernazza [cod. reg. Taur. 59 f. 7] qui descripsit 8 Mai. a. 1806; Romanelli 1, 212; Mazois IV p. 56; de Iorio P. 134 = 89; Gell Pomp. 1821 p. 247; Guarini comm. VI ed. 2 p. 85, fast. ed. 1 p. 143; Avellino op. 2, 246; Zangemeister Bull. dell' inst. 1866 p. 30, cf. de Petra in actis acad. Neap. 1866 p. 82; Niccolini teatri tab. 1; Fiorelli descris. p. 353. Orelli 3809.

Sic ut dedi antiqui omnes. At postquam d. 25 Mai. 1815 furto perierunt ea quae dantur inclinatis, pro OCVLATVS moderante Bonuccio male repositum est OLCONIVS, quo cum supplemento titulus prodiit Mus. Borb. vol. 1 tab. 38 et apud Niccolinium l. c. Supplementum me olim decepit; rem exposuit secundum narrationem custodum Zangemeister l. c. narrantque item furtum quomodo acciderit acta Pompeiana edita I, 3 p. 277.

Idem duovir nominatur n. 955. Videtur esse aetatis renotioris, cum iure dicundo appellatio absit et in altero eius titulo pequnia scribatur.

Figure 3: CIL, X 845.

Figure 4: S. Giorgio al Velabro. Downloaded from beatopadrepuglisi.it.[17]

40718 (= 1123) tit. honorarius imperatoris
  Tabula marmorea ex tribus partibus coniuncta undique fracta, in fronte
  caelo dolata (30) × (44) × ?. Litt. 7. In aede S. Georgii in Velabro ⟨*Urbs*
  O/P 23⟩ descripsit iam Forcella. Extat ibid. a porta ecclesiae introeun-
  tibus a sinistra parieti inserta, ubi descripsi a. 1987, recognovi a. 1989.
  Cum a. 1993 titulum denuo adire et im. phot. sumere volui, clausus erat
  aede post pyroboli diruptionem ab hominibus terrorem excitantibus
  effectam ex parte diruta et cancellis ferreis circumdata.

    Fuit fere:

    - - - - - -
    [Germanico maximo Sarmatico maximo]
    Persico ma[ximo Britannico maximo]
    Carpiç[o maximo, pont(ifici) max(imo)],
    [tribu]niçia [potestate - - -]
    - - - - - -

Figure 5: *CIL*, VI 40718.

iii) Inscriptions can be damaged.

Since the time when the Lanzichenecchi sacked Rome in 1527 and left visible traces of their passage on the frescos of Villa Farnesina,[21] 'barbarians' of every age and place seemingly cannot resist the temptation to use walls and stones—no matter how ancient and valuable they are—to express their feelings and political opinions, providing useful materials for historians, but also inflicting sometimes irreversible damage to our cultural heritage. It is the case of an epitaph found and still displayed at the fifth mile of the via Appia (Figure 6),[22] where the ancient inscription was temporarily covered by a modern 'graffito' insulting Rome's former major Francesco Rutelli.

In all the above instances, having the inscribed texts and the related images digitised and available through one of the repositories aggregated by EAGLE will ensure somehow their survival. Although this cannot prevent further future destruction of artefacts, at least it does increase our chances that information will not be lost, and therefore yields the possibility of reading and studying these documents, thus keeping—so to speak—an open window on our past.

Figure 6: *CIL*, VI 21312. Photo Leonardo Radicioni, by kind permission of the Soprintendenza Speciale per il Colosseo, il Museo Nazionale Romano e l'Area archeologica di Roma.

5 Added Value of new Tools and new Media

New technologies can help us not only to preserve the remains of ancient civilizations from damage and loss, but also to make them more visible, informative and valuable. ICT is playing an increasingly significant role in the way in which culture is perceived and appreciated by the public. Not by chance, according to one of the most famous travel websites, Tripadvisor, the most important 'attractions' in Rome, and one of the 'Top 25 destinations' are the domus under Palazzo Valentini, whose remains have been included in an underground walk full of suggestion, images, lights and sounds that transform a guided tour into an emotional, immersive experience. The narrative structure and the virtual reconstructions meet the needs and the expectations of the modern visitors, stimulating curiosity, amusement and interest at the same time.[23] Why should we not learn from this experience and try to extend such an approach also to ancient inscriptions without being afraid of their apparent complexity?

In order to meet these needs, two flagship mobile apps have been foreseen as part of the EAGLE project:

- The Mobile Application, whose aim is to provide sightseers with on-the-fly information about inscriptions: thanks to a visual recognition system, developed by the CNR-ISTI in Pisa and by Eureva in Paris, all that visitors have to do is take a photo with their smartphone of the inscription in which they are interested. The picture is sent to the EAGLE servers. There, a specific software will recognize the picture from within a database of selected inscriptions and will provide all the information associated with that picture. This image-based application overcomes the difficulty represented by texts written in ancient languages and alphabets and using often abbreviated forms typical of the 'epigraphic habit'. Moreover, this custom developed software can become the base of further developments that can use epigraphic content to reach a different type and level of public: scholars, casual users, tourists, children… In this way, without denying the complexity of this particular kind of cultural object, technology can help us not to abandon the idea of including ancient inscriptions in touristic routes and educational projects.
- The Storytelling Application, conceived to help professionals (teachers, students, writers, historians) to build stories starting from ancient inscriptions and using materials and information collected in different digital repositories and projects (not only EAGLE but also Perseus, Wikimedia Commons and the other members of the "Wikifamily", not forgetting what can be found in the social media like, for example, Flickr or Instagram). Starting from the preliminary assumption that behind every inscription there is an individual story—of a man, of a family or of a community—it's up to us to tell this story in a way that can be both creative and historically

documented. The stories already collected in the specific repository of the EAGLE project website are a good example of what can be done with this material.[24] The storytelling version of a group of inscriptions of the National Museum of Slovenia in Ljubljana has also found a more traditional form in a book recently published by M. Šašel Kos, The disappearing Tombstone and other stories.[25]

But, in this case as well, technology is just a possibility, and not a real resource for cultural development without a vision behind it. And the vision in this case is that, even if it may seem impossible, epigraphy can be fun. Now, as a video recently posted on You Tube has shown, curiosity and amusement can be the way to let people do willingly and happily what they know is important, but seems to be heavy and boring, like... taking the steps instead of the escalator.[26]

You can have fun with epigraphy chasing inscriptions in places where you would never expect to find them. Irene Somà, PhD student in Ancient History and one of the followers of the EAGLE project on Facebook, during a trip to Qasr al-Azraq in Jordan noticed an important bilingual (Greek and Latin) inscription bearing the names of the tetrarchs Diocletian and Maximian; she could not only identify it,[27] but also found it mentioned in the novel 'The Seven Pillars of Wisdom' by Lawrence of Arabia and posted both the image of the stone and the passage of the book on the EAGLE Facebook webpage.[28] Following this example, another novel, 'Isole' by Marco Lodoli, was posted on the same webpage[29] because it contains a specific reference to an inscribed monument too: the long verse epitaph of the young *Quintus Suplicius Maximus*, who died at age 9 after having won a poetry contest, which was found (and is still visible, although in copy form) near Porta Salaria in Rome.[30] Even a real estate advertisement can be used to discover or, better, rediscover an ancient dedication to the god Mithra, seen in the 17th-century by the scholar Lukas Holste during his epigraphic voyages, and since then considered lost.[31] Actually, the stone is still immured exactly in the same country house where Holste saw it three centuries ago, as the web page of the real-estate agency proudly shows (Figure 7) and as Lucio Benedetti was so keen to find out.[32]

Films can also be an unexpected instance where you can find ancient inscriptions not necessarily recognised and used as such. For example, in a scene of Nell'anno del Signore, by Italian director Luigi Magni, an ecclesiastic tribunal chaired by cardinal Rivarola (here played by Ugo Tognazzi) stands behind a 'table' which is actually made of a large inscribed architrave. This is part of a dedication to the emperor Constantine and his sons, found and preserved in the Baths of Caracalla in Rome,[34] where the scene was shot. The ancient text does not play any proper role in the film (although I cannot exclude a more or less conscious reference to the power of the ruling class),

Figure 7: *CIL*, XI 3320. Photo downloaded from duemmepi.altervista.org.[33]

but its creative use in this scene is a very immediate way to show how, in a city like Rome, at any time, past and present always co-exist along each other.

On the other hand, in films based on ancient history or, more generally, set in the ancient world, one could expect that inscriptions should be a significant presence in the reconstruction of the urban landscape, as they actually were. A good choice is given, for example, by the *Rome* TV series, whose opening credits run over ancient walls completely covered by graffiti.[35] But I must admit that, in most cases, inscriptions are not felt as an important element, and the results are often disappointing, as in *Gladiator*, where over the door of the training school for gladiators beside the Colosseum the attentive viewer reads 'Ludus magnus gladiatores', a text that amounts to grammatical nonsense. Or as in the film *Agora*, set in the ancient city of Alexandria, where the local Serapaeum proudly shows on its architrave a monumental inscription: 'M. Agrippa cos. tertium fecit', which is no less than... the inscription of the Pantheon in Rome![36]

The aim of these observations is not to find all the 'errors' in *Gladiator* or in other historical movies, but rather to show, through scattered examples, that even epigraphy can appear in unexpected guises and ways, that can generate curiosity and interest. One might assume—with good reason—that scratched and fragmentary words written in ancient alphabet and languages which are often difficult to read and to understand are not exactly the first thought for those who walk through museums, expositions and archaeological areas. To quote the title of the paper by Laura Löser recently published in the Proceedings of the First EAGLE International Conference: 'Epigraphy, who cares?'[37] Well, the process of user engagement developed thanks to cooperation with Wikimedia is showing that people *do* care: in only a few months, about 800 'external' users have been adding comments, asking questions, collaborating in different ways about the images posted in Wikimedia Commons and identified as ancient inscriptions. So, once again, to quote Stacy Sullivan, Google's Chief Cultural Officer, 'If you engage people, they will amaze you.'[38] In this framework of scientific and civic issues, the EAGLE project, with its concentric organization and collaborative spirit, has the ambitious objective to become, in the field of epigraphy, not just a mere working tool, but a real resource intended for all citizens, be they scholars or not: academic research will benefit of the portal's services and content curation; important parts of our cultural heritage will be collected and preserved in a digital archive; but at the same time EAGLE will also work as social media 'hub', where users can share experiences of personal 'discovery' of ancient inscriptions in unexpected places (books, sites, films).

6 Conclusions

Any form of public engagement, if correctly presented and supported by a preliminary research, is not to be considered just a 'sale' of the scientific knowledge. On the contrary, arising consciousness of the importance of our archaeological heritage, and of the classical studies that help us to understand it, should be part of the academics job. In this sense, the European projects that always require a whole series of dissemination activities are somehow starting to change the traditional approach to this matter.

One may argue that, in times of social and economic difficulty such as ours, ancient epigraphy is not exactly a primary need. But I think that, especially in times of social and economic difficulty, long lasting values like a shared knowledge and a civic approach to cultural heritage maintain and even increase their importance.[39] Epigraphy may be not a primary need, but, after all...

> *O reason not the need! Our basest beggars*
> *Are in the poorest thing superfluous:*
> *Allow not nature more than nature needs,*
> *Man's life is as cheap as beast's*
> (William Shakespeare, King Lear, II, 4)

Notes

1 Vala Afshar: 'Harvard's Chief Digital Officer: 10 Digital Best Practices' *Huffington Post* 01/31/2014: <http://www.huffingtonpost.com/vala-afshar/harvards-chief-digital-of_b_4701663.html>.

2 Europeana EAGLE Project: <http://www.eagle-network.eu>.

3 These databases are: Epigraphic Database Bari (EDB), Epigraphic Database Heidelberg (EDH), Epigraphic Database Roma (EDR) and Hispania Epigraphica Online (HEpOl).

4 Online at US Epigraphy Project, 'Inscription: KY.Lou.SAM.L.1929.17.662': <http://usepigraphy.brown.edu/projects/usep/inscription/KY.Lou.SAM.L.1929.17.662>.

5 Online at Epigraphic Database Roma, 'EDR135710': <http://www.edr-edr.it/edr_programmi/res_complex_comune.php?do=book&id_nr=edr135710>.

6 On this subject see Mimmo 2012 and Pio et al. 2014.

7 For a complete description of the consortium, see 'Who we are': <http://www.eagle-network.eu/about/who-we-are/>.

8 Europeana Collection: <http://europeana.eu/portal/>.

9 Pelagios Project: <http://pelagios-project.blogspot.it/>.

10 Ashmolean Latin Inscriptions: <http://www.ashmolean.org/ashwpress/latininscriptions/>; see also Masseglia 2014.

11 Attice Inscriptions Online: <https://www.atticinscriptions.com/>.

12 As pointed out in The European Charter for Researchers: <http://ec.europa.eu/euraxess/index.cfm/rights/europeanCharter>.

13 Europeana 1914–1918, "Add your story": <http://www.europeana1914-1918.eu/en/contributor>.

14 <http://www.edr-edr.it/edr_programmi/res_complex_comune.php?do=book&id_nr=edr102733>. Compare also CIL, VI 25611 = <http://www.edr-edr.it/edr_programmi/res_complex_comune.php?do=book&id_nr=edr151314>, that seems to have shared the same destiny.

15 <http://www.edr-edr.it/edr_programmi/res_complex_comune.php?do=book&id_nr=edr150240>.

16 On this episode see Cooley 2014: 342.

17 "Le bombe dell'estate '93 e la trattativa con lo stato," available: <http://www.beatopadrepuglisi.it/2014/10/le-bombe-dellestate-93-e-la-trattativa.html> (last accessed February 2016).

18 Corresponding to CIL, VI 1123 = 40718 = <http://www.edr-edr.it/edr_programmi/res_complex_comune.php?do=book&id_nr=edr093098>.

19 Specifically CIL, VI 32164, available: <http://www.edr-edr.it/edr_programmi/res_complex_comune.php?do=book&id_nr=edr151433>.

20 For example CIL, VI 13493, available: <http://www.edr-edr.it/edr_programmi/res_complex_comune.php?do=book&id_nr=edr131538>; or

CIL, VI 7598, available: <http://www.edr-edr.it/edr_programmi/res_com-plex_comune.php?do=book&id_nr=edr131539>.

[21] Orlandi 2013, 335, with images at 336–337.

[22] CIL, VI 21312, available: <http://www.edr-edr.it/edr_programmi/res_complex_comune.php?do=book&id_nr=edr151412>.

[23] On this particular aspect Mandarano 2014, See also Donnini 2014.

[24] 'Stories'; available: <http://www.eagle-network.eu/stories/>.

[25] More about the EAGLE Mobile Application and the Storytelling Application in Orlandi et al. 2014, and Amato et al. 2014. For another application based on image recognition and storytelling, see e.g. Mazzanti et al. 2014.

[26] "The Fun Theory 1 - Piano Staircase"; available: <https://youtu.be/SByymar3bds>.

[27] IGRRP, III 1339 = <http://edh-www.adw.uni-heidelberg.de/edh/inschrift/HD031629>.

[28] Irene Somà, Timeline photograph, available: <https://www.facebook.com/photo.php?fbid=10151978886059331>.

[29] Eagle Europeana, Timeline photograph, available: <https://www.facebook.com/EAGLEuropeana/photos/a.510572815704156.1073741829.368159833278789/605067492921354/>.

[30] CIL, VI 33976 = <http://www.edr-edr.it/edr_programmi/res_complex_comune.php?do=book&id_nr=edr107864>.

[31] CIL, XI 3320 = <http://www.edr-edr.it/edr_programmi/res_complex_comune.php?do=book&id_nr=edr121131>.

[32] Benedetti 2014. Cf. a similar case in <http://www.edr-edr.it/edr_programmi/res_complex_comune.php?do=book&id_nr=edr078389>.

[33] "Il Mitreo di Sutri – tra sogna e realtà," available: <http://duemmepi.altervista.org/blog/il-mitreo-di-sutri-tra-sogno-e-realta/> (last accessed February 2016).

[34] CIL, VI 40772 = <http://www.edr-edr.it/edr_programmi/res_complex_comune.php?do=book&id_nr=edr073541>.

[35] *Rome*, Opening Credits, available via YouTube: <https://www.youtube.com/watch?v=LCaDRlog0Rc>.

[36] CIL, VI 896 = <http://www.edr-edr.it/edr_programmi/res_complex_comune.php?do=book&id_nr=EDR103378>.

[37] Löser 2014.

[38] See also the European project Civic Epistemologies, available: <http://www.civic-epistemologies.eu>.

[39] See, for example, the contributions collected by Parello and Rizzo 2014. See also the presentation 'Challanging the crisis with digital weapons: The DigilibLT case', by Alice Borgna, available: <https://www.academia.edu/15250546/Challenging_the_crisis_with_digital_weapons_The_DigilibLT_case>.

References

Amato, G., Casarosa, V., Martineau, P., Orlandi, S., Santucci, R. & Giberti, L. (2014). EAGLE: Europeana Network of Ancient Greek and Latin Epigraphy. A Digital Bridge to the Ancient World. In Ronzino, P. & Niccolucci, F. (Eds.) (pp. 25–32).

Benedetti, L. (2014). L'Iter Perusinum anno 1643 di Lukas Holste (Mscr. Dresd. F. 191). *Quellen und Forschungen aus italienischen Archiven und Bibliotheken*, 94: 166–218.

Cooley, A. E. (2014). The emergence of eigraphy in the Kingdom of Naples. *Journal of the History of Collecions*, 26: 337–353.

Donnini, D. (2014). Gli strumenti per l'emozione con le innovazioni tecnologiche al servizio di una nuova relazione tra il visitatore e i beni culturali. *Archeomatica*, 3: 26–29.

Löser, L. (2014). Meeting the Needs of Today's Audiences of Epigraphy with Digital Editions. In O. Santucci et al.(Eds.) (pp. 239–254).

Mandarano, N. (2014). *Tripadvisor e il marketing culturale*. Rimini.

Masseglia, J. (2014). The Ashmolean Latin Inscriptions Project (AshLI). Bringing epigraphic research to museum visitors and schools. In O. Santucci et al. (Eds.) (pp. 221–231).

Mazzanti, P., Casini, M. & Caldelli, R. (2014). SMartART: un nuovo modo di fruire il Museo. *Archeomatica*, 3: 30–34.

Mimmo, D. M. (2012). Computational Historiography: Data mining in a century of classics journals. *ACM Journal on Computing and Cultural Heritage*, 5(1).

Orlandi, S. (2013). Le tracce del passaggio di Alarico nelle fonti epigrafiche. In J. Lipps, C. Machado & P. von Rummel (Eds.), *The Sack of Rome in 410 AD. The Event, its Context and its Impact* (pp. 335–351). Wiesbaden.

Orlandi, S., Giberti, L. M. C. & Santucci, R. (2014a). EAGLE: Europeana network of Ancient Greek and Latin Epigraphy. Making the Ancient Inscriptions accessible. In *Lexicon Pilosophicum. International Journal for the History of Texts and Ideas*, 2. Retrieved from http://lexicon.cnr.it/

Orlandi, S., Santucci, R., Casarosa V. & Liuzzo P. (Eds.) (2014b). *Information Technologies for Epigraph and Cultural Heirtage. Proceedings of the First EAGLE International Conference*, Roma.

Parello. M. C. & Rizzo, M. S. (Eds.) (2014). *Archeologia pubblica al tempo della crisi. Atti delle Giornate gregoriane*. VII Edizione (29–30 novembre 2013), Bari.

Pio, G., Fumarola, F., Felle, A. E., Malerba, D. & Ceci, M. (2014). Discovering Novelty Patterns from the Ancient Christian Inscriptions of Rome. *ACM Journal on Computing and Cultural Heritage*, 7(4).

Ronzino, P. & Niccolucci, F. (Eds.) (2014). Horizon2020 and Creative Europe vs Digital Heritage: A European Projects Crossover. Flash News, Pre-Conference Workshop. at *Museums and the Web Florence*. Retrieved from <http://ceur-ws.org/Vol-1336>.